NICE ONE CENTURION

Stephen D. Headey &
Tim Parker

NICE ONE CENTURION © Stephen D. Headey

All rights reserved. No part of this publication may be reproduced, stored in a retrieval system, or transmitted in any form or by any means electronic, mechanical, photocopying, recording, or otherwise, without the prior written permission of the author.

National Library of Australia Cataloguing-in-Publication entry (pbk)

Creator: Headey, Stephen D., author.

Title: Nice One Centurion / Stephen D. Headey

ISBN: 9781925388831 (Paperback)
9781925388992 (eBook)

Subjects: Soldiers--Humor.
Wit and humor.
Psychology, Military.

Dewey Number: 808.882

Published by **Stephen D. Headey** and InHouse Publishing
www.inhousepublishing.com.au

I would like to dedicate this book to all my fellow Rockapes and Penguins, with a special mention to Mick Cundy who helped me come up with the idea for this book.

A special thank you to Tim Parker who has provided the humorous cartoons contained within.

The contributions from our guys made this book possible and I am deeply grateful.

I would also like to thank my wife Susan Baker who, when times were tough, helped and supported me through difficult times and encouraged me to keep on fighting.

I hope we have done our regiment proud, and that we help our readers with a laugh or two to keep their spirits up.

CONTENTS

Foreword vii

Chapter 1: *In The Beginning.* 1
Chapter 2: *An Officer and a Gentleman* 57
Chapter 3: *March on the Queen's Colour Squadron* 89
Chapter 4: *No Rockets in My Pockets* 119
Chapter 5: *Airborne: A Bar Too Far* 233

About the Authors 265

Foreword

What is the RAF Regiment? A question that is often asked and, I suspect in this day and age, looked up online. The answers are various but the common themes are the fact that it is a corps within the Royal Air Force, when it was founded, what it does, perhaps where it is located, and the sort of 'kit' and weapons it employs.

This is all factually correct and informative but I think it misses the key point. To serve in the RAF Regiment, to be a 'rock', is, at the end of the day, about the people you serve with. Rocks come in all sizes and shapes, from all backgrounds, from varying educational standards and together create a kaleidoscope of characters. They have pride, loyalty to each other, a sense of duty, and a common ethos that makes them, together, stand head and shoulders above other organisations.

It has been my privilege to serve with rocks across the globe, in the worst of conditions and in harm's way, and in the best of places enjoying life to the full. To be a rock is to be a member of a band of brothers second to none and I had no hesitation in agreeing to provide an introduction to this book.

Stephen and his contributors have sought to capture some of the essence of the people that make up the RAF Regiment. Some of the humour reflects the age when the events occurred and must be taken in that context—many of the episodes would, quite rightly, not be seen or tolerated in 2016! This collection was never intended to be an academic history but rather an anecdotal record of life on the front line and the personal memories of those involved. The accuracy is only as good as the memory of those writing the input and if any toes have been trodden on or egos bruised then that is regrettable; it was never the intent.

Take this book as it was meant to be. If you were serving at that time then it will hopefully provide a few laughs and take you back down memory lane. If you were not serving at that time then you missed quite an adventure.

Well done to all those who made this happen. The book is a tribute to rocks everywhere but especially in memory of those members of our corps who have made the ultimate sacrifice over the years and will never be able to read it.

Per Ardua
GES
Air Marshall Graham Edward Stacey CB MBE

CHAPTER 1
IN THE BEGINNING

Daviid William Ahearn

You wanted an early tale, so how about this. 1982 I was hitching back from London to Catterick. Stood at a roundabout near Stanstead Airport when I get a lift from none other than Jimmy Edwards (actor, former RAF pilot).

He'd spotted my kit bag and I told him I was in RAF Regiment.

He told me a tale of his early days in the RAF, as he was put on a holding unit at an RAF station in Norfolk prior to pilot training.

This would have been circa 1940. As there was no such thing as The Regiment back then, he was lumped together with a group of other 'spare wanks' (his words!), given rudimentary training with a Lee Enfield, and used as a quick reaction force.

So one night a report comes in of paratroops on the airfield; he and his mates pile into a truck and drive out into the dark.

Soon after they get to the end of the runway 'all fucking hell broke loose!'. Blokes running around like headless chickens, rifles being fired all over the shop, and bullets whizzing overhead.

Half an hour of this chaos later, a voice from the dark is shouting 'cease fire'.

Turns out the 'paratroopers' were an army patrol that neglected to inform the RAF that they were out there.

Jimmy turns to me and says something I found so funny at the time:

"And when you fuckers were formerly formed a couple of years later it wasn't much better as the army had a perfect excuse to get rid of the troublemakers and mad bastards!"

David Hudson

This is a story about a squadron patrol of 15 Squadron.

Kuantan, in the Malayan jungle in 1968. I was in 1 Section A flight and with us was a lad called Jeff. Now him and another were scouting in front of 1 Section and as anybody who has been in the jungle knows, you could lose someone who is just a few feet away. So we in 1 Section was out of sight of the two scouts when suddenly there came a startled shout and the sound of running feet coming towards us.

What had happened was Jeff and the other lad had slowly gone around a bend when they suddenly came face to face with a tiger, and they all looked at each other.

The two scouts then turned and legged it back towards us. We heard something crashing about in the jungle and the flight commander (who carried the live ammo) went in, and he must have seen the back end of it as he came back to confirm the sighting.

Bill Espie

Swinderby, 1970. Derek and I are JNCOs on 5 Flight and the intake is three flights … and is crap. Bull night, and inspection was so bad the flight commander threw their kit out of the window. Another bull night, and guess who gets dicked for the duty? Yep, you live in. Trolls across at 1900 and its carnage. Absolute no-hopers, so I give them close direction and some muscular counselling for the next hour before our intake sergeant turns up to inspect.

He is GD—old school—and throws a wobbly of volcanic proportions, and on they go again. He says to me, "Esp, they are on GDT in the morning, will you pick them up at 0800 and march them there? NP says I head back to the delights of the Perm Staff bar."

Easy night and next morning a bit of a saunter across to the block to find no flight. "Strange," says I, and wanders to the door of the block with, "Ooonnn parade, 5 Flight," and a few other tender words of encouragement. Nothing, nil, nada, not a stir. I was by this time getting a bit leery so upstairs I went and around the barrack rooms. It was like the Marie Celeste—boots with yellow dusters lay on beds, small tins full of water bumpers in the middle of the room, and a thin veil of polish on the floor. I was starting to consider that the truth was really out there when I heard a whimper from one of the old tall lockers we used then. Esp the investigator quickly ascertained that there was a recruit in said locker and it had been locked from the outside.

Fire extinguisher was more than a match for that lock and soon I had the story. Sarge was not happy with the block and kept giving them an hour to get it up to scratch, spending the in-between to consume a copious quantity of his favourite brown-coloured sherbet water in the mess hall. About midnight he really lost his rag and ordered the room leaders to lock them in their lockers, and then the senior man locked the room leaders in their lockers, and then he locked him in *his* locker and sauntered off back to the mess. He only intended to leave them there for an hour but, well, he got as pissed as a fiddler's bitch and went home to his married quarter at around 2:30, knowing he had the morning off.

As a consequence, sixty recruits spent their night in their lockers, causing untreatable mental injury to most but not as much as to Sarge—yet another severe dig and fine, but as he said to me afterwards, "If you have not had at least two severe digs back in the day, the real hard men DS would make you eat with the pigs!"

Robin Flack

Colerne, '73. A SAC (senior air craftsman) wants to get off the squadron ... gets called into the flight commander's office.

"What's the problem Airman?"
"I need to leave the squadron, Sir."
"Why?"
"You, Sir."
"Me? Why?"
"Every time I see you I want to hug and kiss you, Sir."
"What! Flt Sgt, get this man out of my office!"

It's a good job he was already packed ... or he would have missed his bus!

Robin Flack

OK, a starter ... In a place we were never in (Salalah) in 1973 a certain sergeant had a good idea. We had lots of empty oil barrels, lots of used engine oil, lots of polystyrene packing ... OK guys here's the plan: put the barrel at the FPF, fill with old engine oil, pack with polystyrene, attach two thunderflashes to the barrel with wires running back to the hedgehog ... enemy attack ... attach wires to battery ... BOOM!

The commanding officer (who knew nothing about the 'idea') was invited to attend the test firing. It went BOOM! WOOSH! And showered the whole area with molten polystyrene! The whole hedgehog took cover. Commanding officer's comment after regaining his composure was, "Great idea Sergeant ... but if NATO hear about this we could be in a lot of trouble ... in fact if anybody hears about this we will be in deep shit! *Don't do it again!*"

So the GPMG attached to the ZB298 went to the drawing board. But that's another story ...

Humphrey Howell Humphrey AKA Peter

One of them was when he was trying to enter through some crash gates of an airfield in France that the Germans had recently abandoned. The soil on the other side of the gate looked like it had recently been dug over, and they suspecting that the gate had been booby trapped. They decided to tie a rope to the gate, and hide behind a tree on the other side of the road then pull the gate open with the rope. They all hid behind the tree and pulled on the rope, but the gate just wouldn't open.

So then one of the men suggested tying the rope to the back of the Rolls Royce armoured car using it to pull the gates open.

So the rope was tied to the rear bumper, and they all climbed into the armoured car. My dad instructed the driver to put his foot down, which he did. The gates were pulled open and the tree across the road blew up. So probably a good job they couldn't open it, otherwise I wouldn't be here now typing this.

David William Ahearn

Grobbendonk training camp, Belgium. Mid to late '70s, 16 Squadron of sixteen. Doing some field refresher training. Admin day, so we are tidying the site, etc. Pongo sergeant in charge of camp asks me to burn the rubbish stuffed into two forty-five-gallon oil drums. Suggests I use paraffin. But all the tilley lamps have been filled and there's none to spare. So I get a jerry of petrol and splash a liberal amount into each. It's a nice sunny day. Boiling in fact. I light the first drum, and its goes up nicely. I wander off to get a stick so I can light the second one at arm's length, the heat evaporating the petrol nicely. Pongo sergeant wanders up, and decides to help by lighting the second drum with his lighter.

Boom!

Huge fireball, burning litter all around, and one pongo sergeant on his arse minus eyebrows. He storms up to the boss and complains and the boss just shrugs and tells him it's his own stupid fault for trusting us.

Robin Flack

A long long time ago, in a place we were not in, a certain Scotsman was training for something: running between Bravo and Delta ... oh you guessed! Anyway he came steaming into Delta beating his personal best by nearly two minutes. When questioned he puffed, "Got half way, fooking great camel spider jumped up and chased me!" Oh we did laugh ...

Robin Flack

Early '70s, Colerne. Monday, 0830 hours. SACs Eddie Hill and Mark Kirsh are at their normal post (outside the commanding officer's office).

Two minutes later a very angry CO flies out of his office, down to the surface warfare officer's office, barks some instructions, and leaves. SWO assesses the situation ...

All on parade, *again!* Pick elves and any blunt instruments available issued to the whole squadron.

WTF is going on!

SAC Eddie Hill (quite sheepishly): "Oh ... me 'n Mark invited the local Hell's Angels Chapter to a fight this morning at ten to see who was the best ..."

"FFS! Eddie, we've got enough trouble going on without you inviting it here as well!"

Eddie's reply: "Thought it might be good for riot training ... seven days jankers without privileges, march out!

Humphrey Howell Humphrey AKA Peter

Well once they gained access to the airfield in France they found some ordnance the Germans had left behind in their haste to get away, and my dad and his men were tasked to guard it. It was a bitterly cold night and they were trying to keep warm when one of the men spotted a phosphorous bomb, and said, "Why don't we throw this at the ground to set it off? Then we can all warm ourselves as it burns."

So they took one of the phosphorous bombs and threw it on the ground, setting it off. It was burning away nicely, giving off a lot of heat, and they were all standing there, warming themselves, when one of the men said, "I'm pretty sure I read somewhere that these things burn for a while then explode, killing any fireman trying to put out the flames." So my dad suggested they retire to a safe distance just in case, which was probably a wise decision because shortly after they retired to a safe distance, it did indeed blow up.

David Jeremiah

In the early '70s, was on 48 Sqn at Catterick. The squadron was on a major exercise; I was on C Flight. Our squadron 2IC was there—we called him P.E. (plastic explosive) as he liked to use lots of P.E. whenever he could.

We were doing a fly-in attack. We were briefed by our flight commander that when P.E. goes off we were to break left.

We all broke left, but our flight commander, he broke right; got blown up, had his ear drums blown out, and was thrown out the regiment.

He was the air vice marshall commandant-general of the RAF Regiment's son who was a flight lieutenant (can't remember his name as I just called him Sir).

Humphrey Howell Humphrey AKA Peter

Another story was when he had to take a guy to a port in Northern Africa who was going on compassionate leave due to a death in the family. On the way back from the port, they were running low on fuel and called into an abandoned German Airfield to see if they could find some fuel. All they could find was aviation fuel and some oil, so they mixed the two together to thicken it up a bit. Apparently the Rolls Royce armoured car drove faster than it ever had done before. Unfortunately, they ruined the engine because it almost melted.

Chapter 1: In The Beginning

Peter Huntley

I was on Bravo hedgehog during the the wet season in '72, our dunny (toilet) was below the 50 calibre gun down by the wire. It was an old wooden storage container and was very roomy inside. One morning I went for my constitutional and was sitting on the thunder box contemplating nothing really when I heard a buzzing sound coming from behind and above my head. Looking up, saw about 10,000 big nasty hornets making themselves at home. These things could kill so I removed my bum from said box and did a Usain Bolt out of it.

We discussed how to rid the dunny of the hornets, I think it was Gus who suggested firing a rocket flare at the nest, leaving the door open for them to consider somewhere else.

So off I marched with said firework and approached the dunny.

Opening the door I set off the flare and then stood back out of the way. Well the flare ricocheted around the dunny, hitting every wall and also the hornets.

What I didn't know was that the boss had preceeded me and was sitting on the box not having seen the hornets.

Well the hornets became aroused (as you would) and three squadrons attacked the nearest thing that looked nasty; the boss, followed by pissed off hornets, also did a Usain Bolt from the dunny. The language, for an officer, was appalling.

He remained incognito for the rest of the day, nursing several bumps on his head.

No one told him who had fired the flare but all fingers were pointed at me. Well, at least we had a laugh about it—all except the boss!

Robin Flack

It's a long one so bear with me, but true. 1974 GDOC Salalah. I'm Zero. Callsign Zero Bravo is an officer in the hills in a small forward position heavily armed but also with his pearl-handled six guns (no rounds available in this theatre but he liked them).

"Hello Zero, this is Zero Bravo, over."

"Zero, send over."

"Zero Bravo need help, over."

The officer GDOC duty grabs his telephone handset.

"Hello Zero Bravo, this is Sunray, what help do you need, over."

Zero Bravo: "N-need help getting up … over."

(At this time certain voice procedure has gone right out of the window!)

Sunray: "Why do you need help getting up … have you been attacked … over."

Zero Bravo: "Nope … pissed."

Sunray: "How much have you had?"

Zero Bravo: "Hang on. 1, 2, 3, … 10, 11 …"

Sunray: "You've had eleven cans of beer?! Over."

Zero Bravo: "Nope, still counting, they're the ones on the floor, hang on … some more on the table so … lots …" he giggled.

Sunray: "Zero Bravo this is not good enough—where did you get them?"

Zero Bravo: "Hehehe. Not telling! Shall I sing you a song?"

Peter Huntly

It was a freezing November night and we had left Pennaly camp and were driving in convoy back to Bicester. I was the last four-tonner with a gun behind in the convoy. My commanding officer driver, who couldn't drive, was wrapped in his sleeping bag as we didn't have heaters in the old Bedfords.

Our commanding officer decided en route to drive all the way back to Bicester with no rest break. We were about forty miles from Cirencester when down came a heavy mist and I pulled over as the lads in the back were banging on the cab roof for a slash break.

Well I pulled out after about ten minutes and continued to follow the now-invisible convoy. I spotted, through the mist, the four-tonner with gene some distance ahead and tagged on behind.

We had gone about four miles when the convoy pulled over onto the hard shoulder. Good, I thought, a proper stop. Leaving my non-commanding officer driver sleeping whilst I shook off the icicles, I jumped down and walked over to the gene four-tonner where the crew in the back were lighting up.

"Who are you then?" Said one of the smokers.

They were pongos; somehow I had latched onto an RA convoy that our lot had passed. I quickly got going again and soon the boss was passing us going in the opposite direction on the 'down' side of the dual carriageway.

He must be looking for us and I had been going in the wrong direction, I thought; luckily I found a roundabout two miles further on and turned onto the carriageway the boss had just gone down, so I continued in the same direction, only to see the boss going up the road we had just been on.

Back down to the roundabout I had taken to latch onto the pongo convoy and up the road the boss had taken only to see, to the amusement of the pongos as they must have thought we were doing a scene out of *Keystone Cops*, the boss heading down the other road again.

Switching on I pulled up by the top roundabout and the boss pulled in behind me to then assault me with sailor's language for stopping for a slash break and joining up with the wrong convoy.

Back on the road again we finally got to the outskirts of the quietly slumbering town of Bicester at 0230 hours. We were briefed to drop down a gear when entering said town as not to wake the inhabitants.

I duly dropped down a gear and the muffler fell off. A roar like the coming of Armageddon reverberated around the town, sheep in the fields took off and were last seen in Brighton, old ladies rushed for long disused air raid shelters, blokes having their end away with lonely pongo wives were jumping out of top-floor windows like fleas deserting a newly powdered dog.

I drove into camp, thus awakening the entire married quarters where the boss was waiting for me with his opened Manual of Upset Sailor's Language Book.

Bill Espie

Up country Malaya 1969—Kotta Tinggi JWS out at Lombong Waterfall. My friend with the googly eye has the bright idea of increasing the number of beer chits we get by volunteering us for the shitpit duty. "Two shillings and eleven pence a day for objectionable duties is not to be sneezed at," quoth he. So every morning before we bogged off on training we had the honour of emptying the squadron's elsons into a large pit, slinging some lime on it, and depositing the correct amount of that blue poison Racasan into the new useable elision. It could have been the heat or the lack of a copious amount of Tiger (every time 15 organised the airdrop the palette with the beer on creamed it) but after a while Yorky started to take what I thought was an unhealthy interest in the contents of said elisions. So I was not surprised when he appears at my side in the queue for breakfast (another advantage—poo pit team went to the front).

"Quick Esp, come and look at this, I found the World's Biggest Turd (WBT)."

Faced with a mess tin full of powdered milk swimming in some form of liquid, I joined him and sure enough he had indeed snagged a monster. My little inner voice started to murmur when he started to measure it and then, using his gobbling rods, carefully lifted it out for close examination. The only flat surface we had was the bonnet of OC 15 Sqn's rover, all very spruce with a lovely white canvas cover for the spare wheel on the bonnet. Yorky then tastefully arranges the

WBT into an arrangement like an upside-down ice-cream cone on the white tyre cover. At that moment Mick Roberts grabbed me to go and draw the A43 for the day's training so I left him gloating over his prize.

Perhaps my inner voice was turned down too far; anyway after a hard day's training standing in the cook house tent queue that night, minding my business, the squadron warrant officer comes up and looks at me and Yorky and says, "You two, commanding officer's tent, now!"

One didn't argue with John Gorman and so we paraded at the commanding officer's tent. Piggy came to the point quickly. "What sort of insult did you intend when you left that turd on OC 15's vehicle?"

Me, hearing the inner voice hitting the loud pedal, and listening to the gibbering loon going on about how long we had been on the crap house gang—we had taken time to make sure there was no one suffering from any foreign disease by inspecting the bogs every day. Piggy was having a good day, so we got a lecture about taking mundane cities too seriously and we could get out. Result: the inner voice shouted and I got as far as the door before the commanding officer asked Yorky which bogs it came from.

Quick as a flash the crafty one says, "Officer's toilets Sir," to which Piggy had a wee smile.

"Out, the pair of you." I actually got my hand on the tent flap before the loon asks, "Any idea what caused it Sir?"

"For your information it was babies' heads and bacardi and coke," thus confirming it was his—so somewhere in the Ulu north of Lombong waterfall lies the last resting place of the World's Biggest Turd where the sun comes up over China—just across the bay.

As a surprise consequence of the World's Biggest Turd, Yorky and I were removed from the chain gang by the commanding officer on the grounds that he didn't want to see two of his potential NCOs ruined because they were keen. Returned to the flight with a status of rockstars, we got deeper and deeper into our training. People will talk about the hot countries and all that, but there is no shorter nor more efficient way of learning your trade as being in the jungle. Everything carried on your back, chlorined water, piss-wet through all the time (sweat or rain), putting one foot in front of the other, next hill, next tin of Tom Piper stew, next harbour. Our flight commander at the time shall remain nameless, not because he was a total dung head—he wasn't—but because he turned out a great officer, although on the Rapier-side of the house, and has remained a mate over almost fifty years. Well anyway, back to the plot—jungle harbouring drill were an essential for any field fight to master. Contrary to what I saw subsequently in Belize, nobody moved in the Malayan jungle after dark. You went firm, sorted the harbour and comms out, and waited for daylight, perfectly able to scramble the crap out of anybody who strayed into your locale. Nothing difficult about the set-up: three sections in straight lines in a triangle—GPMG at each apex, Flight HQ in the middle. Comms were always line pulls for silent *stand to*, and a vine would be secured at chest height along the perimeter to indicate 'no further forward movement'. Sections sorted out their own stags and, hey presto! Not a problem. We all made bashas ground sheet and some sticks for the night. My problem this night was that I was on the HQ brick carrying the A41 (radio set), rear link back to squadron. Of course it would never work—it never worked at Feldom so there was no chance of it working in the ulu. Anyway, we get set and I share the bashas with the flight commander and the lines come in from the sections just the usual green twine. One tug *stand down*, series of tugs *stand to*, etc. All tested, we fed hard.

Routine: no fires, water and Tom Piper stew cold—eat your heart out Jamie Oliver. Settle down for the night and problem number one emerges: the flight commander had cut the cord to length about three feet too short and they could only come to the radio op just outside the basha. By moving around I could get all three on my hand if my arm was outstretched. Still a minor discomfort.

We settle down, until about an hour after *stand down* I hear a very light southern Irish accent saying, "Halt who goes there?" And a reply along the lines of, "Friend," followed by a very pregnant pause and about fifty rounds from Ted Flint's gun. No need for *stand to*; the world had woken up. False alarm—one of the lemons had wandered outside the vine, been spotted by Paddy C., and challenged. As Paddy explained later, "For the life of me Sor, I couldn't remember the password so I shot the bastard to be on the safe side." Rocks made sturdier choices in them days. Anyway it merely served to unnerve our young boss and throughout the night the flight was up and down on *stand to* like a Penang Island hooker's knickers.

Problem number two: because the cords were a little short, when himself whispered, "Stand 'em to Esp," he leapt out of the basha and with unerring accuracy put his right foot in exactly the same spot every time—on my hand that was holding the comm's cords. Reflex to pain—open your hand, and cord shoots away in the dark and you spend the next half-an-hour finding it again. By the time you have found it it's *stand down*, back in the basha. After this had happened three times, I decided to modify the comm's system, cut the cords about a yard long and tie the ends to the basha structure and the other end to the hand, which was now inside the basha and not getting used as a hog roast by every mossie in Malaya.

Peace, perfect peace, for almost five hours until a couple of loud cries woke me and looking up I saw a large black shape obscuring the lightening sky.

"He's in the basha, Esp, stop him!"

Well you have to, don't you, young fit lad—boxer and quick, everything went into that right hook, which connected wonderfully, like a four off the meat of the bat. Follow up—some nice rib shots, get the boot in and pin it to the floor, yelling like a demented budgie, "Got him, Sir, got the evil bastard here!" punctuated by another knee somewhere painful. Hands in the dark took over and Mick Roberts secured him as I asked Mick, "He got in the basha Sarge, Boss alerted me."

Mick gently soothed me by saying, "Esp, that is the boss."

Oops—a major SpecSavers moment that earned me a night ambush with the Ghurkas. But that's another story…

Andy Ingam

48 Sqn, RAF Aldergrove NI, early 1970s. I was off duty in the GDOC one evening, about to settle down as all the patrols had finished for the day.

The next minute the Hadley Box lights up like a Christmas Tree—this was a direct landline comms system, you just pressed in a button, pressed 'call', which squalked at the far end, and pressed 'talk' when they answered. Anyway everyone was now calling me at the same time; ATC, airport police, MOD police, etc. Each in turn reported an explosion in the direction of the airport terminal (Belfast International, over the other side of the airfield from us).

I went through my checklist, deployed a patrol section, brought the IRF at Hector's House to immediate readiness, dispatched an RAF police patrol, and then informed the commanding officer. About fifteen minutes later the commanding officer and 2IC arrive (in civvies) just as the SITREP comes in from our patrol. They report a large hole in the chainlink fence near a BFI as they cordon off the area and set up a VCP.

The boss looks over to me and says, "Andy, you had better go out there and take charge!" So off I go in the duty wagon with a driver having grabbed the 9mm pistol from the drawer.

On arrival the second commander has everything under control, so I liaise with the airport police, MOD police and RAF police and ensure that the cordon is secure and it is just about dark. The next thing I hear is the sound of an SLR being cocked (one sound you never forget) and the challenge, "Halt or I fire." (Or whatever it was back then on the Green Card.) I look over and one of our Gnrs (a senior SAC with over fifteen years' service—we had lots of them back then, thank goodness) taking aim at OC RAF police (in civvies) who were climbing through the hole in the fence towards us! As I recognised him (he was an LFF) I yelled 'stop' before he was shot! It transpired he had driven around the airfield and decided to have a look at what was going on without checking in with us or his guys—what a plonker! Never heard such back-peddling when I informed him he was almost shot!

Picture courtesy of Barry Love.

Chaz King

A bloody great hole so we could drive the four-tonners in towing the Bofors then drive the truck out.

The hole would have been around sixty feet long with ramps at both ends and dug about three feet deep. Holes were cut out into the walls to hold the C42 radio, which was about a metre squared. We dug another flipping hole to house the Meadows generator. This was 2.5 tonnes on its own chassis. We also dug a hole big enough to hold an aircraft engine box back in the woods behind the gun. I think this measured about 15' by 8' by 8' and we lived in it when on exercise.

The whole thing was underground and we built steps to get down to it. Pop Johnson was my sergeant.

The daft thing was that we only used this site a couple of times then made it a dummy site and moved us outside the wire to a field at the bottom of the runway. Not allowed to dig here so we were trying to disguise a four-and-a-half-tonne gun and generator and tents in an open ploughed up field that some super intelligent young officer decided was a good location. The amount of times we got bogged in and had to be towed out!

Andy Ingam

The sheep turd in the glass! In the summer of 1974, 48 Sqn and 26 Sqn deployed to Otterburn training area for a tactical fighter meet. This was an opportunity for the gun crews and Tigercat crews to practice tracking live targets and for our OP screen to practice reporting. By now I was the squadron adj and signals officer, so my job was to run the squadron CP way out in the training area. As it was summer I thought it would be good to take the squadron motorcycles with us, so about six of us rode them from Catterick to Otterburn and used them during the week as DRs delivering signals, video for debriefing, etc. Anyway, I digress.

We were only required to man the kits during flying hours roughly nine to five, so our off-duty time was spent back in Otterburn Camp. 26 Sqn had come over from Germany and brought a truck full of beer, which we consumed over the week. On the last night we all got stuck in at our officers' and SNCOs mess/bar when the 26 Sqn officers decided they would start ejecting the 48 Sqn junior officers through the windows (this was a regular occurrence at RAF Aldergrove between the Rocks and the helicopter crews). I decided I was having none of this (having been 'windowed' many times before) and with my beer climbed up onto the roof of the building to sit things out. Empty beer cans and then sheep turds (the camp was littered with them) were thrown up at me, but eventually they gave up.

When I came down I decided it was time for revenge and dropped a sheep turd into Dick Moore's (who later became our CG) beer! He was livid and turned on me, but I was pretty agile and ducked away through a door. Dick gave chase, raising his glass of beer to throw over me, when his hand and glass connected with the top of the door frame! Beer, blood, and broken glass everywhere! Hilarity momentarily over while the doc (who was three sheets to the wind) gets out his medical bag and casually sews up Dick's hand, with us all sitting round watching him. Drinking then resumed!

P.S. Dick still has the scar on his hand!

Humphrey Howell Humphrey AKA Peter

Another time, I was coming back in an Anson on leave, and they were flying in thick fog, so the pilot told my dad to stick his head out the window and tell him when he could see the Thames Estuary.

So he stuck his head out the window and was straining his eyes for possible landmarks when suddenly out of the fog appeared Battersea Power Station's chimneys. So he pulled his head in quickly and shouted, "Climb, climb, climb!!!"

Close one.

Andy Ingam

48 Sqn, RAF Aldergrove NI, early 1970s. Once again duty officer in the GDOC late at night. Cup of coffee in hand and settling down to watch a bit of TV when I hear a distant 'crack, crack, crack', the Hadley Box lights up and the direct line to ATC rings. The duty air traffic controller is yelling. "We are under attack, we have just been shot at, I have seen tracer rounds fly past our windows!"

Everyone starts flapping, what is happening? The MOD police guards out on the airfield also report being shot at, the RAF police at the main gate report shots fired. Patrol sections woken up and the IRF alerted.

Next thing the Hadley Box squalks from Alexander Barracks (adjacent to RAF Aldergrove)—their duty officer rather sheepishly explains that one of their ferret armoured recce vehicle crews just had an ND on return from patrol—they must have fired off a burst of three to five rounds from their .30 machine gun right past ATC!

David Bowen

Time about 1977-ish, place doesn't matter. Some Rocks are drinking with our colonial brother of the USMC when a marine turns to a young Rock and says, "So tell, where were you Brits in Vietnam?"

Without batting an eyelid the young Rock replies, "We thought the Veitcong were doing alright without us."

Punch-up now follows, as would be expected.

Robin Flack

Gibralter '74, our first time out there, relieving 3 Queens (oh don't go there … I'm being serious!) from their hard (the gates were shut FFS!) border patrol duties. Squadron assembled in the gym for briefing on do's 'n dont's by snowdrop sergeant, including places/bars not to visit. At the end of the briefing said snowdrop leaves.

Commanding officer clears his throat. "Ahem! OK men please give a round of applause to the snowdrop ... he's saved you a lot of time looking. You now know where to fight, fornicate, and get pissed on the cheap, without having to ask! Well done and thank you Sergeant PRATT!

Robin Flack

Germany, in a wood, mid '70s (if I told you where I would have to kill you so shhhh). Rumours are rife that there is a local call girl centre not far from where we are hiding. Sure enough on day two, OC site gets a visit from a representative from school expressing her concerns as to safety, etc. OC site draws himself up and states, "Madam, you have my word that no member of this site will at any time put your girls in any form of danger or compromising situation." (Yeah right!)

Madam OC centre's reply: "Thank you for your assurance ... but ... ahem, I'm more concerned for the safety of your men ... it's a corrective school and putting it delicately, a lot of the girls are not tame! Oh that was a great site briefing the next morning.

Richard Sharp

Spearpoint, 1976. I was on 18 Sqn with Wallace, Smith, Roxburgh, and others. Geordie was on shit pit duties. He followed the wing commander to the pit. After the wing commanding officer had finished and departed, Wallace scooped up one of the wing commander's 'deposits' on his shovel and took it to the mess tent where he placed it in front of the officer and said, "Is this one of yours, Sir?"

That man could get away with murder.

Robin Flack

1974, somewhere in the sky on a C130, three hours' low-level flying before the jump. The ex-Rock turned PJI—I will call him

Digger—blows his cheeks out a couple of times, produces a sick bag from his pocket, covers his face, and makes lots of 'huweee' noises. Looks in the bag, shouts "Ooh, carrots!", grabs a handful of diced carrots from the bag and eats them.

The 'huweee' ripple effect up the kite was incredible! Glad to get the door open that day and get out!

Robin Flack

Another true airborne story. Mid-70s, hankley common night, descent sim 31s with containers. Due to a timing error, another and I meet under the aircraft and one goes through the other's rigging lines (still disputed to this day as to who went through whose!) the following conversation ensued:

Moi: "We are entangled."

Him: "Shall I cut my lines and pull my reserve?"

Moi: "No! They might be mine!" After a quick assessment: "We are OK … coming down a bit quicker but OK."

Moi to ground staff: "Two men entangled, both OK, coming in a bit quick."

Ground staff, shining torches to the sky: "We can see you, carry on!"

Moi to ground: "Turn them fecking torches off, can't see a fecking thing!"

Moi to the other guy: "OK, release your container then, I will do the same."

Him: "OK …"

Moi to him: "We are coming in a bit quick, when you hear a thump and me moan, brace yourself, 'cause you're next!"

Thump, moan … followed by *thump, moan* …

Moi: "You OK?"

Him: "Yep."

Moi: "Thank feck for that!"

Officer IC ground crew to moi: "Well talked down Airman. But next time could you make the language a little less colourful?"

Moi: "Sir! With respect! I do not intend to make this a feckin' habit!"

Johnny Ballantyne

Completing a 'Jungle Survival Course' in Malaya, I made it clear to the chief instructor that I had a great fear of snakes.

On one exercise acting as advance patrol scout moving up a jungle track, I came across a dead tree blocking my route forward. How I worked up the courage to continue, I do not know. I checked all around, under it, and leaned over the tree to ensure no snakes were present on the other side. Gingerly I lifted one leg over and checked again; nothing but great relief. Preparing to proceed I looked up and there across the track was a spider's web with a spider the size of a dinner plate.

One look and I about turned, cleared the dead tree, and was off down the track. Reaching the rest of the patrol, I was rugby tackled by the chief instructor and my OG trousers stripped down before I could say a word.

"Where did the snake bite you?"

Eventually I managed to explain to him that nothing had bitten me, and about the spider. He then went off to investigate whilst I recovered my OGs.

His explanation to all on his return: "It would have given a sore bite but not lethal."

Thankfully that was my last advance scout duty on the course, which I did pass.

Vyv Walters

So it was spring 1972: I had just done few weeks at Colerne and failed miserably, so they posted me to 63 Sqd, who were just arriving in flights at North Luffenham from Singapore. I went to stores, got a set of greens, then went for a nose in the hangar. There was a long line of Rocks ... yep, one long line, and at the front was a warrant officer, Tilley (think that's correct), shouting at the guys so they were in a straight line. Stood in the background with flying off Tim Martin (RIP) was a female medical officer, and a CPL (corporal) from the med centre. The warrant officer shouted out, "When I give the order I want to see your trousers down to your ankles ... release belts ... trouseeeerrrrrrrs down!" and like a QCS drill movement, trousers were dropped to the ankles. At this point I'm shaking my head wondering what the hell I had let myself in for.

Then a Scottish CPL, one Willie Harper, crept up behind me and said, "WTF you doing here laddie?"

I explained that I was just joining the squadron then enquired what was happening.

He looked and smiled at my innocent face. "It's the SMO just checking the boys for gonorrhoea and syph."

I said, "Oh! Of course," and drifted back towards the block.

I had never seen so many suspect willies stood to attention in one place. Then my career started, ha ha!

Bill Hayes

I recall in about 1969 myself and the late SAC Alan McQuiston were returning from a *big* night in Singapore where copious amounts of Tiger Beer and local brandy Sam Soo (that wasn't fit for human consumption) had been guzzled. Two very pissed and happy Rockapes sitting in a taxi talking absolute shite when Alan suddenly opened the door to the, by this time, low flying cab. I initially thought that he was going to jump out and practise para rolls but thankfully instead he had a good chunder. The door shuts and we continue on with the verbal diarrhoea. We travelled a few more miles and I was becoming more and more puzzled with something that didn't seem to be right, but I couldn't work out exactly what it was.

Then I realised what it was.

When we started the night Alan had sported a wide, toothy grin, but now there was a large gap where his four front teeth used to be. It looked like he had left them on the Bukit Timah Road when he had his chunder.

The funny part was that they stayed like that until the last time that I saw Alan in 1972 when he was posted to 34 Sqn Cyprus.

RIP old mate—we did have some great laughs. More tales for a later time I think.

Robin Flack

1975. The well-known Airborne Sqn are due to move to Catterick (boo!). I'm on the advance party. We arrive, sign over married quarters (observing many a twitching net curtain ... ooh they're comming! Hide!), and I and three others retire to the Angel for a quick few.

"Are you 2 Sqn?" the barman enquires.

"Yes."

"OK you're barred!"

WTF! Same at the Bay and the Twig! Banned from all three pubs before we even got there! Well, that soon got sorted! Duty rumours from 48 were rife.

Chris Deponeo

1978, The Berlin Tattoo, in my room at Gatow, was Stew Fern, Terry Midgley, Roy Jones 347, JC Conneley, and we were rioting loud and drunk. A CPL came in full of anger to tell us all to shut the hell up again! But in minutes he had a bottle of Blue Nun tipped down his gullet and Midg had him standing against the wall with a traffic cone on his head and a matchbox on top, and Midg was trying to knock it off by throwing golf balls at it. Then Terry decided he was going to show us some kendo, so he pulled the head off a broom.

We were all in bulck with laughter anyway but just at the exact moment Terry was raising his 'sword' over his head to perform a downward blow, just at that very moment, Trev 'The Fryery' Ford walked into the room in his grundies (Y-fronts, by the way) with an unlit fag to his lips pinched between finger and thumb. With raised pinkies, he was demanding light for the CPL! Light for the CPL. I think he had been acting for the Tattoo—and fuckin' wallop! Down came the broom shank right on top of Trev's bonce, we pissed ourselves.

In the morning, all very much the worse for wear, 0700 *bang bang bang* a German worker was knocking a hole in the wall under our room. 347 hung himself out of the window to bollock the workman and he shouted so loud at him he made himself throw up—all over the German worker! The powers that be were not amused.

Then we invented a drink called The Bismarck! But that's another story.

David Hudson

This is a story about digging bogs in the field, which we all must have done at one time or another. The bloke in question is Yorkie Pilling of A Ft. 15—F Sqn, in about 1968. This photo of a bog was taken in the jungle of Malay. The reason this photo was taken was because on this day it was Yorkie Pilling's day to dig the bogs and digging bogs in the jungle was no easy matter due to all the tree roots. So on this day the squadron halted and Yorkie duly dug a Fts. bog. No sooner had he finished than the commanding officer ordered the squadron to move.

Later we stopped again and the same thing happened. So you can understand that by the end of the day Yorkie was not a happy chappy. So at the end of the day he decided to build a bog to end all bogs. So here is a photo of the best dug bog in all the Malayan jungle.

David Bowen

On 21 July 1977 it was my 21st. I was in a side room in the surgical ward at Wegberg with my forearm strapped to the bed to immobilise me. First, mid-afternoon my girlfriend of the time, an RAF nurse, walked in wearing an overcoat (strange for July). She dropped it and was wearing only heels, stockings, and suspender—what a start to my birthday! When she had given me my present the boys from 16 turned up and we proceeded to drink in true Rock fashion.

I got charged four times that day all while immobile, strapped to a bed in hospital, so all I can say is thank you to Rosemary and the boys of 16 for a birthday to remember.

P.S. Half the boys who came were on the Sqn Nijmegen team who were shipped back and banned from Nijmegen for life—but that's another story.

Robin Flack

OK standby, it's the big one: Salalah 1974 (oh my God, I said that place's name in open conversation! Oh sod it, we were there, OK?). Our Barnes Wallace of a sergeant has another 'great idea'.

Sir! Sir! If we connect up the GMPG in SF Mount to the ZB298, when contact is made the gun is already pointing at the target, therefore saving time. The number one gun can just squeeze the trigger and job done! All the drawings won't cost anything ... can I try it Sir, can I can I, pretty please!"

OC flight, sighing: "OK sergeant, carry on."

the day arrives and the two items have been cobbled together with metal bars, rope, and black bodge tape. It works ! The CO is summoned and after a long briefing on how he got the idea and the principles of use, we are set for the first live firing. The radar head moves to the left with the gun, then traverses to the the right; the gun follows, eyebrows are raised in an 'oh my God, he's got something here' type way.

"Contact as indicated!" shouts the sergeant. "Rapid fire!"

Number one gun squeezes the trigger and lets of twenty rounds, at which point the radar head shakes free of its mounting, falls on number one gun's head, causing him to squeeze the trigger again. Thirty rounds are sprayed all over the place, at which time smoke is coming from the radar base.

Sergeant, stands to attention, says, "Needs a bit more work, Sir, but in theory it works."

Sharp intake of breath from the CO, who picks up a large stick followed by FL.

"You can do the fecking paperwork for this one! And if he has any more 'great ideas', hit him with this! You have my word you will not be charged."

Patrick Turner

Gerry Graham was the number seven on the gun near Butcher radar—correct me if I'm wrong, I think it was Bravo. He decided to have a BBQ and invited the rest of the squadron. After getting the fire lit in the forty-five-gallon half-drums and getting all the snap ready, he decided that said fire needed a boost, so using the five-gallon jerry cans, he heaved it on the BBQ and had to jump back, suffering singed eyebrows. Consequently the airfield crash crews were called to put the roaring inferno out.

When the boss was bollocking Gerry he said, "Well CPL Graham, what have got to say for yourself?"

To which Gerry replied, "I have to say I'm sorry Sir."

"I should think so CPL—are you truly sorry?"

"Yes Sir, I'm sorry, I didn't have the chicken a bit closer, it would've been done a treat."

Ian Boyce

Late '75, young Ian has recently been promoted CPL and has been sent to SCHINF Warminster. All NCOs in the regiment are qualified instructors to conduct/supervise on ranges comensurate with their rank. Not so in the infantry; NCOs must attend SCHINF InfDiv JNCO Skill at Arms course, a fairly intensive course run over two months. Whole course is around 150: all cap badges; loads of paras, guards, and gurkas; and two blue-jobs, me and George Bray (who was an SI on my FT1 towards the end). The course is split into two divisions and several syndicates. In mine were a sergeant LI, two L/sergeants from foot guards, and remainder were CPLs of various seniority. I was probably newest. Our SI was Paddy Byrne (Eniskillen Fusilier), who went on to be the corps sergeant major of SASC.

Luck would have it, I had to take the first TP (teaching practice), so when I was ready to begin, I slammed to attention, made the class "Sit UP!" and asked for permission to carry on, in best 159 fashion. Paddy nearly dropped his pipe and spilled his tea; once he had calmed down, he stated;"CPL Boyce, this is Warminster, *not* Pirbright, now relax and carry-on."

I was nearly as taken aback as he was, so I re-evaluated and continued the lesson. The course progressed favourably, with myself and L/sergeant Scott (Coldcream) vying to be top of our squad. I remained keen for the first four weeks. Sadly, after the mid-course break, when we had a weekend off I lost some of my competitive edge; I was getting bored seeing all the same presentations/demos that I had just seen on my FT1 and I just wanted it to be over. I have never been one to go to the squad room at night to 'rehearse' my lessons—I would prepare it and go through it in my head and that worked for me.

I had a TP one day, got a C grade, and was happy that I would not get another the next day. We had three TPs to prepare each night, one of which this night was IWS fitting/use with the GPMG. Next day I was sat in the class and Paddy told me I was up, with the IWS/GPMG (which of course I knew inside-out). Lesson went well, till it came to the part where I showed the class how to remove the IWS from the gun ... it would not come off, oops! Paddy asked if I had 'rehearsed' the lesson, the obvious answer was no, so I now became known as 'Boyce The Cuff' (as well as Biggles, as I was a blue-job).

The course ran its course. Towards the end, one sports afternoon we did 'Shoot-Lauf', a long orienteering course around Salisbury Plain, wearing belt kit, carrying an SLR, with the assault course culminating in a falling plate shoot. I was paired up with Scotty, my arch enemy on the squad, and we pissed it, winning the event by a mile.

End of course, in the training theatre, we were given our results. George gets an A grade, I get a B, Scotty gets a C; which is a pass, but he does not get to wear the Warminster crossed rifles over his stripes. He was livid. To make things worse, we should have been presented with 'The Commandants Prize', for winning 'Shoot-Lauf'. That year it was not presented, as a blue-job won it—ho-hum.

Robert Booth

A Flight 51 Sqn, '74. Deployed to Hong Kong in company with Taff Tyndall, Ginge Roffey, Mike (Dobbin) Kerswill, Curly Connelly, and Chris Chandler, to name a few. One fine day we set off in a landing craft for a football match on a distant island. Turned out to be a prison island. We got ready and were warming up when the whole inmate population were brought out and lined four-deep around the pitch. After the first half and losing pretty badly, Ginge encouraged us to be friendly and have a chat with the opposite players. So being the conversational types, we asked, "How are you doing? What are you in for?" Answer, "Oh, professional football player, taking bribes."

"Right, and how many in the team are professionals?"

"Ten."

"Oh—who is the odd one out then?"

"That's the centre forward, he is in for three axe murders."

We lost badly. Later after a BBQ on the beach with the warders, we set off on our return journey in the LSL. The guy taking us back offered to go via all the islands on a pub crawl. This was an interesting trip, which included hitting the jetty three or four times before docking as the guy steering had drunk as much as us. After we left the dock some returned to Kai Tak, others went off downtown. One of our number was adopted by some American marines and taken back to their ship in port. A no-show at parade the next morning. Sometime later that morning a helicopter from the ship that had sailed in the early hours of the morning brought him back.

David Hudson

This is about a convoy I was escorting on, which was ambushed at army checkpoint Bravo at, I think, Al Mausure in Aden.

In 1967 about Sept/Oct time. I was on 1 LAA Sqn. This checkpoint Bravo was at the end of the causeway that went between RAF Khomaksar and Slave Island. We were escorting a few busloads of Penguins back towards the RAF Base. There were three of us in the land rover and our job was to drive ahead of the convoy and then stop the local traffic at road junctions to stop them from splitting the convoy. On approaching the roundabout where checkpoint Bravo was, I was the first one out stopping the traffic from Al Mausure. So I was nearest the buildings but on the opposite side of the roundabout to checkpoint Bravo. As the convoy was approaching the roundabout the ambush started.

At first I was busy trying to stop the traffic from intermingling with the convoy as it picked up speed, going past behind me. When the convoy was nearing the end I turned around in order for my land rover to stop and pick me up. Unfortunately it sped past me, leaving me out in the open. I then heard an army lad shouting, "They're on the roofs!" At that moment all hell broke loose from the army GPMGs. I turned around and saw movement at the edge of the roofs and fired a quick shot before they disappeared, driven back by the army firing. As I was nearest the buildings I could not see the roofs, so didn't fire again.

I was still standing out in the open as all this happend very quickly and felt very foolish as an army lad who was in the GPMG tower in the middle of the roundabout shouted for me to take cover. To this day I have no idea of how long I was there, as the firing stopped and started a number of times. I know it stopped once and I put my head up to notice women in those black burka robes come walking across the road behind me, and once they had gone it started up again. I also saw while the firing was going on a pongo from the GPMG tower started sliding down the ladder like firemen do and running towards the checkpoint. Then he was running back, loaded up with ammo boxes. To this day I don't know how he managed to climb back up the ladder with those ammo boxes. Finally, a long while after the firing had stopped, I ran across the road and roundabout to the army checkpoint, where I waited for someone to come and pick me up.

It must have been bad at the squadron as the commanding officer himself came to pick me up. I was not debriefed and no one told me what was happening at the squadron or what was being said over the radio net.

While I was stuck at checkpoint Bravo, I put photos on another regi. site, and when I put my Aden photos up I also put the story up, hoping someone would tell me what happend at the squadron. But as yet no one has. The photo is of checkpoint Bravo taken from the causeway with the GPMG tower in the middle and the buildings on the right. The map is the airfield, the causeway, checkpoint Bravo, the roundabout, and Al Mausure.

Robert Booth

51 Sqn, singly barrack block, '74–'77. A fine AOC (air officer commanding) parade day, or not. Wet weather program. Guin sent by SWO to stores to sign out the Wellington boots for use on the inspection, only to be told, "Sorry, the Rocks have them all signed out." SWO turns up at the block and finds all the boots lined up in the air raid shelter under the accommodation. Turns out the tunnel beneath the barrack block and the WRAF block was flooded with rain water.

Wouldn't have wanted to dirty the floors.

Bill Robbie Robinson

Always lumbered with carrying the A41 when out on foot patrols in Aden. Always dreaded having to use it during a contact as it was not that reliable in built-up areas; without line of sight, chances were you wouldn't get through. Remember, we used to use the battery to power the radio mounted on a shelf above the door in the defence section accommodation in Troodos.

One night when we were locked away the troops decided they were going to have a session on the Ouija board. They eventually got a response from a French knight who they tormented until the A41 battery flew from the shelf into the window at the other end of the room, bursting the shutters open. Needless to say, Ouija board sessions stopped for the rest of our detachment. Spooky, but I was there to witness its truth.

Robert Booth

51 Sqn, 1975, Hedgehog Bravo, Salalah. 'Contact Contact', all hell broke loose. 81mm opened up, the .5, the SF GPMG.

Someone was hollering to cease fire when it all calmed down and we could hear properly again.

Turned out the person operating the ZB298 had called the contact from the hits on the screen but then discovered the azimuth brake had unlocked and he was looking at the town behind us.

This was the same bloke who decided to protect himself in the ZB tower at night by wiring up the metal staircase to several A41 batteries. That ended badly when an officer doing an unannounced inspection got burnt hands.

David Jeremy Wilson

On 72 Sqn RAF Odiham in August 1976. We didn't have seperate blocks for Rocks as most were in married quarters so were thrown in with a mix of Guins, Army Navy, and Royal Marines.

In my bed space, I shared with two army lads from the signals regiment. We all had different bull nights just to add to the confusion. One night the two army lads were privy to the equivalent of AOC inspection, so had bed packs, the lot, but it was my night off. Us Rocks, however, wore the same DMS as the pongos and I was lying on my pit with my shirt off reading a book. We still had to come to attention, however, when an officer appeared.

The pongos colonel arrived and we all stood to attention. He looked at the army fella and then at me and immediately asked his sergeant to take my name, and said, "You're a slovenly soldier, aren't you? I've seen you before somewhere haven't I?"

I said, "I have no idea Sir."

"What regiment you with—I'll have you on a charge for this!"

I said, "I'm David Willson Sir, RAF Regiment."

His face went red. "What's a bloody Rockape doing with my lads, Sergeant? Get him moved at once!"

It was so funny—I was sure he burst a blood vessel.

Richard Hawkes

On exercise when 16 Sqn was a gun squadron, we were on Stamford training area when the squadron silverware came out for the officer's dinner. Six of us were volunteered to be waiters for them.

Well, all was going well till one of us had to go and take their orders for the first course. Someone goes out and instead of going round the table, he stood there and said, "Hands up who wants soup."

A couple of hands started to be raised until they saw the squadron commander's face. The warrant officer went off his head at him. I can't remember who it was but the commanding officer was MJ.

David Jeremy Wilson

Salalah, Oman, 51 Sqn, 1974. Life on a tour for myself. I was on B Flight; our section comprised of myself and Ronald, chappy who manned the GPMG in the pill box on HH Bravo. Thomas Carr,

Smudge Smith, J. J. Dave Bowen, Beano, Steve Morley, Paul Kelly, CPL Robson, CPL Evans, and FO Piggy Barns are the names I remember. Roll call on the rest.

We worked a three-day rotation first day on; the hedgehog would be to arrive in the morning and change batteries. Spend most of the day lazing around, but two men on duty on lookout. Some SAC training. At about 1600 we would have tea cooked by our chef David Bowen. At 1700 we stripped and cleaned and lightly oiled all guns; at 1800 *stand to*. And for one whole hour we would have fire missions laying down fire on enemy positions radioed in by 22 SAS, or a free-for-all shooting at anything we fancied. Stand down and guard duties and Zb 298 duties.

The next day we had off we would sleep, and spend time in The Crazy Camel club getting drunk on double double rum and coke for a hundred baizers. Spend our dosh in the NAAFI or at night in open air cinema. Trips to the markets or swimming at the beach, fresh coconuts filled with rum. Or in the swimming pool.

The mess served the most delious camel steaks and ice cream to die for! The dobi waller washed your clothes.

Day three for SACs was an admin day; usually education LACs did training. This was our life for four months, broken only by the odd fire fight or attack.

But the best sight of all and what I remember most was watching the tracer fire lighting up The Jebel at night, followed by the camp artillery opening up with the 25-pounders or the 55 tom tom. Oh what a lovely war. Ha ha.

Bill Hayes

Picture a mad drunken night in the Malcolm Club in Tengah, early 1970s. Dozens of us there getting blind after a trip into the Ulu for a few weeks. The usual hijinks were happening: singing our ditties about tearing across the donga at ninety miles an hour, Zulu

Warrior, and doing the dance of the flaming arseholes. Taffy Pugh decided to put out the fire that I had lit doing the said dance, but threw his pint at my head instead of my arse. The glass had slipped out of his hand due to (a) his hand and the glass being wet and (b) him being paralytic. The end result was me copping a nice semi-circular cut on the forehead that bled like buggery due to being soaked in piss. Someone called the scuffers who arrived at the mayhem and the young LAC acting CPL just about went wobbly at the knees at the blood and the crowd that he was walking into. I told him to fuck off nicely and that I had hurt myself by practising origami or some such shit. I never saw a more relieved young man when he realised that he didn't have to lose his life to the drunken rabble, at least on that evening.

Down to see the MO, stitched up, and back on the piss with Taff the next afternoon.

Move on to 2005 and I have an itch in the lumpy part of the well-healed scar. I scratched it and was a bit amazed to pull out a piece of the pint pot that had been there all those years and had worked itself out of my head. Told my present missus how it had got there and pissed ourselves laughing.

Good days and wild times with the best mates you could ask for. I wonder where they all are now?

Robert Booth

51 Sqn Harrier exercise in Germany. Early to mid '70s. We had been deployed to a WWII German hospital site. No digging because of the potential of finding bodies. Lots of incidents; one tent burned down when the paraffin heater or Tilly lamp fell over when the guys were asleep. No drinking, but the officers all went out on the piss; one fell asleep on the portaloo. Cue squadron warrant officer with broom handle pushing him over, *and* the loo—the stench was not pleasant.

Then five of us were selected to be enemies for the day, to test Harrier site's defences. We were given free choice as to weapons. We all took GPMGs. Dropped off about a mile from the site, walked through all the outer defences—they didn't even see us. Got to about fifty yards from the aircraft and opened up with all our weapons. That finally got their attention. The DI staff wanted to see the site prisoner handling so they deemed us captured when we ran out of ammo. First man up to me tried to take the GPMG from me by the barrel, off to the medic with him and his burnt fingers. Then after no search we were taken to the site CP and told to leave them anything they hadn't found. Smoke grenades were left, minus the pins, as we legged it.

We later received a bollocking by the site wing commander for taking things too seriously and disrupting his flying and causing all sorts of FOD hazards.

Chris Pacey

RAF Lossiemouth '94 TACEVAL, the station commander wants 48 Sqn to play enemy for the Jaguar and Nimrod forces at Lossie and Kinloss. OC 48 decides to use his gold medal-winning Cambrian Patrol team as a Spetsnaz unit. Using big Tell Reeves as a heating engineer using a gym card, flashes it at the control-of-entry Guin who opens the door into the main WOC entry point window.

Out comes a 9mm pistol to the lad's head and I am in like a robber's dog into the outer COE and through the small window with the agility of an oiled squid! Tell passed me a pistol and I opened the main doors with the magnetic switch. We took the war operations centre in one minute and thirty-eight seconds, storming into the main briefing room when the station commander and all his execs were in their initial 'O Group'. OC 48 was in the room slow clapping as we told Harry Staish to 'put the fucking phone down'!

OC 48 was a very happy man; Harry was not so much. Exercise lost in forty minutes of a two-week TACEVAL. Reset, start again! In fairness, a week after he asked for a beer call at the squadron where he came to congratulate the lads, he said, "All I can say is I am glad you are on our side, twats."

Robert Booth

Christmas '75, you could have Christmas or New Year for leave. Being Scots we chose New Year. So fire piquet for Christmas. Doing the rounds and we get to three, I think squadron Harrier's officers' crewroom.

Having a nose around, we find all the items we as a squadron had been accused of stealing from ferries and bases on a recent exercise in Germany. As we had already served our penance we had all the goodies as well. Their crewroom was a bit bare after but we never heard another word about it.

Michael Marsh

26 Sqn deployed on the spit gun Changi Creek circa 1966. It was evening and we were just about to go to *stand to*; the hut was decorated for Christmas and everyone was in good spirits. Suddenly over the radio came: "Stand to, stand to, bogey fifteen hundred Echo unidentified!"

All hell broke loose and we manned the gun, pulled the yoke over so the barrel was pointing towards Echo marker, and waited. Over the radio: "Reference, unidentified bogey Echo now identified, Santa Claus and six reindeer, out!" Lots of smiles and childish giggles, but lots of arseholes had stopped going half-a-crown thruppeny bit!

Robert Booth

51 Sqn, Salalah, '75. AOC parade. It was more important to provide the guard of honour. All members of the guard were provided with

new DMS boots, which were sent to the bomb dump and the toe caps painted in gloss black. On parade, middle of the day, and it's scorching hot.

The staish decided that it would be good to meet the Herc on the pan with the parade in place. So there we were at the present, paint now melting off the toe caps, and the Herc taxis in and turns its arse to us and covers us all in sand, leaving us all with desert boots again. Still, at least the AOC brought all his young female aides with him.

Robert Booth

27 Sqn, Leuchars, '77 or '78. The Squadron Eng Guin officer after a few and feeling brave is waxing eloquent about how Rocks shouldn't be allowed near technical equipment. Surrounded by Rocks about three-deep, when out of nowhere a fist appears and punches his lights out.

Stunned silence, we look around to see who to congratulate, and there is the squadron warrant officer casually sauntering away with a full pint still in his other hand.

Robin Flack

Salalah, '73. The off-duty lads are parking in a few wets (to keep the dust out of their throats), NAAFI manager decides the bar's closed. As he pulled the shutter down, a large arm stopped its downward travel and in a thick Scottish accent, the words 'we haveny finished yet' were said.

"We're shut!" he screamed, and ran away!

Up went the shutter. A certain large Scotsman vaulted the bar and announced, "Free bar lads!"

Then the Feds arrived with their dogs. All hell broke loose, with Feds and dogs flying out of every possible exit minus lumps of flesh. Happy Christmas to all ... hic!

Ian Boyce

1974-ish, young Ian has been on II for a couple of years, no longer a total sprog. Life at Colerne has a routine: every Thursday is Top of the Pops, then into the NAAFI for 'Zoo Night'. This particular week goes as planned; get to bed late-ish, fairly well pissed, station alarm goes off around 0300, squadron call out.

Stagger over to squadron hangar, really big flap, folk coming and going, get the order to pack containers, no worries, it is only an exercise …

Later on the squadron Pantech truck turns up full of parachutes, we draw and fit and leave them lined up in stick order. Later still, two Andovers reverse up to the outside of the hanger, tail-gates open (they seem to be taking this exercise thing a bit seriously?). 'Black Jack' Palmer, squadron warrant officer, calls us into a hollow square to brief us.

"Gentlemen, we are jumping into Uganda." What! (This was during the Idi Amin Uganda Asian thing.) We were to jump in, take an airfield, then other regiment units would TALO in and we would assist UK citizens out.

Happily, we were stood down towards midday. Could have been a little bit nasty.

Michael Marsh

GDT at RAF Honington, early 1973, got some pilots coming through for pistol training and my brief is to teach them to fire in all positions including the prone position—that's lying down, for those Guins reading this.

Anyhow, the training goes well and the boys are keen as mustard, including their Wingco (wing commander).

So now for the shoot: five shots lying, five shots sitting, change mag, five kneeling, and five standing. Give my usual speil about the slide coming back and not to get too close to the weapon with your face, give the order to fire, and the slide comes back and catches the Wingco right across the nose, splitting it and sending blood in all directions.

I stop the shoot and ask him if he is okay. He tells me to continue and he completes the rest of the shoot without any problem. Afterwards, I tell one of the zobs to drive him to sick quarters to get his injury sorted, and off he goes. I fill in all the books, including the accident book, and tell the guys they have all passed.

My boss sees me later to say that the flyboys were extremely impressed with my instruction and that their Wingco would always remember my teaching; especially about the slide.

Later that year I was promoted to sergeant and posted to 4 School of Technical Training as a driving instructor. Someone was having a giraffe, surely!

Michael Marsh

In 1972 I was posted to RAF Honington, then a flying station for buccaneers, which is in Suffolk. The GDT section consisted of a flight lieutenant, one flight sergeant, and one corporal; me.

So it is the annual shoot for the plods and I take them for dry training and assist the FS with the range. Final shoot going through and Chiefy gives the order to load. One plod loads then makes ready, so order to unload is given. Chiefy points out the error and gives load order again. Plod loads and makes ready so order to unload is given and once again Chiefy explains plod's error and also what should happen. This is repeated four more times and on the final time Chiefy loses it big time and yells at the plod, asking him what the fuck he is thinking, when, *bang*, plod puts a round between my legs. So picking up the flag I whack him with it and grab the pistol, unloading it and telling everyone else to unload.

In the meantime, Chiefy has plod by the throat against the back wall of the range, demanding to know why plod had shot at his corporal and did plod know how much it cost to train a gunner to the rank of CPL. Plod shit himself and for six hours I took him through the pistol, but he still insisted on loading and making ready on the command load.

I failed him and he was retraded. Chiefy asked me why had I spent so long with him as he would have binned him after the first hour and not bothered with the other five!

David Jeremy Wilson

In 1975 on 51 Sqn in Hong Kong we did a simulated beach landing with the 6th Royal Gurkha Regiment and their mules, then hiked up a mountain range in the new terrotories. Each squaddie was laden down with equipment, which consisted of full battle dress. In our jacket pockets were two-inch mortar bombs and a variety of hand grenades. Looped round our necks, like Mexican bandits we carried belts of GPMG ammo, four mags of SLR in our ammo pouches. On my back as well as a large pack and an entrenching tool, I had two bombs for the Carl Gustav, plus tin lid. Personal weapon in right hand and box of GPMG ammo in left. One lad, Mick, had an A41 radio as well.

When I reached the top everyone else had rested. I was last up 'cause in all that terrain I was the only one to find a well, and fell down it.

The CPL said, "Right, Wilson, you can fire the Gustav first, seeing as you carried the bombs."

I complained but got nowhere, so in a prone position with Bob as my number two, we proceeded to load. The target on the other side of a ravine was a mocked-up tank.

Well, after the smoke cleared away, the officers and SNCOs were scanning to see my fall-off shot, but could see naff all because there was no target left to see. First shot I blew it to smithereens.

My wonderful CPL said, "I think we found our marksman, Sir."

So I ended up carrying that bloody thing all the way down that bloody mountain.

Len Hames

So it's my last night in Her Majesty's forces, I am stationed at RAF Hereford (Credenhill), I decide to go on a mega piss-up in the NAAFI. Best civvies on, back pocket full of demob money, beer chits, wait outside for the doors to open and in I burst, order a pint, and wait for the rest of the lads to join me. Seven o'clock and we're off, I buy the first round, buy the second round and off we go, four or five pints later we start having a go at all the Guins, most of them sprogs and new entrants, did not know what they had walked into. Now I am not saying I'm a party animal—more like just the regular Rock animal.

2100 hours and we start the party antics; Rock party games begin with 'Down in One', followed by 'Down in One and a Short', then 'Dance of the Flaming Arseholes', followed by 'Pints of Puke', followed by all the usual Rock songs. The young sprogs had never seen the likes before. Then the mod plods and snowdrops turn up, take one look at me, look at the rest of the Rocks, turn round and feck off and leave us to it. More merriment, plenty of beer, shorts, and mega mixes, getting slightly pissed, but a true Rock and carry on, having a great time, talking over my great journey in the RAF Regiment, who I've met, where I've been, what we got up to.

Getting late now and the NAAFI is due to close. The girls behind the bar start lining the drinks up, there are pints from one end of the bar to the other ... *Bang!* The shutters come down and we carry on. Now I am feeling a bit for the worse, outside I go and I eject all the shit out of my stomach—well the colour was amazing: green, blue, black, red, the grass outside the NAAFI had never looked so good. 2345 hours I decide to go down the village to the pub, leaving everybody inside wondering where I gone, but no search party follows. After a long swaying, weaving walk, I get to the pub only to find it's fecking closed. After banging on the front doors for about five minutes and a lot of shouting and screaming from both me and the landlord, I decide to go back to camp,

Bearing in mind the walk from the pub to camp would take around fifteen mins, I finally arrive after around an hour, only to find the main gate closed. After contemplating what my next move is I decide the best plan is to scale the gates. I look up at the gates, look down at the ground, and off I go.

Now you would think that one pissed up Rock versus one pair of big metal gates won't go, but I scaled them in one easy flow, more of an up and over, only to find the duty CPL and some sprogs on the other side. Shit, here we go, scuffers on the way, the duty sergeant turns up followed by the SWO, feck, I am in for it now! Last night and I am going to get arrested!

They all take one look at me, look at each other, and the SWO turns round and says, "Hames ... in my twenty-two years of service that's the first time I have seen an airman trying to break into camp on the last day of their service—normally they can't get out quick enough ... get in that feckin' guardroom!"

In I go unassisted, straight into the cell I go, collapse on the bunk and fall into a drunken sleep. I was awoken at 0730 hours by the duty sprog.

"Excuse me," says, "do you want breakfast?"

"Yes," I slurred back at him, only to find a full English waiting for me and copius amounts of black coffee.

The orderly sergeant turns up, he was a Guin, he says, "OK Hames, off you go, go get your ID card handed in, collect your kit, and you're free to go."

Free to go? Feck me, I am off, a feckin' civvy!

Hand my ID Card in, collect my blue RAF hold-all with all my worldly possessions in, along with my only suitcase, and make my way to the main gate for my final time. I am aiming to get the bus to the town so I can get a train home to Nottingham.

Standing at the main gate just contemplating my next move when an LR turns up. "Where you going mate?"

I turn round to see a Rock driver. "Town," I say, "railway station."

"Get in," he says.

Throw my kit in the back of the Landy, get in the Landy only to find out that the said driver was Colin, who I served with on 58 Sqn when I left basics. Ironic—one of the first Rocks I met was Colin and the last Rock I see is Colin!

Well, long story, but I hope you enjoyed the irony of being a Rockape. Per ardua guys. Long live The RAF Regiment.

John Stowell

16 Sqn Wildenrath. Late '70s. The squadron has been there a few years and postings in/out were happening and sections were changing round. We got Sergeant Billy Kerr as our new Det Cdr. As you will all know—new boss, change everything! He wanted the Rapier bay changing around and part of that was to move all the noticeboards to different walls. Andy (Big Jock) and I were given this job. So off we go to Eng Flight ('the wizards cave') to get what we thought we needed. After we had drilled a few holes we discovered that the wall plugs we had were too big to fit the holes. So typical Rocks (Jacks of all trades and masters of none) started to make the holes bigger using a screwdriver. It was at this point that OC Eng walks past and eyeballs us through the open bay doors.

"What are you two clowns doin'?" he asks.

Quick as a flash, Big Jock says, "Screwing these holes onto the wall Sir."

The look on his face was a picture. You could imagine a scene like the Terminator scanning for a possible response. What we got was, "I should have known better," as he walked off shaking his head and muttering to himself.

The good thing is, I don't think them holes ever fell off!

Robert Booth

51 Sqn, A Flight Salalah, '75. Our flight commander has volunteered us to remain behind as the rear guard. Not that popular; as we wave goodbye to the rest of the squadron, we find out that, two months into a three-month stint, it's been extended to four months.

He now has to find things to occupy us, as we are only manning HH Bravo. So various activities are dreamt up. Swimming with wild dolphins at Raysut beach, where we cut our hands and feet on the razor-sharp coral. But the funniest was the day that we were dropped off at the HH and told to march back in full kit to Umm Al Gwariff.

So off we go out into the bondoo, toddling along. We have been told cold drinks will be waiting as they set us off on our journey at the hottest part of the day.

A shout goes up from tail end Charlie 'Camel Spider' as he starts overtaking everyone. We looked back and the biggest monster any of us had seen on the whole det. is bounding towards us; it must have been jumping six to eight feet at a time. That was enough for the rest of us. Cue ten Rocks with our bravest faces on running like hell across the desert.

We arrived at our pick up point twenty minutes early—I don't think anyone mentioned why, but we really needed the cold beers.

David Hudson

1966, 26 Ind LAA Squadron Airfield Gun position under the command of one Sergeant Minchelle.

I had been into the squadron compound with RL Bedford to collect some gear, and returned and drew up next to the garage ready to drop said gear off. Minchelle however wanted me to back the truck into the garage and told me to leave my door open while he guided me back!

"Go on, go on, go on," shouts Minchelle as I reverse back slowly. "Straighten up, go back, back, back, back—" *Crunch.* the driver door connected with the wall and was torn off its hinges.

Minchelle started cursing and swearing and jumping up and down, asking why I hadn't looked and why I had not stopped. He was marshalling me and I was following instructions!

Filled out FMT3 and Minchelle went before OC and got a bollocking for not paying sufficient attention to what was going down.

I was then called forward into OC's office and it seemed that Sergeant Greenwell wanted a layer on the spit gun. The squadron warrant officer had kindly volunteered me; seems he was worried about Sergeant Minchelle's high blood pressure and weak heart!

So I went to the spit gun, which was on the sandy area across from Changi Creek.

Sergeant Greenwell greeted me with, "Do you fish young man?"

"Yes Sergeant I do," was my reply.

"Ah! Good, you can grab the gear and put it in the canoe, we are going fishing."

Brilliant! I can drive anything, me, including boats and canoes.

No more garages to reverse into, as the only buildings on the beach were the dormitory, radio shack, gun pit, and the ammo dump, all of which were wood and sandbag construction. Spent the next six months on the beach, then posted to 63 Sqn!

Bill Hayes

At Stamford PTA in 1973 doing infantry tactics and generally running around like unregistered dogs. Towards endex (end of exercise) my section were tasked with setting up an ambush at the junction of a track in the early hours of the morning.

We navigated to our position by compass and set up the ambush in a triangular configuration. This let us cover the L-shaped junction as we were unsure as to what track the 'enemy' party would come from.

It had been a good summer so the grass that we were laying in was dry and about three feet high. I was tasked with springing the ambush by some genius who instructed me to trigger the ambush when the enemy patrol entered the killing ground by firing two schermoolies.

So there we lay for several hours until I heard the enemy coming from our left. I rolled over onto my back and at the relevant time fired the rockets. Large bangs and flames, followed by firing as the section kicked in. Trouble was, long dry grass and flames equals a raging fire, with me lying in the middle of it.

Needless to say, self-preservation kicked in and we—us *and* the enemy—legged it like Bugis Street Kai Tai's being chased by a proctologist.

Funny thing was, we never heard another thing about it.

Ian Boyce

1976, 2 Sqn no longer share the roulement in Dhofar with 15 and 51, so we get to do the NI roulement instead.

In preparation for our first trip to the province (since the 60s), we undertake a fair bit of training (not quite Hythe and Lydd but fairly intense). We sent three search teams down to Chattenden. I had the A flight team, Tom MacKay B, and Mick Gant SW.

Fairly busy for all of us; loads of new shit to learn, but our three teams were far better than the army teams we were training alongside, including the REST teams (RE search teams who are called in when unit teams think they have found something). The course was progressing at pace; we had moved to a row of old terraced married quarters on the outskirts of Canterbury to conduct unoccupied house searches, each team dealing with the houses in the terrace at the same time. Those of you who have conducted unoccupied searches will be aware of just how meticulous and cautious this search is. (Not quite as dodgy as the occasonal *bang!* when someone trips, or releases a trip-wire, or steps on a pressure plate.)

We become used to them blowing themselves up and keep ourselves focussed on our own houses, until Mick Gant decides that his team is not progressing fast enough and decides to 'clear' the stairs by running up them. His team were *very* unimpressed ...

Steve Scott

Age seventeen, young LAC sets off on his first adult trip outside the UK, to the heart of the Caribbean basin. Having been posted to a mini gun squadron, his job as with all sprogs was to shut up and do as he was told while out there we completed LAC and SAC training on the L40/70 bofor gun under the instruction of Sergeant Ray Kidd.

We were taught all the roles to man the gun. As such, we also learnt how to clean the thing.

Unlike today's modern forces, to change the barrel was a four-man job, the heavy end being nearest the main body. In good old regiment tradition, practice makes perfect—and changing places all the time!

Near the end of the day me and a so-called friend (still is) had the front of the barrel cmdr lift given we take the weight edge forward barrel clear of body of gun.

I look to my right. My ex-mate looked at me and just said 'fuck it' ... and let go, leaving me to take the full weight. I can hear the nice Irish voice saying, "Don't you dare." Rocks being Rocks, no one rushed to my aid as the barrel was slowly lowered to the ground. Every vein was pumping. Eyes popping. Knees were buckling.

Managed to put the barrel into its rest position on the ground, then hit the floor myself. An Irish voice said, "Well done laddie, you've passed," followed by, "I never believed in the Hulk until today."

Richard Hawkes

Who remembers the old C42 radios? Well, on this day Geordie was tasked to check the ACCs (batteries) well in the back of the Land where there was a piece of rubber matting, which was there so when you disconnected them the fittings didn't touch the metal. Well, he forgot to put matting down, and next thing there was smoke coming out of the back. Then Geordie came out of the back; he was coughing and spluttering, and instead of holding one of the connectors he put it on the floor. The connector was welded to the floor of the land rover, the other one still connected to the battery, so someone had to go in and disconnect the one that was still connected.

We all had a laugh over that incident.

Bill Espie

Back in the day, November '69, the corps had five squadrons in theatre in the province. 16 Field had Fermanagh on the border operating out of Enniskillin and FOBs at Linsneskea, Beleek, and other holiday areas. Troops did thirty-six hours on and twelve off for six weeks at a time and then went on reserve at Omagh, which meant twenty-four on, two-minute readiness to move. Twenty-four on, two hours off, twenty-four on, twelve hours off. Chopper patrols were the order of the day and boat patrols on Lough Earne; the usual stuff that never changed.

Got a heli task with a Wessex one day from Lisneskea, an hour's jolly up and down the border paying attention to the concession roads—in reality, normally a chance for an hour's sleep.

Section commander was the mad rugby man Ralph Smith. Ralph didn't lose his marbles as a warrant officer, they were gone long before that. Great bloke and a very close friend.

We get a call that a post office in the republic has been held up and the baddies are heading north on the concession road, so away we go.

Ralph selects a DOP and down swoops the Wessex, pilot lands arse-about-face with the bird between us and the road.

Never registered that we were on quite a steep slope. Tear down the road and set up the snap VCP and the car heaves into sight, sees us, and U-turns away back to the republic where the scuffers lift them.

We get the lift signal from the pilot to go to a follow-up location in case they try to get out on foot, and in he comes. Trouble is, he comes the other way so the disc is too close to the ground and sits in a low hover with the door at least seven feet above us. No problems—young, fit Rocks, adrenaline pumping, on to each others' backs and into the cabin, helping the next guy up.

Last man of course, the section commander. Two of us lying flat and reaching for him, managed to grab him by the webbing straps, when some clown in the chopper called 'up up up' to the pilot who did just that, and the Wessex was up fifty feet before you could blink, with Ralph hanging on for grim life, legs pedalling like a demented spider vowing all forms of death and torture on us. We were laughing so much we couldn't pull him in, but eventually we rescued him and to this day the guilty bastard has never owned up. Ralph always asks me when I see him, but that's a secret that one of us took to the grave.

Robert Booth

How some things come home to roost. 51 Sqn, mid '70s.

The barrack block is visited one night by some officers looking for a few volunteers. Turns out that the ATC cadet camp were having an escape and evasion exercise that night—would we act as the captors and interrogators?

Would we? Of course, anything to oblige and get a few free pints.

So off we go, rounding them up in a nice LWB. Sand bags on the heads, lie them down in any available puddle, land rover revving up close by, and the spare wheel being rolled up against their heads as we questioned them. An hour-and-a-half later, plus a fair few extra puddles and brown stains, we are told that's enough for the night.

Roll forward a good few years and having to retread to air traffic. Posted to Gutersloh, arrive, and meet one of my new junior bosses. Yup, for some reason he had never forgotten his night in a sandbag.

Peter Huntly

While not the same, when our gun detachment was out in the ouloo in Libya, Paddy Manning filled a large empty kero tin full of sand and poured some petrol in. I, thinking there should be more, poured in another half-gallon.

Danny Worthington thought it was time for a brew and stood next to the Benghazi burner and threw a match on. Well, while the rest of us had tailored our shorts so they showed off our manly thighs, Danny's resembled a marquee; the flames flew up his shorts at MACH 10 and burnt all the hairs away from his scrotum, as well as frying his dong.

His rain dance was something to behold.

Mark Kimberlin

16 Sqn, Ireland, '74. General strike and they're expecting a bit of agro at Aldergrove. So the brains of the unit decide some anti-riot training is in order. We didn't have tin lids with us so they issued us some from stores. Minor problem; no inners!

So to prevent the spike inside the helmet being driven into what little brains we had, we were told to use towels! Picture it: four sections of Rocks with riot shields, batons, and assorted coloured towels dangling round our shoulders!

The 'rioters' they got for us to practice against were the civvie workers from the camp and airport, who would have been the actual rioters if the fertiliser had hit the air conditioning in the following weeks.

So all in all a result: riot control trained, and the term 'towel-heads' hadn't even been invented!

CHAPTER 2
AN OFFICER AND A GENTLEMAN

Barrie Griffiths

I joined my first sqn, Sqn 48, with a pilot officer who was always in more shit than I was and deflected it off me. He is now the commandant general of the RAF Regiment.

The IG was delighted when said pilot officer did a recce of all of the sites with the very delicate surveying instrument, the artillery director, thrown into his Bergan and bounced around as he tabbed around the sites. Needless to say he was then posted to CVRT! He was always a favourite though in those days. Must be a message in there somewhere!

Neil Horn

Now the Oktoberfest I remember. It was our J Course against the ladies. Not being proper trained gentlemen yet, we were determined to win! Until Charlie V burst in, revving away at a 20" husky. Same Oktoberfest that Jez Parkinson turned up in head to toe tin foil with a number on his head as an 'oven-ready Jew'. Taste, diplomacy, and gentlemanly conduct not yet bred in!

Nick Newman

RAF Leuchars, duty officer, 1986. I've just arrived on 27 Sqn fresh off JROC—19 years old and looking about 14—and I'm station duty officer. I get a call that there's an incident in the guardroom and could I come down urgently. Apparently the RAFP had arrested a gunner who was drunk and disorderly in the NAAFI and had gone beserk. I put on my best blues and head off the guardroom where I find one of the lads hurling chairs around with all the cops taking cover behind the furniture (I'm pretty sure it was Tim Thwaites but he was probably too pissed to remember anything about that night!). Anyway, I walk in looking like I've just stepped off the square and Tim snaps to attention. I calmly ask him if he wouldn't mind marching himself off to the cells and he shouts, "Yes, Sir!" does a smart about turn and locks himself up! So I turn to the cops and ask if there's anything else they need. They're all looking a bit shame-faced when I head off back to the officers' mess!

I always wondered what would have happened if Tim had decided to give me a kicking too! I was just mightily relieved he decided to look after his own!

Barrie Griffiths

OA on 63 Sqn, took a VIP out on a tour of the Rapier sites without realising he was on permanent send and proceeded to broadcast all our secrets … on the BATTLE NET! Of course if you have never served on Rapier, the significance of the 'self-jamming' of the second to second 'fighting' net by the sqn commander may not be immediately apparent.

"This left turn on the march is proving difficult for us to crack isn't it sir?"

Kevin McGee

1988, 1 Squadron, Llaarbruch, a new Pilot Officer was due to arrive, Edward, or as he was known to lesser mortals, the Right Honourable. It was decided that he should have some sort of initiation as befitted his title. A goat was borrowed from the school and put in a pen in the compound, I think it was Kenny Claxton who was goat orderly, and Edward was told the goat was his responsibility and that if the squadron was on parade, he would have to march with the goat. Edward had no idea how to march with a goat, so I was tasked, ex QCS sgt drill pig, to put him through his paces. Not wanting to embarrass him, I took him and the goat around the side of the flight lines onto a strip of grass which, unbeknown to him, the troops could overlook from the high windows. After about 30 minutes of being beasted by me, butted in the groin by the goat, he eventually marched the length of the grass in a fairly smart manner using the correct goat drill, made up by myself. Ed, as he became known then, went to lunch. The goat was then returned to the school, and after a short while, the station tannoy requested 1 Squadron goat officer report to the guardroom as the goat had escaped and had been reported running around the airfield.

Ed was sent on a wild goose (goat) chase for a couple of hours and the goat had apparently disappeared when someone told Ed that the school had goats, which was where the mascot had been bred, and that he may have returned there. The next act was Ed telling the head that his goat was in the school herd to be told it was the mascot's twin. Ed then tried to buy said twin for a vast sum of money. Who eventually told Ed this was a windup I don't know but it kept the guys amused for a few hours.

Neil Horn

OC GD Flt in 89/90 at W/R was a complete tool and despised by 66 officers. Always trying to drop us in the shit, but under-estimated the vindictive nature of the regt.

Mess had a single phone for private calls with extensions in the bar and one private room.

He was on the phone to his bird one night. A certain rock picked up bar handset, set the tannoy to 'send', and broadcast the 30 minute dirty call all around the mess.

Said OC GD went on leave for a week. Broke into his room, soaked it with fire extinguishers and poured a B&Q store of watercress everywhere. He came back to a 2 foot deep paddy field, duvet, wardrobe, everything.

Dining in night, in the bar after dinner, we kidnapped him, stripped him, plasti-cuffed to a chair, and put outside the patio doors. Left him for an hour then turned on the patio light. The fucking mess erupted with laughter and then just carried on drinking. Apparently he was not popular with anyone. Never fucked with us or the sqn after that ... strange, huh?

Neil Horn

A memory of WO Taff Bruton (RIP). Organised the sqn fishing trip as part of AT in the Hebs.

Boat loaded with about ten of us chucking lines in. Well we couldn't stop catching fish, hundreds of them, the boat deck looked like a trawler. Well, in great regt fashion, Taff took all the fish and went blaggin. The messes, the DI, everywhere. Best free sqn BBQ ever. He traded the fish for meat, beer, buns, the lot. Great man.

Nick Newman

101 uses for a dead air marshal. It's 1991 and I've just been appointed aide-de-camp to AOC 1 Group—AVM Dick Johns, later to become our honorary air commodore. He's been invited as guest of honour to the regiment dinner and the PSO—another Rock (Sqn Ldr Ian Jenkins) has left early for the pre-drinks. His parting words to me are, "It's a quiet afternoon—there's nothing you need to worry

Nice One Centurion

about." The AOC's last appointment of the day is a meeting with a retired Air Marshal who lives in the local village. I show him into the boss's office and a few moments later Dick Johns bursts out of the room looking ashen and says, "I think he's dead!"

I calmly phone 999 and then go into the office where I put my GDT first aid into practice—ten minutes of mouth-to-mouth and CPR while we wait for the ambulance, with the boss pacing up and down his office looking helpless! Sadly, I can't revive his guest (turns out it was a massive heart attack) and once he's been taken to hospital, the boss says, "I'd better let the CinC know what's happened."

As ADC, I had to set up and monitor his business calls, so I'm listening in as he tells Air Chief Marshal Sir John Thompson what's happened… "Oh my goodness, Dick—it must have been awful for you," says the CinC.

"Not really," says Dick Johns, "My ADC is a Rock Ape and he knew exactly what to do!" A couple of hours later I'm in my black tie and sitting down to the regiment dinner where my colleagues try to come up with '101 uses for a dead Air Marshal'—lie him down and use him as draught excluder, prop him up and use him as a hat stand, etc. Sick bastards! Still, I certainly went up in the boss's estimation that evening!

Neil Horn

66 Sqn deployed at Lakenheath, John Cloughton and I turn up at B Ech for an O Group. See two techies leaning on a wagon having a brew. Normal pleasantries, "How ya' doin', fellas?"

"Good, boss, and you?"

"Great, fellas, where's your gat?" (SMG back then)

Techie went ghost white, looking at his Landy, "Fuck, I left it just there," Landy bonnet, "When I was at Brigie's site, fuck, fuck."

It was found on the main drag outside Lakenheath and handed in to USAF guardroom by a civilian. As I recall, in standard 66 fashion of the day, the techie got a bollocking, some gash jobs, and nothing on record.

The joys of 814 and going to RAF Newton for SY training. Two weeks of my life I will never get back. Anyhow, had to clean wagons after an 'exercise'. All lined up, one of the big open vehicle washes with the big, blue, spinning brushes. FS and cpl copper had obviously not checked their Land Rover tilt. They drove in, the thing started and within seconds ripped the tilt off the wagon. We were rolling on the floor nearly pissing ourselves as this thing just kept whipping around and wet bitch-slapping the pair of them! Not sure how long we left it before hitting the emergency stop.

Barrie Griffiths

Definition of 'loyalty'—reassuring the sqn cdr that the chants of, "Who is the hom' on the bike?" from the sqn bar as he left to go home from successive sqn beer calls … ON HIS BIKE … was but a coincidence.

"Besides, Sir, 'hom' is short for 'homie', which in many ways would be very much a compliment!"

A fine grasp of the irrelevant. DSC briefing sqn cdr on a Sunday afternoon, at a base in RAF Germany in the 80s.

DSC: "Sir, you need to know that I have just read in the News of the World that one of our gunners is about to return from two weeks summer leave with a new wife." The sqn WO advises me that SAC C had not met this woman before he went on leave two weeks ago. In the paper it has reported that he is now returning to duty with a new double-barrelled surname, after adding hers to his, and they are expecting to see the families' officer on their return tomorrow and march straight into a married quarter.

Sqn cdr: "What were you doing reading the News of the World?"

Neil Horn

Another inventive nickname was for LAC Woodcock on 66. No-show on a Monday morning, so OCA and FSA did the normal call the home number.

"We're friggin' snowed in boss, I'll get in as soon as I can."

The muppet (as every LAC and pilot offr is!) lived about a mile from Catterick, did he not think OC A would call the depot … Beautiful, sunny winter's day, not a snowflake in sight. Woodcock charged upon his return and forever known as 'Frosty'.

Steve Simpson

Taceval in Germany 84/85ish, orbat comes out, I am oc B Flt veh CD-R and Ken Page is driver. OC B in the shit more than most, radio msg: 'pick me up at officers mess'. We go, he turns up in pressed green shirt, gleaming boots, and pressed dpm. Take me to Sqn tax hq, co wants a word.

Ambling along in Spartan, turns of perri track to tax hq, huge puddle up ahead, oc b dreaming taking in the beams, Ken puts the boot down, I duck inside, and bang! Shit hits the fan.

Ken and I are on intercom, boss ain't, I could hear him cursing Ken from inside the wagon, stood back up and he was covered in thick, slimy mud—he was feckin' raging.

Got to ha he, debussed, we feckin' pissed ourselves, and he went off to face the music. He came back in high spirits, in the shit again, sqn duty officer again, 28 days straight I think he did, feckin' priceless!

Alan Thompson

RAF Honnington was having an AOCs and the airmans' mess was on his hit list so naturally they cracked out all the good stuff, cutlery, crockery, and even the best food—so steak was on the menu.

In trots the AOC with his suitable clingons, baggage, and station photographer. Taking his life in his own hands, decides to approach a table of gunners chomping on best steaks. "And how is your steak?" he says to one gunner, who is looking slightly disgruntled.

"Well, Sir, it's not that good to be honest," says the gunner, with that being said, the AOC picks up a fork, sticks it in a piece of steak, and immediately starts to eat it.

"Rubbish," says the AOC, "That's the best bit of steak I've ever eaten, lovely and tender!"

To which the gunner says, "Well, Sir, that piece should be, I've just been chewing on it for the last five minutes." Exit one AOC followed by scowled looks from the stn cmdr, SWO, and the rest of the cronies.

Barrie Griffiths

Must have been something about 63 Sqn in the Falklands and officers catching fish. A certain flt lt was very upset that what he caught—his prize Mullet—disappeared one day.

Cue a day of Mullet-related record requests for him on BFBS. Seem to remember it was 'Mullet of Kintyre' being requested that send him ballistic! Anybody remember this and/or the other requests he had that day?

Neil Horn

J1/88, OC was Flt Kim Balshaw. Kim was getting married to Eve and so as a course we had to make his stag do memorable. So a plan was hatched. After copious amounts of alcohol, Kim was bundled into Ed Codagan's car with Dave (the cardboard box) and myself as minders to prevent him jumping! Hot foot to, I think, Newcastle Airport, with the rest of the course in convoy.

Much protesting from Kim, "WTF are you doing?"

At arrival at airport (pre 9/11 security) a recce team was sent forward to square away security and crew about this 6'11", pissed bloke. Kim was stripped of all but passport (thanks for supplying that, Eve) and the contents of an RAF holdall—train timetables, spare shreddies, tour guides, and enough cash to get trains/buses to UK about 3hrs before his wedding. But not quite enough to fly (pre Ryan Air). He was then bundled onto a plane to Spain.

Next morning all of 159 were looking for Kim; Mick Knight came into the class fuming, "Where the fuck is the boss?" Kim was meant to be teaching us.

"Oh, we sent him to Spain." Cue Mick Knight explosion! Kim got back for the big day, I think he blagged a cheap flight … took it really well. Fun times.

Albi Pinnion

At Gutersloh, early eighties, I was asked to go find the flt commander on a Monday morning, after a no show. I drove down to the mess, knocked on his door, nothing. So tried the door, he was fully clothed in his pit, pizza boxes all over the floor, and his room looked like the whole flt had a party in there.

Anyway, he got up, got dressed, could not find his beret, so wore his No1 hat—boy did he look rough! I took him to the sqn, none of the other officers would lend him a beret, so all day he was wondering around in his ogs boots, shirt, and no 1 hat. I don't know what extras he got, but I never told anyone else about the pigsty. On following room inspections, he walked in, said, "Very good as always," and walked out. He was a good officer, what became of him I don't know, he was a champion hurdler, great runner, and not bad at rugby. Initials RH.

Neil Horn

There of course is the tale (true or folklore?) of the career bachelor (officer) known for being a little eccentric. Anyhow, after many years as a devout bachelor, got married—as it was the done thing. Driving with new wife in the e-type, stopped for petrol. About three hours later, reaching the final destination … oh shit. New wife had gone for a piss at the service station, but had not got back in the car. Marriage over.

Andy Ingham

A certain OC training wing was visiting Ex Omega and laid into me that the trainee gunners hadn't been taught properly. He had asked to see their 'trench cards' and was given blank looks by the lads. I took him over to a trench and asked to see their 'range card' and a fine example was produced!

Neil Horn

Puggy (my driver) getting chased and 'counselled' by JC. We left Puggy at a kit to cook Flt HQ breakfast when we went to morning 'O' Grp. Arrived back at kit to be served full English, looked a bit undercooked but hey-ho. JC tucked straight in, spit, cough, splutter, nearly puke. JC's normal tirade of Anglo Saxon ensued, Puggy then clocked that the carton of cooking oil had the faint letters 'TPOL' on it. The muppet had used washing up liquid to cook with! JC went nuts, while I (not eaten a thing) and the crew nearly pissed ourselves.

In FI there was a Rocky Horror party. Me and Chris Thomas got the boss (in UK just before) to bring out suitable ladies attire, wigs, etc. Full rig on, stockings, suspenders, etc. Chris and I leant at the bar and two jockies in flight suits wandered up, one grabbed my arse, got the shock of his life when I turned around and threatened to put his lights out. They got shit from the army birds for the rest of their tour. Funny as.

Barrie Griffiths

I have always loved, admired, and respected the ingenuity and imagination of the RAF Regt gunner, except when it comes to nicknames. There were/are just so many Jocks, Geordies, Scouses, Taffs, Brummies ... you get the picture. Imagine my joy to meet Dave (Daggers) Lang. At last, a nickname to convey something more exciting than a region of the UK. *He could be pretty handy with a switch blade*, I thought, *Better watch myself.*

Maybe he is an ex-commando, or maybe he has done the all-arms cdo course, even more respect accrued, I considered.

Maybe he has won awards for his writing from the crime writer's association ... Shit, this guy could be really interesting.

"So, why are you called Daggers then?" I asked expectantly, in between the CP banter in the wee small hours.

"Cos I'm from Dagenham," came his disappointing reply. I will qualify however, that was the only time that he ever disappointed me! Top Man.

So officers' mess tales huh? Names, sqns, and dates nameless! Sometime ago in the FI there was a do attended by the sqn junior offs in the FI mess. After dinner and a couple of pints of 'spicey and coke', things started to go south. For whatever reason, dancing on the tables ensued—those tall bar tables that have no balance at all. Well a certain sqn adj started to topple, so grabbed the (false) roof for balance. Like a scene from road-runner, he came crashing down, along with the table, all the best mess crystal that was on the table, and about 100 square foot of ceiling tiles, metal, and wire. *Ah well, that should buff out in the morning.* A couple of guins not impressed with the officers' behaviour got slapped and ejected from the mess.

Drinking and fun continued. Early the next day, the likelihood of trouble hit home and all apologies, offers to get fixed, etc. were made and accepted. All good and done … Not.

At Sqn O Grp, the boss: "CBFFI is fuming, apparently the mess was vandalised, ceiling torn down, glasses broken, and there was a fight, if you hear anything let me know."

"It was us, boss."

"What, the fight?"

"Erm, no, all of it."

The rest of the one way conversation is kind of blurred, but basically, "Fix it." Anyhow, the bill amounted to about 1,500 each. However, being enterprising officers and using initiative, they were aware that OC work services (army bird) had hots for OC eng. It was requested that he do the honourable thing. It was never confirmed, as officers are gentlemen like that, but all repairs were done within days, and bill was never seen, and no more was said.

Worst was going to the officers/SNCOs' drinks the next night, supposed to be in offs' mess but had to be moved to SNCOs' mess due to damage. All sqn offs on an alcohol ban being asked by SNCOs, "Wtf did you lot do this time."

Chris Pacey

On the corps concentration competition at Strensall, the visiting AOC was invited out for a night in York with the lads. It was a high tempo drinking affair and fair do. He ended up in the gallery night club at the end of the night. There were two mini buses—an officer's one, and a lad's one—somebody decided that were not going to wait for the AOC and the first bus left without him. Good career move for some JO. So he ended up waiting in the second bus and fell asleep waiting for a lift back, the lads stacked on, and we started rolling

Back to camp. Five mins in, he wakes up to find a gunner in the next seat getting noshed off by a wench from the club! His eyes sprung open and he said in a jovial chirp, "Good to see romance isn't dead," and went back to sleep! Top lad.

Robin Flack

One of the joys and sometimes downfalls of being on the station rugby team and doing the officers' mess discos is that first names are used quite a lot. On one occasion, I was walking down the road at Catterick on my way home when approached by a sqn FO, and a few paces behind him the station CO. I threw up a smart salute to the FO, "Afternoon, Sir."

He returned the salute, "Afternoon, Rob." A scream from behind him stopped him in his tracks, "Flying officer! Stand still! Airman move over there!" Oh shit. After a brief 'chat' involving officers and other ranks addressing each other with the FO, he was sent on his way a bit red-faced.

The station CO then walked over to me (*Oh shit, shit, shit!*) I saluted and it was returned. He then leaned forward and said, "Sorry about that, Rob, not your fault. Stupid junior officers need pulling up every now and again … On your way … Oh, don't let him do it again."

Phil Swales

Big Briggy at Warcop, Field firing on 66, in the bar. "Let's have a 'who can hit the softest' competition." Step forward OC Eng, a young thin lad, new to the sqn (think his own guys egged him on to do it cos we all knew the game). Bar hushes, Briggy says, "Seeing as you're an officer, Sir, you can have the privilege of going first," so up stands OC Eng, clenches his fist, and touches Briggy on the arm with the softest of a hit … you know what's coming don't you.

Briggy says, "My turn," and wallops the officer in the arm with such force it knocks him sideways and says, "You win, Sir!" Cue the guffaws around the bar … and cue the scream from OC Eng, bless him—that would cost him a dead arm for quite a while and I bet the bruising didn't go for ages. But least he got a 'well done' from everyone, even the CO who must have been glad it was only the arm and not the 'chin' side of the game.

Anthony Rogers

Walking past officers' mess St Mawgan myself and Paddy, hot female officer is walking towards us. Paddy is closest, so salutes, but as he does so, he comes out with a gleamer, "Are you alright, darling?"

She is slightly taken aback by this by her face but she cracks a massive smile and says, "Fine thank you, airman." Think her day was made as she passes by with a bit more of a wiggle in the hips.

Shortly down the road, I turn to paddy and say, "Do you realise you called her darling?"

"Aah no," he replies.

"Well you got away with it. I say, shit never sticks to you does it?"

Neil Horn

The most testing of one's metal in the corps. It is not to be brave and fearless under fire as many may think. It is to be gunnery staff in the Hebs and maintain a straight face, whilst urinating oneself, as a missile goes nuts, and all the lads on the firing point (under shelter … NOT) go scattering for the bunker. Then having to regain composure, trying so hard not to belly laugh, as BAe, MBDA, the Hebs staff, and all 'investigate'.

The answer of, "The missile was obviously fucked," was never really seen as scientific, so all these highly paid scientists spend an hour looking at the traces and stuff to come up with, "The missile was probably fucked."

The 'Polaris' always being the most sporting, especially when launching out of the sea towards range control.

Left 66 Sqn, a now matured fg off to the operational theatre of RAFG. Time to change, grow up, and be punchy! Well, first Friday night in the mess bar, drinking, chatting with officers from 33 Wg, 63 Sqn, and Harrier Force (Luton, John Todd, Laybourne, Thayne to name a few).

Mess window was suddenly opened and one of 63's officers, "Guess the OC," note: not 'boss', "Has outstayed his welcome … again," to be followed by a regt sqn ldr being thrown at Mach 3 out of the window into the bushes, dusted himself down, got on his bike, and on his way.

Thought no more of it but realised that perhaps RAFG is not going to be the 'maturing ground' that I anticipated … it wasn't! Anyhow, next Friday, exactly the same occurrence and every f'ing Friday from then forward.

A small gathering of various officers in Gut for a few drinks at one of the OMQs. All going well, wobbly and schnapps getting consumed at a good pace. One of the young daughters brings her new pet for all to see, a wee little hamster. Aaah cute! Hamster let loose on the living room floor to everyone's oohh, aah how cute!

All good until someone decides to open the patio doors... in rushes a super playful, big German Shepherd just runs in and bounds straight on the hamster, squishing the darn thing....dead!

Kids screaming, chaos and a few rocks, not related to said kid and a bit pissed, trying so hard not to laugh!

Phil Pringle

Time to try and recall the fateful night of my first exchange drinks in the officers mess at Honington (it even gets a short mention in

Harry Foxley's book!) It was after attending a 20 Squadron function in the British legion, and after a cracking night, we all went for the transport provided and boarded for the return trip to camp, quite pissed. During the said trip Robbie said he needed a piss! He was bursting, surrounded by wives and girlfriends of squadron members, rather than piss on the floor decides to sit there, take his knob out, and piss in his mouth, and drink it, allowing him more time to get back for a slash! Well it was entertaining watching it go everywhere.

We arrived back to camp after dropping off at the various married patches, and the junior officers invited some of us to go back to the officers' mess for a drink, happy days thought! Off we went me, Spike, Robbie, Gus, Spin, Andy, and Fraggle. We gets in the mess and went up to a room (Kev Lewis') and drank him dry of what he had. We were then told that a room a few doors down had lots to drink, and he was in Saudi and wouldn't mind! So we went there, the door was locked. We promptly kicked it open and entered, only to find paradise—a huge room with sofa chairs, TV, and a damn big drinks cabinet (thank you, squadron leader pilot type) so we commenced drinking the said cabinet's contents. 2's OCA asked Robbie about his party trick! So Rob showed us all how to insert Lumocolour permi pens, etc. down his Jap's eye, making the officers gag and us roll around laughing.

We then started scouting missions around the mess on our various trips to the toilets, finding moving officers' shoes waiting to be cleaned! Swapping the tying knots in the laces, pissing in them, and then taking the odd dump in some—Robbie also ventured into a WRAF wing commander's room and was caught going through her dirty underwear when she woke!

A few scuttle runs and safely back to the sqn ldr's room to carry on drinking—it was around 3 a.m. when we found out that OCA PO Wigglesworth (RIP) could play the trumpet, so we actively encouraged him to play for use culminating with a fine solo performance of the Last Post on the officers' mess balcony at 3 a.m. which seemed to cause excitement amongst other residents of the mess! And by this time, it was getting late so we decided to bomb burst through the fire exit and back to the block.

Then Monday morning we got charged for being out of bounds! We protested our innocence, but to no avail, the powers that be wanted to court martial the officers so we had to take the hit! A damn good night.

Neil Horn

All the old comments about officers with maps, blah, blah. Well there is actually something much, much worse—a gaggle of officers with no map or compass, but, "We know the way."

One sunny Sunday morning in the FI—recovering from the night before (shocker)—it was decided that a good rush of fresh air should cure things, "Let's do tumbledown!" A quick run to the NAAFI set us (them, I meant to say them) up with Irn Bru and a bag-rat. Best Rohan's on they set for the CP to grab the battlefield tour script. Hit the road, park at the tour start point. How hard can it be, beautiful sunshine, and an f'ing great hill to aim for.

A few hours pass, lots of bitching and moaning, falling over boulders etc. one reading the script, which for those who have not done that tour is actually pretty amazing. Go through all the various 'sangers' looking at all the abandoned argy kit. Finally reach the memorial at the top and each pay our respects. All of a sudden, like fecking instantly, it was pitch dark and foggy as feck. No map, no compass, and actually no real idea where the LR was. *No probs, let's just follow the trail back.* Well, after passing the argy field kitchen for the second (or was it third) time, we worked out that we may be slightly unsure of our location! It was at that point that aircrew navigator, Lloyd Barrett (shit where I remembered that from, never met the guy before or since) announced he had the new Gucci digital compass on his watch! Result, implement emergency route plan and set bearing for the Stanley Road, then turn right and head for LR. Off we trot, not able to see a fecking thing … not a torch amongst us. Again, tripping, falling, bitching, moaning.

Climbed over a barbed wire fence and onward, just short of the road climbed another fence, "What does that say?" looked at the sign with a lighter—big ole red skull and 'DANGER MINEFIELD'. Walked about a mile through a minefield—oops! Slogged down the road for miles, got to wagon, and back to MPA. Ahh well, all those mines are old and deep in the peat anyway. Until last year when I just happened to read an article about the FI mine clearing that was just completed a couple of years ago—'Most of the mines we found were in amazingly good, operational condition, preserved, it appears, by the peat'. Moreover, despite our initial thoughts that most of the mines would have sunk to a depth that would have rendered them safe, this was not the case. The majority were still at their operational depth of 6-18 inches!

Paul McCarthy

An officer story now. No names but it's my flt cdr tour on ADS and a night shift. Walking through the crew room to the back office in the early hours, I find it packed with the troops laughing like fuck and giving constructive criticism to someone's sexual technique. I absentmindedly glance over at the TV to see one of the troops shagging his girlfriend on camera. Mindful that this is the late 90s, and OC P1 or the stn cdr might not see the funny side. I made discrete enquiries with the FS and sgt to determine where the video came from, and was the UT porn star aware it was on general release. The matter was handled efficiently as one would expect but I found it difficult to speak to the gnr in question for a while without struggling to laugh.

Phil Pringle

Jed's stag day in Bury St Edmunds! Jed was due to get married while we were all on 20 Sqn, and his best man Andy Dalton was tasked with arranging a stag do! So rather than a stag night, he would have a stag day. It was arranged for on Saturday morning the week before the wedding. We all met at around 10:30 by the main guardroom to get the 'shopping bus', there was a very good turnout, helped by most not being able to go away due to the Orbat requirements—we virtually filled the bus. It was quite a sombre atmosphere, a bit like a black and white war film where they are all going on a high risk mission with little chance of return! But in reality it was due to the hangovers from the night before!

Off we set and arrived in Bury at just after 11:00 and headed straight for the One Bull, our favourite drinking hole, things started off quite quiet. After a couple there we headed to the D&P for more refreshments. We then wandered up to the town calling in all pubs on the way. Our first refusal for entry to a pub was the Nutshell! But that was due to the number of us! We then went to the Cupola, which was a favourite amongst the ex-field types who would always tell you the intricacies of a Scorpion turret! And so it went on pub to pub until 3 p.m. when the pubs closed and didn't open until 5 p.m. (allowed to open early on market days). So at around 3:15, when asked to leave, we had a chat and decided to go to the off-licence and get some tinnies and go the park. Tony Pickard, I remember, got himself a party 7, so armed with our carry out, we headed to Abbey Gardens to sit in the park and drink until the pubs reopened. On the way there, we passed a tramp playing the mouth organ. We offered him some beer and a couple of pounds to come play for us in the gardens and off we all went. We found a secluded spot and sat down drinking and singing to songs like 'It's a long way to Tipperary', 'Salome', and others, and having a dam good crack.

Spin Dry and Andy Barlow said they needed to go for a slash. Off they went to the bogs and about five minutes later came running round the corner! "Quick, lads, we have got trouble," they shouted. They had just met the Bury St Edmunds National Front (who were renowned for beating up Guins) and had a quick exchange of blows were Spin was hit with a steel Crazy Golf pole! The Skins were in pursuit of Spin and Andy but had a shock when they turned the corner to see Spin, Andy, and about thirty other jolly gunners. And so it kicked off, evenly numbered, we attacked. The tramp grabbed a few tins and made a hasty escape. Feet, fist, and foreheads were been exchanged readily, the mass brawl started to spill into the more public areas with people running in all directions.

It was around the gates, I was punching this skinhead on the face as he was putting him to the floor when I was grabbed from behind—in what I thought was a strangle hold—panicked slightly, so threw my head back a couple of times, reached round, grabbed them, pulled them to one side, at the same time dropping my forehead hard, squarely on their nose, dropping them to the ground, only then realising that it was one of the Skinheads girlfriends!

The fight carried on and spilled on to the main road stopping the traffic! It was shortly after this the police turned up, got between us, and stopped the fight. Our chief negotiator explained to the police that they had started it and they accepted this and told us to go back to camp. The Skins shouting they were going to get us later as we laughed at them. We headed towards where the bus picked you up, then detoured back into town, and back on the beer. We kept drinking and having a good time ended up in the Wine Loft Club at about 21:30 as it was free to get in before 22:00. A beer fight started and a couple of the lads got soaked so removed their shirts, Al Bunce was wandering around topless, and trying to impress and turn on the women by rubbing his nipples in front of then—but only managing to offend them and turn himself on!

It wasn't long after that we were asked to leave the club. We were going to kick off and take out the doormen when we were told we would then have no club to drink in! So off we went again, back to the One Bull. We were happy drinking in there until closing and we left only to be greeted to something you saw on TV during the miners' strike! A wall of policemen and dogs, many called in from surrounding towns and cities! It looked as things were going to have a very bad ending as Andy Dalton at the time was having a dump in the Indian Restaurant doorway! But thankfully he wasn't seen, but he did walk to the front and say to a dog handler that he would, "Put his left arm in the dogs mouth and grab its front leg with his other and rip is heart in two and kill it," pulling his Welsh war face (picture a constipated sheep from Merthyr Tydfil). The policeman said he wouldn't let him hurt his dog, and moved away! The negotiators (jnr NCOs) started their work! We were asked for our ID cards and we said we didn't have them! Then they started taking our names! Virtually everyone giving false names, according to the list, all the officers from the CO down were there, it was hard to think of names as someone would use the one you had thought of! I settled on Dougie McRae (my FS). One of the lads said, "Rip Hare," and then was asked not nicknames, so he said it was Italian and short for something I can't remember.

There were at least three Karl Radfords (he was on his FT). We were then told to go to the bus station/taxi area. We were walking up the hill, followed by the police. About halfway up, someone shouted, "Bomb burst, every man for themselves!" and we all ran in all directions. It was like something off *The Fugitive*, running full pelt and diving down alleyways to avoid capture (turns out police didn't even follow us). I ended up at a kebab shop and met a few of the lads and a sober type from camp getting a kebab, so we asked for a lift back to camp, we squeezed into the car three in the passenger seat, five in the back seat, and three in the hatchback.

Off we set, on the way back, Ross chucked his half eaten kebab out the window and it hit the car behinds windscreen, they then cut us up and forced us to pull over and out got four burly chaps! The driver opened the boot and we all got out the car, they were shocked to see twelve of us, so ran back to the car and drove off at speed! We got to the camp and stopped short of the gate and got out and let the driver go on. We could see there was a commotion at the gate! So stayed out of sight, putting our training to good use. Spin Dry was there and a few others so was our 2 IC FL Parsons, he didn't take kindly to Spin saying he did not realise that he was on gate guard! At that point we scurried off to a point where we could scale the perimeter fence. Which we did safely, then to bed.

A few had spent a night in the cells, but most of us thought we were in the clear. Monday morning comes, and mid-morning a squadron parade was called, the CO addressed/bollocked the squadron and informed us that he had just come from the station commanders office, and he and every member of the squadron including wives were banned from Bury St Edmunds for a month! He said that he wasn't at all happy that he could not take his wife shopping in Bury! Then the Squadron WO Harry Foxley said, "The following names fall in outside the exec briefing room …" Every one of us had been caught! Serious.

Neil Horn

Gulf 2, I was attached to 1 Division HQ as an air liaison officer. What fun that was—being the only Rock in an army divisional HQ as a flt lt. Walked into one of the bde HQs to a bit of 'liaising', and in true Rock fashion, "Parker, you useless wanker, what the fuck are you doing here?" Oh you could have heard a pin drop, anyone who's been into a brigade HQ tent knows the noise and hive of activity—not this moment!

Ya, see this guy was on my J course, Pete Peter Kelly knows who I mean. The biggest waste of space on the course, failed pilot, failed Js. However, the army loved him obviously, as at this time he was a col. in the 'desert rats', and chief of staff to the bde cdr. Went red as a fucking beetroot, "Erm, er, hi, Neil." Troops and officers sniggering left and right.

'Winterised' Land Rover Wolfs! How well that worked. Studs on anti-fod tyres, kind of like walking on marbles. Never forget Chris, Kev (OC eng), me, and a few troops in Norway, nipped out for a day's skiing. Top day out, until we departed in the evening. Sheet ice on roads—*no problems, we have studs ... really!*

Pulled out from the car park, down road (straight downhill), Kev hit the brakes at first set of lights, nothing, nada, zip. We actually started accelerating in full Torvil and Dean fashion. Through lights unscathed, still no traction or steering, another set of red lights ahead, traffic streaming across, straight through. How, I do not know. Then about 1/2 mile ahead was lights with a T junction and a really busy dual carriageway, surely we will have traction ... nope.

How the hell we made it through four lanes of non-stop traffic doing 70, I do not know. But, life flashing before my eyes, Wolf with eight bodies, skis, etc. We plowed into a snow drift at the far side of the carriageway. 4WD, low ratio, diff-loc, and we crawled out and crawled the ten or so miles back to camp.

The sport of drinking games. Flaming Sambuca to be precise. Think it was West Raynham (may have been Honington), memory is faded on the location, but the names (still serving) are clear but to remain classified. Anyone who has done any flaming liqueur type thing knows that one of the tricks is speed (amongst others). Well the tray of said flaming drinks was on the bar and all rapidly drunk and glass placed on forehead for proof positive. One, however, deep in conversation and being goaded by the rest, "I'll get to it." A few minutes passed, young officer grabs his drink, does the necessary (without the hot glass touching his lips). However on placing to forehead the little old liqueur glass, with the smell of melting flesh, welded itself to his forehead. I am wincing just remembering the look on his face. This was around twenty years ago, I still recall the officer bearing that scar when I left the mob eight years ago.

Stuart Balfour

I was sent to 48 Penal Sqn in the mid-80s as a shiny new pilot officer—boy was I out of my depth. On HQ Flt with such 'characters' as Stodge McLean, Sid Clark, and most of the Smiths and Williams on the Sqn, and yes, it was a baptism of fire.

One incident that sticks in the mind is what happened in the NAAFI one evening: one of the guys decides to get naked at the bop, lies down on the floor, and proceeds to give himself a golden shower. *How do we make this more fun*, thinks one gunner, *I know* ... and grabs the prone gunner by the ankles and swings him around, thereby giving everyone the good news ... You know who you are! Every posting since was a breeze!

Neil Horn

All this talk of officer totty reminded me of (yet another) from West Raynham. We had just been across to RAFG for something or another and returned with the standards of Wobbly, Brats, Curry Ketchup, and German crisps. Upon return, the plans hatched for an impromptu OM Octoberfest. The mess being pretty much ours, the mess manager et al set about and put on a great spread.

Anyhow, a certain sprog officer on 66 was two sheets to the wind (probably four or five sheets, actually) attempting to trap a young filly from 85 Sqn (Bloodhound) at the bar. Feeling a tad nauseous, he beckons the barmaid (SGT PTI's wife, awesome girl) who hands him a giant empty bag of chips (edit: 'crisps', darn, been in USA too long). Without a flinch, he pukes in the bag, hands it to the barmaid (she thought nothing of it, was used to worse from us) and continues his advances on filly. Pure class and, by all accounts, this impressed the 'lady'.

Nick Newman

Thought it was time to join in with a tribute to 'Paddy Mac' MacDonald—my first flt sgt, who taught me how to be an officer. Paddy Mac #1 of 3—LS&GCM. As a young pilot officer, I arrived on 27 Sqn at Leuchars in September '86 and took up the post of sqn adjt/OC HQ Flt, where the SNCO was the legendary Sgt 'Paddy Mac' MacDonald. He always called me 'Boss' in front of the lads, but in private I was always 'Kiddy-O'!

One of my duties was to look after the sqn photo album, and one day I noticed the picture of Paddy receiving his long-service and good conduct medal from the OC—Sqn Ldr Roger White. For some reason, the photo had been folded in half so you could only see them from the waist up. I unfolded it to see why the bottom half had been hidden, and found two JNCOs on their knees, holding him upright. Apparently, Paddy was so pissed he couldn't stand unaided, but the OC decided to go ahead with the presentation anyway, after they'd managed to prop him up!

Belize Skill-at-Arms meet 1988. 1987/88 Belize SHORAD Det and Flt Sgt 'Paddy Mac' MacDonald enters a 27 Sqn team to compete against 2 PARA in the Skill-at-Arms meet. The Paras were the first unit to deploy with the SA-80 and had kindly loaned us some to train with. That is, until the rehearsals, when we beat all the army teams. The paras panicked and got the rules changed so that units could only compete with personal weapons—so Paddy's team entered the next day with their SLRs and no rehearsals. They managed to hold their own, and by the finals it was all down to the falling plate competition.

The Paras sprinted down first and started blatting away—but the 5.56 rounds were bouncing off the plates. With a few seconds to go, Paddy shambled calmly up to the firing point, took aim, and dropped all the remaining plates with his SLR! Humble pie for CO 2 PARA when he handed over the trophy.

Benbecula Archaeological Survey—1987. 27 Sqn were preparing to deploy for missile practice camp in the Hebs, when a new squadron clerk was posted in. He was a big Geordie lad who was struggling to fit in. The OC thought it would be a good idea to take him along and asked the DSC ('Mad' Mike Daly) to find him a 'project' to help him feel part of the sqn. Mike called 'Geordie' in and handed him an admin order for a special mission on Benbecula.

According to Mike's imagination, the previous sqn clerk had been a keen amateur archaeologist and during a previous MPC he had found the remains of the only hairy mammoth to be discovered in the British Isles, which was now on display in the 'Museum of Mankind' in Edinburgh. Geordie's mission was to collect the 'archaeology' pack from stores and link up with Lady Felicity Duckworth-Chad in Benbecula (President of the Scottish Amateur Archaeological Society) to receive instructions for continuing the survey—and then to make a video diary of the dig. My task (as sqn adjt) was to source a convincing 'Lady Felicity', a dig site, and support team.

On our first night in the Hebs, the officers were invited to the station commander's house for drinks, so I asked his wife if she would be willing to play the role. She readily agreed and the next day Geordie was invited to afternoon tea where she gave him a load of BS about archaeology and wished him good luck. I'd found a hidden strip of land that I'd marked out with mine tape—and got the lads to form a roster to help with the dig. Geordie spent the next week digging in a muddy hole with a metal detector and a toothbrush. The lads spent their days sourcing bones and junk that they could bury and then help him 'discover'. Each day, Geordie would record his progress—discoveries of 'prehistoric bones' (from catering flt) and even a suspected 'Viking belt buckle' (found in a scrap metal yard). The lads maintained a continuous support team throughout daylight hours and I made regular officer's checks. As the week went on, none of us could believe Geordie hadn't realised it was one giant spoof.

When we got back to Leuchars, we got the whole sqn together for a film evening where we showed his video diary. 120 men crying with laughter and the poor bloke still didn't twig it was a spoof—not the sharpest knife in the block!

1987/88, 27 Sqn, Belize SHORAD Detachment, and 'Paddy Mac' MacDonald had been promoted acting flight sergeant. He'd discovered that the admin officer was paying a special allowance for units who conducted construction work to improve the quality of life at airport camp. Paddy proposed building an Attap palm shelter for an outside detachment bar, and had got agreement for a few hundred dollars funding. One morning I found him loading up the 4 tonner with out of date ten-man rat packs. I asked him what he was up to and he just winked and said, "Baksheesh, Kiddy-O," before driving off.

When he didn't return the next day, I began to wonder if I should report him 'MIA', but decided to give him another night before I called out a search and rescue. The next evening Paddy drove back into camp with the 4 tonner piled high with freshly cut poles and palm leaves and a grinning Mayan Indian sitting on top. For the next few weeks, this guy built us an Attap shelter whilst eating and sleeping on Rapier Site 1, where he lived like a king. When he was finished, he 'signed' a receipt for the work and Paddy dropped him back in the bondoo, before cashing in the allowance, and using the money to pay for a booze cruise for the lads out to the Cayes.

It turned out, he'd found the guy in the jungle and had paid him in ration packs, so the whole enterprise had cost us nothing—and we'd ended up with a new bar and a great weekend R&R!

Alistair Bidwell

While on TSF. 1990, I think. Anyone remember the JRoc Saudi officer who buried the GPMG on finals because he couldn't be arsed to carry it on the final tab?

Got back to RTSA, did the weapon count, and one said GPMG missing. DS demanded recount. Again, one GPMG missing. "Who last had it?"

His reply to being asked where it was? "I bury it! No worries, I buy new one."

Neil Horn

Okay, on the theme of officers and maps, but not RAF Regt specific. Gulf 2, I had the awesome privilege of being attached to HQ 1 Div. D+1 after the break into Iraq, the behemoth that is a Div HQ was to advance. The advance party already moved forward, we load up the 120,000 tons of other kit and wait for orders. On the bus, off the bus, not enough buses, etc., for a few hours, then pile in. About 40 to the back of a 4 tonner, on top of kit and Bergens.

Anti-ambush orders given by some Siggycapt …like that will work, it'd take us about twenty mins to even get the tailgate open. Any old how, we go trucking off into Iraq 'led' by a young Siggysubbleton. About two hours in, we stop. Thinking it was a piss break, we all literally fall out the back of the wagons, what a shambles. Only to find that we had taken a wrong turn, the entire convoy gone up a dead end in some Iraqi village! Subbleton was trying to get directions off a couple of villagers—outstanding. "We are the British Army HQ, we are trying to get here, that is where we will be located." Twat!

Then to watch the carnage for the next hour as about 200 of us milled around while they turned all the trucks around. I felt perfectly safe with my 9mm and 10 rounds, everyone with an 185 had 20 rounds. So we were good for a wedding celebration but kind of screwed for anything meaningful and no CBA (had to donate that to combat troops). What an utter cluster.

Jerry Riley

Many of my colleagues have heard me recount this. PCBC, Warminster, the course is in a steep-banked auditorium, Paras at the front, taking notes to try and win the course binos; the likes of us behind them, trying to keep up the corps' reputation, guards asleep at the back; whilst some army colonel whips up the fever with a firebrand lecture about, "The lot of the infantry is to close with the enemy—eyeball to eyeball, blood, guts," etc. You get the picture.

"Has anyone here been shot at?" asked Col Blimp. A few hands went up (it wasn't unusual in those days for subalterns to go direct to their battalions in N.I etc. and only come back later to complete PCBC). The big man's chest swelled with pride, "And you men who were shot at—did any of you see the man who shot at you?"

The hands all went down, bar one, at the back, where the guards officers usually dozed, pyjamas poking out from under lightweights as they were too late back from London to properly get changed. "Splendid …and what went through your mind when you looked into the eyes of the man who shot at you?"

Cue the wonderfully laconic, dry Irish guards officer's voice, "Well, Sir, I thought it was rather odd—it was my staff sergeant at Sandhurst." I honestly cannot remember where the lecture went after that as we all dissolved.

CHAPTER 3
MARCH ON THE QUEEN'S COLOUR SQUADRON

Gary Horsfield

The 'Edinbrugh Tattoo bang' will fit one of the most talked about stories I know of during early 80s. Six beat drum roll, we started the sequence, marching up the Esplanade. Within the first few opening mins of the show, we go to the trail arms, and the famous carrying handle of mine snapped at the neck followed by one loud bang! My SLR falls to the floor scared and apprehensive of what's going to happen to me when I get off the Esplanade. The lads are advising me, "Just carry on, Gaz." Keeping calm, I do exactly that, the only drills man having to continue through the whole show with no weapon.

We finally gets to the end of the show for the present arms then a spotlight shines intensely on my brow and the speech reads, "Ladies and gentleman, tonight you seen a very rare sight for the sqn, and we're happy to say that the airman concerned will not be in the guardroom."

Six beat drum roll, we march off. The WO doing a double quick pace to see me, followed by the lads. I hear WO voice, "Gunner Horsfield!" I show him the carrying handle. His face went from a pulsating vein red to a calm pink and with plenty of pats on the back from the lads. I was overwhelmed by the sheer feeling of professionalism not only by my own action but that of the sqn as a family. To this day, every time I see the tattoo, or even stand on the Esplanade, I know that I did my job as a drillsman on this sacred tarmac! Edinbrugh Tattoo. 1982.

Dean Montgomery

Uxbridge 80/81ish leaving the NAAFI bar late meant running a gauntlet of abuse and water from fire hydrants to get back into the block! One particular evening, with girlfriend in tow, was approaching a very quiet main entrance to the block when jets of water appeared out of nowhere. Managed to avoid the water and

Chapter 3: March on the Queen's Colour Squadron

Edinburgh Tattoo 1982

head for the fire escape, up to first floor, into corridor, and fortunately my room was second right. Just managed to unlock and get into my room as a jet of water came shooting down past my door. Anyway, feeling pleased with myself 20/30 mins later, all eventually settles, and lying in bed, I hear the squeak of my sash window being raised, before I could even move, the end of a fire hose is snaking around in my room, we got effin' soaked. Turns out the bastards unwound the fire hose, climbed out of another window, and disco kneed it along a small concrete ledge! Don't know for sure who it was but the origins of the BHG were afoot back then …

Gus Dunning

QCS, about '82, sat down for Christmas dinner in the Uxbridge mess. As usual, we were the largest contingent in there. Some bandsman got a little brave and started flicking pea or sprouts at us. Huge mistake as on the tables was a selection of fruit, which contained the largest oranges you've ever seen. Incoming and carnage on the bandsman tables as they all got Jaffa-ed while the Rock officers tried to restore calm to the rabble.

Neil Horn

QCS, Sqn 'do', in early 90s. Not sure the occasion but it was fancy dress. Boss told all officers, "No fancy dress—officers and spouses must be in dinner jackets and cocktail dresses."

He never said who in what, so me and Mrs H turned up, her in DJ and me done up to the nines—I looked quite hot actually! Give Dave his due—he just looked at me, "You fucker, nice one."

Picture courtesy of Tim Parker.

Phil Cameron

On exercise with QCS, in the mid-90s, around the time boil in the bag and Peak stoves were being issued. The lads were all getting scoff and brews on. About 10-15 feet away, one of the sqn officers was looking at all this new 'Gucci' kit with a puzzled look on his face. After we've shown him how to get his Peak stove going, we notice he's got an open bag of rolled oats in his hand, but is still looking bemused, we just carry on with what we're doing. Next thing we see is said officer placing said bag of rolled oats directly onto the flames! You can imagine the suppressed sniggers.

Dave Capps

During an exercise in Germany, QCS was deployed to defend the Heli force. As part of that, the Tactical Strike Force (TSF) formed a third flight. The OPs are set, and three gunners in a remote position observe a Lynx (enemy) helicopter deposit four hostiles in a field to their front.

This is duly reported by radio and landline to the deployed helicopter site. The helicopter sits idling awaiting the bad guys return.

During the initial activity, a member of the OP team has disappeared from his post and is suddenly observed by his *compadres* approaching the Lynx, weapon in hand. At the edge of the rotor disc, he takes a knee and gives the thumbs up to the bemused aircrew, who, suitably impressed by procedure, return his signal, inviting him to join them. Not being one to pass up on such a kind offer, our intrepid hero duly boards the helicopter and sticks hid SLR in the pilots face requesting, "Fly me to Cuba."

Four hostile ground troops captured, one lynx and two very upset AAC pilots chalked up to a three man TSF OP ... Sorted.

Fraze Barkway

When on QCS, an old SNCO mate of mine paid a visit and reminisced about his time in the block whilst he was there. QCS had a three storey block, as they all were at Uxbridge. The WRAF block was opposite. This was long before the invention of VHS porn, so the only way to view it other than in a book was to get the Sqn's 16mn projector and watch it by the reel. Not exactly a private affair. Some genius had the idea of waiting for it to get dark and then projecting it from the rock block onto the WRAF block opposite. Effectively making everyone's rooms on that side of the block into a wanking booth. The old legend explained that it worked brilliantly, apart from the odd WRAF opening a window and asking what the hell was going on.

I laughed at his story but it wasn't until the next morning stood looking at the block that I really got the giggle fits. All the WRAFs must have seen was a wall of windows with gunners' heads pulling the Japanese sniper face at them and shaking shoulders.

Mark Dorward

During my time on QCS, we got into the habit of having firework fight inside Doiran block. On one particular evening, a few of us were gathered in one of the lad's (Martin Ashford, I think) rooms, deciding how best to deploy the contents of the huge box of fireworks he had bought. One of the other lads (Andy Rowlands, I think) decided it would be a good idea to light a firework and lob it into the box. The result was, as you can imagine, 'impressive'. We scattered from the room, leaving the box of fireworks on the floor to do their thing, and watched the display from outside the block—smoke and sparks flying out of the window.

On checking Ash's room afterwards, it was trashed, but he still managed to laugh it off. The entire block had to be re-carpeted after that crazy weekend. Mick Austen and Kev McGee went banzai when they saw the devastation. I will never forget that night.

Chris Backhouse

I remember Roy Blake (RIP) once telling a story from when he was on QCS. It was a weekend and he was out for a run when he was pulled by two cops in a squad car for 'fitting the description' of someone who had recently robbed something (?). Anyway, they don't believe he's in the RAF because he had no ID on him, (and he's black so must be guilty, right?). So they haul his ass down the station and leave him to sweat a while before questioning him. Eventually he's brought into the interview room and asked his whereabouts at the time of the alleged crime. Apparently the fact that he was at Buckingham Palace, guarding the Queen, at the time of said crime took some convincing but after calling the OC at his home address, untold quantities of shit flew towards the largest fan ever! Nice one, Roy.

Gus Dunning

QCS, 1982/83, public duties, Buckingham Palace. Sat in the guard room with Sgt Alan Dobson (RIP), about late o'clock at night. In strolls FL R. Booth who had attended a function at St James Palace in the mess—which is something of a requirement, as all the senior offices at RAF Uxbridge who usually detest the sqn get invited for a jolly. Anyway, back to the story. FL Booth is rather the worse for wear, and drops his parade shoes on Al Dobsons desk and tells him to make sure they are prepared for the guard dismount in the morning. I do think there was a bit of history here because as soon as Mr Booth has disappeared, Al Dobson says, "Does he think I'm his friggin' batman," and tells one of the lads to drop the shoes in the fire bucket full of water. There they stayed until the morning, were the said officer sheepishly recovers them from the fire bucket and had to slip them on for the guard dismount. I can still hear him squelching across Buckingham Palace forecourt now. I understand after that he did his own bloody shoes, and always carried a spare pair.

Joan Stuart Currie

Some left-wing, fanny-munching, save-the-world women decided to lie in our pathway as we were getting the five beat drum roll to do a show. The warrant officer ordered, "Just go right over them." We did, wasn't a pretty sight, but they never did that again.

Andy Prynne

Mid-1980s at Royal Tournament. Last night and the squadron is marching on for the display led by the warrant officer, when a rubber chicken is dropped from the roof by the Royal Marines and hits the WO on the head. He was staggering slightly while I was chewing my lip trying not to laugh. Good times.

Chapter 3: March on the Queen's Colour Squadron

Picture courtesy of Tim Parker.

Tony Ryan

I was going to save this until Halloween but I thought I best share this with you, as I still to this day do not know who carried out this heinous crime upon myself—which I believe led to me becoming a little unhinged at times.

It was at Uxbridge, during my penance at Queens Cuddly, late seventies, I was in Bagdad block on the third floor and I was making my way to the ablutions for my usual 7:30 poo, last trap on the right, armed with a paper and a fag. I entered my usual trap and prepared for the business of the day.

I was by this stage in uniform and all was going well until I sat on the toilet. As my arse impacted on the seat, this caused a decent-sized lump of poo to be ejected into the gusset of my pants, catching the back of my right calf on the way down, followed by the fag that I was smoking, at the shock at what had just happened.

I sat there for a while thinking, *What sick, inventive genius had thought and researched this?*— if you cut at empty toilet roll in half, block one end up, and fill it with poo then pat it down a bit, and put it under the toilet seat between it and the basin then the natural process of gravity will do the rest.

As I sat there having a little blub to myself, asking questions like, *Why me, Lord? Where do I start my search for the twat that done this to me?* I then realised that we had so many shit specialist in the block at the time—Royston Jones, Slasher Smith, Cot Death Goulding to name few—this search would go on for months. But I tell you now, there is nothing more disappointing in life than pulling someone else's poo out of the gusset of your own pants.

Neil Horn

QCS, either late '93 or early '94. I was ensign and we had to do a colour party march on for 'This is Your Life' for Sir Michael Gradon, CAS at the time. The older guys will remember the Michael Aspel show, and all was secret until the big day. This was to be held at RAF Halton. I recall Ray Hughes was SWO, cannot recall rest of the colour party. Anyhow, lots of rehearsals on the day, with us, a small band contingent, and a bunch of BBC 'lovies'. Space was really tight and we had to be a bit 'interpretive' with AP200. Band in front, we march down a tight corridor with colour on the shoulder (low roof), then as we enter the auditorium, whip the old blue flag up into the carry.

In typical QCS fashion, timing was perfect, that flag was up as soon as we entered; as if by magic. Then, the live performance. Show goes great, then the big finale; 'dut dah dutdutdut dah' and on we go. Whip the flag up … WTF! I was nearly flipped backwards! Some friggin' lovey had decided to drape a friggin' RAF banner over the entrance, reducing door height by a foot, and the crown on the colour got snagged. Was all I could do not to shout, "Fuck!" on live TV. Managed not to break step and held the colour until it broke free of the damn banner. It literally took all my strength to keep it upright. Not one person noticed until I told them and we 'ran VT', and it was obvious by the venomous look on my face and the fucking banner looking as though it is about to bring the house down.

John Stowell

Yet another one from Germany late 70's. Some of you guys out there may be able to relate to this one. They decided for whatever reason to form an escort for the Queen's Colours for RAF Germany, and made it a joint effort between 16 at Wildenrath and 37 at Bruggen. I don't know if they did it for the other two bases. For some unknown reason, I was selected to be a part of this. We did some parades for some interesting people, usually at Bruggen—such as the then German chancellor Billy Brandt and our own Prime Minister Jimmy Callaghan. But the subject of this story is Fred Mulley, who at the time was the British Defence Secretary. In case you don't know, he had been photographed by the press sat next to the Queen at the Royal Jubilee parade at RAF Finningly *fast asleep*! The photo was splashed all over the news.

Anyway, back to the story. The parade for him was again at Bruggen. We were marched on. Formed two ranks. He was on the dias and the present arms done. As the officer IC was moving forward to give the usual invite to inspect the troops, Pete (Grub) whispers, "This will be the fastest inspection you've ever seen, coz if it ain't, the cunt will fall asleep!"

It's at times like that where you see your career going down the toilet as you so desperately need to laugh but can't. The watery eyes, the bulging neck veins, and the feeling that the contents of your head is going to burst out of your ears. But somehow I/we held it together. Pete was called a few names after that one.

Picture courtesy of Tim Parker.

Glynn Ford

Chaps, a timeless classic. Every couple of weeks, new intake to QCS were summoned to the NAFFI to get to know the sqn Rocks, and of course buy us beers. The ploy—I would sit on my own, staring into a glass of beer, Bill Billingham would advise one of the sprogs to get to know me by asking, "How are your sister's piano lessons going?"

I would then sit bolt upright, stare at the poor sprog with a vengeful look of death and say, "You know my sister's got no fingers!" Oh, the joy as the blood drained from their little faces.

Rip Eyre

Whilst on QCS in the 70s. At the Berlin Tattoo, we'd been taking flak from the loggies when we came off for leaving mags and bayonets on the arena. Last night we'd had enough, whilst leaving the arena, the outside rank passed their weapons in one, and as the first man reached the last loggie waiting to go on, we gave them a good thumping—they went down like nine pins.

Kev Grimshaw

After a visit to Catterick by the QCS body snatchers, 9 'willing volunteers' were duly dispatched to Uxbridge to start the six week QCS drill course! We were politely informed that until we passed out of training flt, the Thursday night bop was out of bounds, and considering the size of some of the sqn enforcers at the time, we duly kept the fuck out!

Six weeks later and the final assessment was given in front of the entire sqn, who were watching us like hawks for the slightest wrong move or gash drill movement—which would usually end up with a proper good hiding! However, all went well, and we successfully pass, which meant one thing—Thursday Bop! Shirts were dug out and pressed, best kecks and polished shoes, and off we went, only to be halted at the door by a couple of the old sweat SAC's!

"Where the fuck do you lot think you're going?" we were politely asked!

"To the bop, we passed out of training flight today!"

"Not without your hats you ain't, sprogs!"

"Hats?" we enquired.

"Yeah, hats—go and fetch your tin lids!" Well as we all know, straight from Catterick and your steel helmet has yards and bloody yards of hessian scrim halfway down your back!

So off we go and all return wearing our 'hats'. "Okay, lads, in you go, have a lovely night!"

So all night we cut around the bop, sticking out like a dog's nuts, and stinking the place out with half of Catterick training area on our heads—until we hear the DJ (Jock Slug Veitch) call us all into the dance floor! Dance floor clear and nine of us in scrimmed-up tin lids are told to dance! At this point we should've clicked by the fact 'Disco Inferno' was being blasted out, that more was to come before we were finished!

One by one, the hessian scrim was lit by over-enthusiastic volunteers, and we had to remain on the dance floor until it had burnt out! Scrim being rather long, shirts were starting to smoulder, and our dance was getting extremely frantic, throwing out moves that even Michael Flatley would've found hard to keep up with, as we patted and beat the flames off each other's clothes! However, now being accepted members of the best drill unit in the world, our comrades, now lost in a thick black stinking smog, kindly 'extinguished' us with approximately 80 pints of lager and Guinness, thus cooling the steel to a comfortable 120 degrees! Funny thing is not one of us pulled that night and helmets remained on till bedtime! Happy days!

Picture courtesy of Tim Parker.

Scott Ramsey

QCS were doing something bone and 2 Sqn got tasked to complete a sun down parade—can't remember where it was and we were not known for our left rights. Anyway, this was being taken very seriously by the commissioned types on the sqn and had some quite high-ranking attendees. It was that important that they had arranged for a Harrier to hover above us during the parade. So we march on, and take our place, stood, all going smoothly, at ease, and then it's time for the finale. March past the 'royal box', eyes right, and Steve Jones as right marker steps off on his wrong foot, resulting in the entire sqn having to skip a step like a Mexican wave as we are marching past the 'royal box'.

John O'Rourke and Steve Parker

The last performance of the Royal Tournament Shows for 1972. The show runs for a month and is an opportunity for the military to show to the public what they can do besides their military duties. We do a show every night for a month and it includes two on Saturdays. Sundays we have off (thank God, it was a killer on your uniform). However you did get paid for doing it—50 pence a show.

The drill squad consisted of seventy-two guys, plus a parade SNCO, and a parade officer. Over the past few years, the last show of the tournament has always been fraught with fun, which means that all the services try and screw the others on the show, lots of piss-taking, and this year was not going to be any different. A member of the British Royal Family in the royal box, Prince Charles, as the reviewing officer. On this day, we did a small guard of honour for him with a flt lt as our officer.

Now going back to the job in hand. It was getting close to our time to march on the arena. We formed up at the rear of the arena behind bloody big doors out of the public gaze and also behind the central band. So Steve and I decided we would put our own stamp on things. We were all formed up when the band started their five beat drum roll. It was at this time that Stevie and I passed our rifles to one of the guys and delved into our uniform jackets—we had hidden these wigs that my missus had got for us. We quickly took off our hats and stuck on these wigs—I had a beautiful, blonde bob, and Stevie had this wonderful-looking, shoulder length auburn one. We put our hats back on and they would hardly fit due to the hairy wigs, but we made them fit. All the guys were pissing themselves laughing at us, smut, innuendos, everything. It was all in good fun and we loved it.

We marched out into the arena knowing that we would be in the shit. But what the hell! As we marched out, we fired blanks from our rifles at the port arms. Unknown to us, the marines were up in the roof of the arena throwing feathers down, they also threw out little, yellow ducks on parachutes, which came floating down, and at the same time, marines came out of the side entrances in white coats and stretchers picking up the ducks. But that's not the end of it.

Stevie and I were getting wolf whistles, cheers, and laughter from the audience, it felt great.

Then as we marched past the parade officer—which just happened to be Ted Chadwick—we could see the rage building up inside of him as he looked at us both marching past and us just smiling away as if butter wouldn't melt in our mouths. As the show was coming to an end, we marched out back to these big arena doors, no sooner had we got through these doors when the officer was all over us, he shouted to an SNCO to have us both arrested and marched away. Tony grabbed two SACs who just happened to be in the way, and had us frog marched and thrown in to a waiting Land Rover. We were then taken to RAF Northolt, about 20 miles away, and thrown in the brig. Northolt was the prison cell for holding prisoners until they were heard.

We spent the weekend in the nick, and on the following Monday we were collected from Northolt, and again under escort, marched in front of the station commander at RAF Uxbridge SHQ, being our parent station. He heard our side of the story but was having none of it, because of his rank he could give a more severe punishment. And he bloody well did, he gave us another seven days in the nick at Northolt for bringing the RAF into disrepute. However, all in all, both Stevie and I have never regretted what we did, it was all in good fun, but the RAF didn't see it that way.

Well having been invited to a sleep over (for seven nights) at the Northolt Plaza nick (it would have been rude to refuse), we were whisked away to detention for the week. When we arrived, we were straight into denims to start our punishment—in fact our punishment was already underway, as whilst being banged up on the Saturday, we had missed the end of tournament piss up and lost out on receipt of tournament pay.

I can't recall how long it was before John and I had bundled up some socks to make a ball, and got a game of footy underway in the exercise yard—the only flaw in the game was that there was a wire roof which in no time at all had grabbed our football—oh, I mean socks—and was determined to keep hold of them. The cpl of the guard spotted us on the camera and entered the yard and realised what we were up to (must have thought we were trying to escape, ha, ha).

Steve was permitted two cigarettes a day; one in the morning and one in the evening. He had to approach the cpl on duty and say, "Please, Cpl, could I have my cigarette now?" However, if we had visitors, we were allowed to smoke if offered whilst they were there visiting. Luckily John was going out with Jo a W.R.A.F. (whom he later married) and she came with cigarettes in abundance which kept me supplied while visiting (did I ever thank you, Jo?).

John had asked Jo to pick him up some shreddies (underpants) on her next visit. Well, she brought in leopard skin ones—not the sort of things to wear in the nick!

We were joined by a Penguin, who I believe had gone AWOL, if memory serves me right.

Now the downside of this kind offer of accommodation was going for meals, one of us had to go and collect meals from the mess under escort and in denims! It felt like you had a big arrow on your back saying, "He did it," so we sent the Penguin as often as possible. We were given little jobs to do, like cleaning the gym. On one occasion, Steve was sent to help clean a married quarter, and it was disgusting—even more so when he was told it was an officer's home. Those where the days!

Andy Taylor

Remember being on 1 Sqn, mid 70s, I think. Dave Bryant was given the task of whipping us up into a QCS-type display unit for an open day at Wildenrath—weeks of being total, double-left-footed, one-armed pillocks. Night before the open day, told that our aged grannies could do better than us, with one leg in plaster and an arm in a sling. Next day, ready to march on, bloody proud as hell. Two displays: one a.m. and one p.m., both done 100% spot-on. Loudest applause, like thunder, not only made me proud to be a Rockape, but also to be able show that Dave Bryant was a master craftsman when it came to turning shite into shine. Per Ardua, RIP Dave.

John Eric Unsworth

Well, here we go, you have asked for some QC stories from the 70s. We went to Liverpool for the flower festival, as normal, we had practice at Uxbridge, all was well. Got to Liverpool, again practice, no problem. On the day of, we went, band playing, us swaggering, going through the drills, no problem. Then we came to the fix bayonets on the march, not a problem you would think, all going well, except Frank Kinder he got his glove thumb stuck in the bayonet lug, next move up into the recover, Frank quick as a flash hand out, glove, up it went! Loads of gleaming bayonets, one pure white glove blowing in the wind. You should have seen it, so many bayonets bobbing up and down with laughter. Needless to say FS Baraclough and Cpl Bodymead went apeshit; Cpl Pink got a bollocking too for laughing. Back at Uxbridge, WO had his say too.

Simon Pogson

I seem to remember being on a Harrier exercise, late 80s, in Germany with QCS (yes we did do some green stuff), I think 1 were playing enemy. Anyway, we had been out for a couple of days and had returned to the site for replen. We timed it so we could have scoff on site and then out we would go again. At the time, section commanders were SACs, as the sqn only had about four to five JNCOs, so we had nobody of rank with us—not an issue, until a gobby Guin SNCO comes up and starts having a go at us about having cam cream on in the mess tent. We take the bollocking and think nothing more of it. Scoff finished and we had just mounted up, ready to go back out, when said Guin walks past, giving us the evils. Big mistake. Next mistake was to head off into a portaloo. As soon as the door closed, three lads from the other fire team ran over and tipped over onto its door. We stayed just long enough to listen to the curses and heaving, and then we made a quick getaway, never to return to that site. At endex, we heard bits about the incident but there were so many rocks in the field (QCS, 1, 63, 16, I think) nobody could be pinged for it.

Paul Johnson

More stories from the Queen's Colour Squadron. The squadron was tasked with so many jobs, its hard trying to keep track of them, however here's a few.

Some jobs that the sqn gets tasked with are funerals. Whether it's a member of any royal family, politician, or a member of the armed services. We were told that we were going to do a funeral at some RAF base for a member of the military that had an accident and died as a result. We arrived at the base and did our rehearsals for the job. When we were at the cemetery, the firing party was moved off to one side of the area to prepare for the ceremony. As the bearer party was lowering the coffin into the grave, the firing party came to attention for their part. As they were bringing their weapons into the high port, the grave that we were stood on (there wasn't room to move), one of the guys, Kenny Lomax, slammed his foot into the

Chapter 3: March on the Queen's Colour Squadron

attention position and the grave started to give way. Apparently, the coffin under the grave collapsed with the weight; the thumping of Kenny's feet was too much, and the old coffin broke up. He started to sink into the grave with every movement; it was so funny when he started shouting and cussing about being taken too early. We had our fair share of mishaps during funerals.

One of the tasks we did as the burial party was to stand either side of the grave, and six of us (three either side) would take up the slack on the lowering ropes (white tapes really) and the grave party would remove the bars going across the grave holding the coffin up. They then would slowly lower the coffin into the grave. However, on this occasion, the coffin was heavier than normal and as the lads took the strain, the ground on one side edge where the boys were standing started to give way and dirt was falling into the hole, being slowly followed by one of the guys, where the ground under his feet gave way.

Stevie Fern

While serving at Swinderby, he was tasked with a funeral and the funeral party was being trained by the SWO who was a Penguin. After some of the NCOs tried to add their 10 peneth worth of advice, they were told to keep quiet, as he knew what he was doing and he was the boss. On the bus to the cemetery, Stevie told him that had he forgotten anything and was told to keep his advice to himself, again he knew what he was doing.

When they were at the graveside, the firing party asked for their blanks for the weapons, and were told by the SWO that he had forgotten them, what a fricking numpy. Don't know what came of the funeral.

One day at the cemetery, the hearse pulled up with the coffin inside. The funeral people came round the back and removed the locking peg that stops the coffin sliding out the back. The boys all assembled at the back of the hearse, ready to accept the coffin, there they were looking at each other, and as the funeral people moved out the first part of the coffin for them to hold on to and then to continue to slide it to, the rest of the boys, who were all lined up ready to receive it, the hearse started to move forward with no one in the driver's seat. The bloody driver didn't put the handbrake on, and it started to roll forward, the coffin was half out the car. The boys hurriedly passed it from the one to the other quickly so that the whole coffin weight didn't fall on the first two men. Never seen white gloves move so fast.

The one that Mick Sandle did was the bomber commands commanding officer during the ??? War and was none other than ???. As they turned up to collect the coffin, Lady ??? stated that, "Wouldn't it be nice to take him through his garden once more?" Mick and his men looked at the garden and came to the conclusion that there was no way he was going to get through the gate at the end of the garden without turning the coffin on its side. With a little conversation with the sqn CO, that's exactly what they did—however they did it without anyone noticing that they turned it on its side.

Another one that the sqn did was at St Clement Danes in London, which is the Royal Air Force's church. The coffin in question held the body of some big officer and had been embalmed, and as the boys were carrying him out of the church, the front men must have been slightly smaller in height than the rest of them and for some reason there was fluid dripping very slowly on the two front men. It seems that the coffin wasn't entirely sealed and the fluid was finding the lowest point, the front of the men's uniform—when they got back they were stripped and uniforms burned.

Paul Johnson

One character we had on the QCS was a gentleman by the name of Carl Styler, what a guy. When we went on detachments, he was often mistaken for a Zob because he had a cut glass accent. But he was like the rest of us an SAC. One day, he came out on parade and marched out onto the parade square with the rest of us, we could all see what he had on his feet. We were all standing in three ranks and stood to attention for the daily inspection from the flt sgt who came around the ranks for the check. However when he approached Carl, he did his nut. Carl was standing there in his blues, ready for the inspection, and on his feet was a pair of brilliant, white, issue plimsolls. The flt sgt went loopy, he shouted at him, "What the fuck are you doing with those things on your feet, Styler?"

Carl coolly replied, without a flinch, that his boots were hurting him and thought that he could wear his plimsolls, and he could have a good day on the square. He was told in between shouts to, "Get the fuck off my parade square and get into your AP boots!"

Carl would sometimes knock on your door and say, "Excuse me but I find that I am financially embarrassed and would it be possible for a small loan."

To which we would say, "Tell us you're skint!"

He would stand on the fire escape at times dressed in his quilted smoking jacket, silk pyjamas, and slippers, looking down on us as Cpl Nicky Carter took the roll call, and would scream at him to get dressed and get the fuck on parade.

Funny thing is, the last I heard, he was doing time for embezzlement.

Peter Bate

As a young lad, after leaving basics, having been posted to QCS, I hated the thought of being a tick tock trooper, so decided in my wisdom to swing the lead and fail QCS—this I eventually managed to do. My reward was to do every gash job going. I was down London talking to an attractive Australian bird one weekend, she said, "Why don't you come and visit me in Sydne?"

Me thought, *Why not indeed, I'm only getting f'ing around here, and the weather is definitely better over there.* There was one big party pooper in my plans and that was the lack of funds, until I came upon the splendid idea of have cheques. Have cheque card, let's go and bounce 350 quid in cheques, and foxtrot oscar to oz land. Oh, yes, must get a visa first. That was no probs, partner in crime Des Kennedy no less accompanied me to Heathrow and off I jolly well went.

Had one hell of a time in Sydney for six weeks, then handed myself into the British Embassy in Sydney, got taken by two city detectives to a navy base in Sydney, whereupon got put in the guardhouse and told I'd probably be more comfortable in the bar till 2300. Sat in there drinking, and suddenly two yank sailors said, "We know you."

Me thinks, *Yeah, yeah.* "Yeah. How the fuck?"

"You were on Manly Beach yesterday. We saw a photo of you surrounded by fifteen cracking girls."

"Err, yes, you're right." A school group—accompanied by their teacher, so I had thought—asked to be photographed picking someone up on the beach. The teacher wasn't their teacher but a local newspaper photographer, hence the picture. Never mind three days later my liver probably wouldn't have held out any more, I was taken to Sydney Airport and flown to Melbourne—nice city—again, tow more city detectives drove me to an air force base. Damn again, locked up in the guard house for all of ten minutes, and as it was a weekend, the RAFP didn't man the guard house but on base personnel did. The cell door opened, "Hey, pommy, you want a beer?" Me thinks, *Am I dreaming this?* I got taken out of my cell down to the room where there was a TV, mini kitchen, fridge full of beer, and steak—what a weekend!

Monday morning, in cell, door was open, those cunts from QCS turned up. Suddenly cell door was locked. Thirty minutes later, in walked WO, can't remember his name, and back to reality. "Get against the wall, you cunt!" was screamed at me. Blah, blah, blah and off he stormed, the Aussies came out and said, "Fuck me, he's got a pair of lungs on him, we'll bring you a couple of beers but the door better stay locked. If you need a steak or bacon sandwich just shout."

I got let out, was lent a beret, got issued a pair of grey overalls, and put in transit accommodation, and every morning went to help clean camp HQ, what a life! Started at 0700, the sun was up, blue sky, and finished at 1500. The flt lt in charge of me was a WRAF, got marched into her office by the camp WO who was—wait for it—an ex sgt rock. She introduced herself by her first name, "My name is Julie.

"Yes, ma'am," I said.

"No my name is Julie."

"Yes, Julie."

During the next week or two, you should have seen our lot's faces when I walked past and she was there. Didn't salute, just said, "Good morning, Julie."

And she said, "Good morning, Peter." Well as usual in life, all good things come to an end. Flew back, accompanied by a sgt from the pay corp from the embassy, and ended up in Colchester for a month.

David Jeremy Wilson

When I arrived at QCS at Uxbridge in 1978, Sgt Ron Barnbrook had me in and out the office at the double some twenty times and I didn't have a clue why! But his attention to me faded when another SAC arriving from Germany walked straight across the parade ground. He had him doubling around it some fifty times with full kit.

Chapter 3: March on the Queen's Colour Squadron

Tim Parker

I'm not sure why the culture arose whilst I was on QCS for pleasuring oneself whilst on post. I was always too chicken to try it myself, and a little scornful until I was shown the inside of a colleague's greatcoat, which bore clear evidence of such activity.

Anyway, I found myself on post one night at the Tower of London, having changed into green after the ceremony of the keys. Rather than a static beat, it was a requirement to carry out a patrol, and it was possible to meet at corners and briefly converse. I was asked by another colleague to keep watch as he planned to indulge himself and I duly turned to return to my post.

Coincidental with my arrival there, officer's rounds commenced and I reported all was well to the flight lieutenant, a namesake of mine, thereafter answering such questions as he had to ask me. Routine stuff. However, I knew that I had to stall him, and attempted to make small talk because I didn't want him turning the corner to be confronted by a tubby jock abusing his tumescent member. Clearly irritated and tired of my attempts to waylay him, the officer and senior set off on their rounds. I then set off in the same direction, attempting to overtake them and warn my devious colleague. I was sharply rebuked to get back on my post.

It wasn't long before I discovered that my monkey-spanking compadre had been caught red-handed. He attempted to tear a strip off me for not warning him until I pointedly explained that I had tried and got in the clag for that, but more to the point, that if he hadn't been polishing his crown jewels when officer's rounds were due (or at all), none of us would have been bollocked.

As it was, he had explained his masturbatory follies away by claiming that he was tucking himself in. I wonder what the officer made of the bizarre behaviour of his sentries that night. Amazingly no-one made off with the real crown jewels.

Nice One Centurion

Paul Johnson

The QCS. One guy we had on the sqn was well known to a lot of us, and that would be the great Ian Bellis. What a guy, he was always well turned out. He joined the sqn and was on the same training flt as me in early '71.

One day, I was knocking on the door to his room to ask him for something (not sure what it was I wanted). Anyway, he said it was in his locker. I looked in his locker and noticed a No. 1 jacket hanging up, full of qualification badges and medal ribbons that he could no way achieve. I asked him what the bloody hell this was doing in his locker, he coolly replied that it was his drinking jacket. After asking further, he said that he wears it to the pubs, and when the old boys at the bar start talking about the good old days, he never buys a drink as they always buy him one for his service—what a cheeky bugger.

One day, we were on the square, practicing for the Albert Hall, and he kept screwing up. The sgt in charge was the brilliant Davy Bryant, he wanted to get a better view so he went onto the balcony at the front of the sqn building. Ian was still screwing it up on the cross over. He was shouting and bollocking Ian from the balcony when he started to slide down to the floor and started to squeak. After we all stopped to see what the problem was, we noticed that some of the other SNCOs were running up to the balcony.

An ambulance was called and collected him from the sqn. As he was being stretchered out of the building, he was heard shouting, "I'll fucking get you, Bellis. I'll fucking get you!" We found out that all that screaming and shouting had given him a hernia, and he popped it out on the balcony.

Robert Booth

Memories being stirred up. We had an oddball character on 51 in the '70s. Surname of Fitzhew or something like it. He never fitted in, no pun intended. He then went off to QCS where he was caught and charged after propositioning another SAC. The other SAC, after the event and dirty deed, went to the police and reported it. Both were done for homo activities. At the subsequent investigation, P&SS discovered that Fitzhew was eight years older than his passport/birth certificate claimed, he was actually Canadian, and he had a wife and two kids. So much for PV clearances.

CHAPTER 4
NO ROCKETS IN MY POCKETS

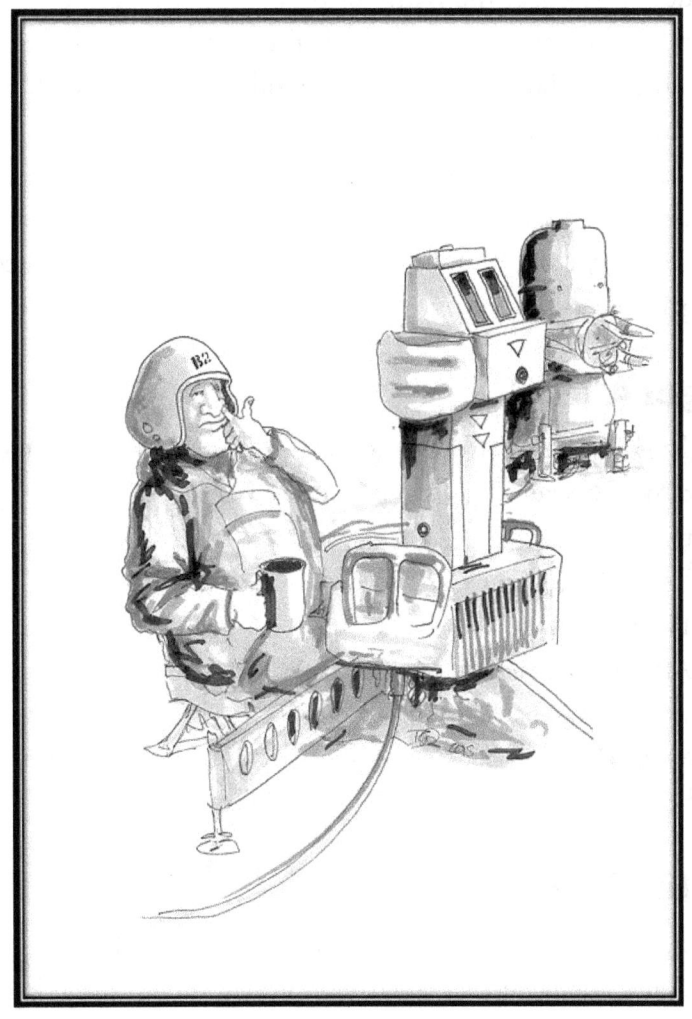

Wayne Holliss

Now when pissed, gunners tend to do stupid things, on this particular night I was in the squadron bar in Belize, along with a few of the lads, Chris being one of them. For what ever reason we started a game which involved the ceiling fan and who could do the most stupid thing with it. So I started by throwing a box of dominos up into it, which didn't really do a lot. Then Shep decided to re-enact the Battle of Agincourt and promptly chuck a hand full of darts up into, bloody things when everywhere, how nobody got a Harold still baffles me today. We even tied blue roll to it and set it alight.

Then he challenged me to stop the fan with me head, so putting a chair on the table, I stuck me swede up, two hours and three stitches later, I was back in the bar looking like I'd just joined the Bengal Lancers.

Nigel Allen

Whilst sitting across from Dean Ogley at breakfast at the mess in Belize one weekend enjoying breakfast. Dean said, "Nige, guess what?"

I said, "You haven't."

He said, "I have."

After a little laugh to myself, he pleaded with me to walk behind him on the way back to our accommodation. The sight of a little brown mark on the back of his shorts had me laughing even more on the walk back …

Peter Carr

Belize, Xmas '84, 27 Sqn. One CPL (can't remember his name), farted and completely followed thorough in the squadron bar. The bar cleared as quick as if someone had tossed a grenade through the door!

Kevin Bell

This is back in the day when on our travels around the world, all the NAAFI shops sold white towelling socks. Everyone wore them. The sergeants' mess looked like one massive Michael Jackson Tribute Act.

Belize, the Upstairs Cafe Bar. There were a handful of us drinking away on the balcony overlooking the bustling street scene. My turn for the toilet. It's very hard to describe Belize toilets, but I'm sure you can imagine. So Ron Hills down, and adopt the 'hovering squat position'. No air and the sweat streaming off me. Finished, oh, no bog paper. Need some, badly. What do you do? The bin which is full of used paper, aaarrrggghhh, no! Okay, sacrifice the socks. A sweaty balancing act to use the first sock, and before thinking, threw sock into the bog. Oh well. Next sock, just to complete the job. Threw that in the bin.

Rejoin the lads swilling rum and coke. A little while later, it was the turn of one of the lads to use the lav. He rejoins the group and says, "Do you know, some dirty bastard has used his sock to wipe his arse, and the knob has thrown it in the bog!"

It was like a well-rehearsed drill movement. Everyone's head and eyes down to look at ankles. Bling! Between my Dezzies and Ron Hills, skin. Busted.

Just as an after thought ... It was many, many years after, before someone was moved up to the sergeants' mess who was cool enough to realise the awful spectacle of the over short black trousers and white towelling socks issue. It still had to be put into SROs/SSOs to ban said socks from being worn in the mess.

Peter Carr

I once fell asleep in my sizzling steak at the Chateau Caribbean, burnt a smile-shaped blister into my forehead that hurt like hell and lasted for months. Was later the only white bit on an otherwise tanned face!

Maz Dutson

Belize, '93, the Shorad CP Rocks used to help run the Battle of Britain bar, or BOBs bar as it was known. A normal weekday night and a good few lads were getting ratted on Belikin beer, rum and coke, rum and pineapple, rum and rum from plastic cups, you know how it goes. Anyway, in walks a pongo SNCO, slashed peak, pace stick, and informs everyone that they are contravening station standing orders by selling spirits which are only allowed to be sold in the sergeants' and officers' messes. Whilst being heckled out of the bar, he says he will be back the next night to ensure all spirits have been removed from the bar list.

Next night, in walks matey boy to see pretty much the same crowd drinking copious amounts of rum. He immediately goes into a rant threatening to lock everyone up. As he gets ever more irate, the duty barman, cool as a cucumber, points to a sign above the bar—'Plastic cups: $1 each. FREE rum with every cup purchased'. Close to bursting with anger, he about turns and marches out never to be seen again.

Derek Wagle

We had a similar thing one night about 2300 at night when a major came in ranting about how the bar should be shut at that time. At that point, he noticed we were all in shorts and t-shirts and went mental because of the dress code, RE mozzies. No sense of humour these pongo types.

Stephen Headey

When we were down Stanley for the first time, we all took it in turns with a VHS recorder we could watch films on ... Well, the very first night said VHS arrived, it was placed in the mess tent and we received the latest batch of videos from somewhere in Germany. Expectation was high as we all sat there like cast members from

M*A*S*H as the engineers were working their magic to get it to work. Success, it was working. "Lights off," commanded our commanding officer. First tape inserted and we all waited as the machine started to play. Amongst the tapes, the wives had sent their messages after a few more wines than normal at the squadron bar. Suddenly, a picture flickered on and we could see the squadron bar. The wives seemed to be enjoying themselves a little too much.

Then shock-horror, the commanding officer's wife confidently showing us all how to eat a bratty was there for all to see. I must say Linford Christie would have been proud at the speed the commanding officer got up raced towards the machine and turned off the VHS all in darkness.

Dan Archer

I remember when I was on 16 Sqn and the then boss Gareth Evans was leaving. He decided at his dining out that, rather than make a speech, he presented a nine-man squad all ex-QCS to perform a display in the anteroom! It went down exceptionally well and the station commander said the lads could have a quick drink in the Scruffs bar before leaving.

After about twenty minutes, OC Ops decided to go and thank them. I went down with him and as we walked in, he was met with the scene of a certain gunner placing twelve bottle tops down his fore skin! It was at this stage they were asked to leave! Great days!

Jim Shanks

On 37 down at MPA, SAC Kev Donoghue (RIP) was tasked with going from the Rapier site to man camp supply to collect a refill of radon gas for the kit. He appears at supply, and signs for a large bag with hazard warning on it, and is told to report to the coppers for escort, and must drive at no more 5mph all the way, with four ways flashing ... oh, how we laughed.

Alan Lomax

Gutersloh, 63, about 1990. Had another run in with someone at the NAAFI bop. Ended up flooring the geezer. Went to buy a drink, only to be told by the lads the police were on route and looking for me. I couldn't escape through the main exit so made myself blend in. Spoke to Al Gardiner. No alibi, so he suggested that he punch me in the face to cut me a little. I agreed so we went to the toilets where Sanch gave me a good dig and split my lip.

Sorted, now I can say the bloke hit me first when and if I got lifted. So I waited for the coppers to arrive with a beer in hand. Ten mins went by, then twenty mins, then half an hour. Where were the police? Guess what? They never turned up. Sanch got a free one on me. Talk about funny though. It's fair to say in all likelihood, I wasn't playing with a full deck.

Barrie Griffiths

Remember the 'Phantom Scratcher' of the 63 Sqn. Sqn cdrs board on the stairs of the 63 Sqn HQ Building. It appears that some ex-squadron commanders were less popular than others and over time their names appeared to get scratched off the board. Imagine my delight when I bump into a visiting ex-OC 63 Sqn Cdr who asks if it is possible to pop over to the squadron to have a look around, "for old times' sake."

"Of course, Sir," says I. As we enter the building, intending to go up the stairs with said ex-OC, I catch sight of the latest OC board vandalism and decide at the last moment to divert towards the security bubble, "Let's have a look around the compound first, Sir," said I. As we passed through, I said to one of the lads there, "FFS, find the warrant officer and get hold of some gold Letraset quick and fix that board on the stairs."

Unsurprisingly there was an immediate understanding of the situation from said lads. Miraculously, by the time we came to leave, having used the second staircase to go upstairs to see the HQ top floor first, he observed the said OC's Board and commented how nice it was to see that the board was being so well maintained. He was clearly referring to the shiny new lettering of his own name and tenure. Thanks guys.

Mac McCarthy

48 Sqn, Belize, 1992, after being dropped off at the police station at the bottom of Cadenas OP by our willing Guats, there is now plenty time for admin. Needing a bath, I pop into the Sarstoon River and go for a wee swim. Before I know it, I'm on the other side, yep, Guatamala!

Seeing as there was no follow-on forces to help secure the county, I simply claimed it for Her Majesty to add to her commonwealth states. Apparently, my nakedness means my claim to Guatamala was null and void, so it remains an independent country.

The following morning we were rudely awakened by a lot of automatic fire at about 5 a.m. Turns out there was a Gaut Army camp just round the corner from my landing point. Two good 'oops' in one day!

Wayne Holliss

Now 48's tour of Belize from Jan-May '89 was memorable for many reasons. Dagger's dear john, zeus on batty's bus, and the infamous valentines card incident. It started after a good session in the sqn bar, as so many do. I left the bar and headed back to the block. On reaching the blk I notice that some guin had had the cheek to park his land rover in front of it. Well, being a Rock, I just had to have a look in. Inside I found a white box, address, and waiting to post, picking it up, I walk into the block. The next thing my brother Rocks had taking the box off me and proceeded to open it. Inside was a lovely valentine's card, oh dear! On looking inside, we decided that the verse was shite and we could do better, and we did, so we thought. We put the card back and forgot about it. Several weeks later, we're up the 'J', all of a sudden, we get a signal telling us to return, asap.

On return, we're greeted by the FS with a, "What the fuck have you lot been up to? The Raf pigs want a chat." Off to the cop shop we went, me in first. After the formalities of name, rank, and number the interrogation started.

"Do you recognise this?" showing me the card.

"No, should I?"

"Is this yours?" showing me my next of kin card, "Yes, why?"

"Do you agree that this writing matches the writing on the card?"

Oops, the penny dropped. Bang to rights, I had little option but to put me hands up, as did the other three. One week after we got back to Lossie, all four of us are up in front of station commander, me in first, said me piece, given fourteen days detention.

Mick Cundy

At Rapier firing cam,ps there is always the competition between crews to be the first FU to declare, so all vehicles and kit are left ready to go from the hangar as fast as possible. One night on shift in the hangar, another engineer and I parked all the vehicles so close to each other and the doors, and in such a manner that not one could move until someone had climbed in and out of the windows or over them, all from one end of the vehicles to the other and wriggle into the cab to be able to drive one of them out, thus releasing the others.

We also mixed detachment vehicles up too (got in a bit of shit over that actually).

Mac McCarthy

Falkland Islands, late '80s, 48 Sqn, Poon Hill. We receive, "Battle Stations," over the net. No probs, up we go, gun out, missiles connected, radar on, chill. Soon after, over the net, we hear, "Hostiles, 100 mile west, incoming." No problems, they've done that before.

"Hostiles, 50 miles west, incoming." Hmm, bit close.

"Hostiles, 15 miles west, incoming." Shit! This isn't right.

Seconds later, the kit to the NW at the quarry calls, "Rats west, rats west," (tracking hostile aircraft for the non-shorad types) Shit the bed, surely not. As I look to the quarry, my kit alarms and slews onto two Tornados popping up over the mountains then dropping right down to the deck to attack MPA as part of a routine exercise!

My radar tracker is locked on and my operator has them, all safety interlocks are off (same with the other kit), all it takes now is a drop tank to go, or sunlight on canopy misconstrued as cannon-fire and we can engage. Operator says, "Erm, Mac ..."

"I know, turn everything off, FFS, don't touch any launch button!" A new OC ops had decided to call, "Battle Stations" (real) on a routine exercise to see if we'd react any quicker.

The muppet hadn't realised that we either plug in real missiles, or a test box, there's no difference in reaction time! The HQ lads told me later that the OC ops (wg cdr) received a one-way briefing in our IGs (flight lieutenant) office for endangering two aircraft, one of which had the stn cdr on board!

Mick Cundy

In the Falklands '82, I attended a FU for yet another fault. On arrival, I was asked to 'go along' with something. I was told that someone had some marking on their neck and was concerned about it so I had a look at it. "Good God," said I, "You've got ringworm on your neck." The person looked very concerned and asked my what that was. I told him that it was a growth that would spread around his neck and, unless treated, it would then contract and strangle him. The 'pebble' was now very concerned and asked what he had to do to stop this happening, so I told him he had to wash it thoroughly and to avoid further infection, he had to shave off all his body hair to prevent more eggs being laid. He was about to start doing that when I just couldn't keep a straight face any longer but he would have shaved it all if I had not then burst out laughing along with all the other crew members.

John Berwick

1983, at call sign 31 Bravo. We had just been delivered our rations dry and fresh, and it was my turn to cook tea, main meal was a joint of beef and veg, and as we have been given some fresh eggs, I thought I would make some pancakes. So went into the store tent, as that's where we kept the flour, made up the pancake mix with

UHT, milk, eggs, and flour, started mixing it all together, and a wee black bit floated to the top, picked it out and flicked it away, kept on whisking the mix, and more black bit came to the surface. I stopped, picked one out and look to see what it was ... mouse shit. I got fed up trying to pick all the mouse shit out, I just made the pancakes and said, "Fuck all."

By chance, the kit went down and a big fat engineer was sent out, I put the pancakes in front of him, told him to help himself. He ate all of the fuckers, even said the raisins were a nice touch. I never told him to this day they where not raisins it was mouse shit.

Chris Pacey

While on JMC at Loch Ewe, some of the 48 Sqn lads noticed an inflatable mock boat (rubber duck target) sitting on the loch unattended. It had a mooring rope on the beach so with normal gunner curiosity, they began to pull the rope to see if it moved the duck. It did.

Quickly it was pulled in, but as it got closer, it was clear that it was quite a bit bigger than they thought, about 30-40 foot in fact, and came in two parts bolted together. Having had experience with rubber ducks before on Rapier, the lads knew there was a plug somewhere to let it down; it was quickly found and unscrewed. It came down like the giant in Jason and the Argonauts! Feeling suitably content that they had scratched their bored gunner itch, they left it there deflated.

A few days later, several admin runs past the now very flat boat, the end of the exercise was upon us, noticing that the boat was still there, the lads found room in the back of a four tonner and re-homed the Matelot pretender into regiment service.

This service was to take the form of the Lossiemouth Raft Race, where it was inflated with the exhaust of a four tonner and floated, renumbered '48' on the river Lossiemouth at the sea front. Towed out by the RAF dive team boat to act as marauding pirates, attacking the rafts with eggs and flour as they came past. This went down well with the occupants of Lossiemouth drawing cheers from the crowd and cameras flashing everywhere, including the Moray Times and the Northern Scot photographers, where it subsequently made a centre page double spread!

Feeling very happy with this, it was removed and placed on the wall in the canteen. It was until a flash signal game in from the RN saying whoever had stolen their £75,000 radar reflective minesweeper decoy, would they return it under amnesty or be charged, as it was vital to the defence of the fleet!

John Berwick

In 1982, just after the war finished, there was what was called 'Galtieri's revenge'. Where you shit and puked up at the same time. There was thoughts that it may have been liver fluke, but turned out that there was some dead Argies floating in the reservoirs, so they ended up shipping drinking water from New Zealand.

David Jeremiah

When in the Hebrides, they kept the piss-stained mattresses in the basement of the SNCO block. Can't remember whose idea it was, but it was decided to get as many as we could and set them up outside Geordie Hardy's room so that when he opened the door, it would spring him back into the room like a jack in the box.

Albi Pinnion

A gunner of Scottish decent was told one Friday he couldn't knock off until the land rover was painted. He asked, "Which one?"

He was told, "All of them," referring to one section/fire unit, he painted them all, but a little too well. He painted everything as instructed, including the windows. A flight 63 Sqn early '80s! I do not remember the outcome! But I am sure somebody does.

John Berwick

A LAC, thick as shit, on 63 Sqn he was on permanent shit burning duty all the contents of the thunder box's would be carried up Canopus Hill to in a black bag and thrown in the shit pit to be burnt, until we started dumping 20mm anti aircraft rounds and 35mm AA rounds by fuck did they not go off with a bang in the shit pit and shit flew everywhere and all over the LAC.

Another time he was burning shit he forgot what the ratio of petrol and diesel think it was 50/50 anyway he poured 3 jerry cans of petrol to one jerry can of diesel and it went up with an almighty flash bang again NAPP was covered in shit

Albi Pinnion

A techie on 63 Sqn decides he has had enough of the commanding officer, and instead of sleeping on it, in his drunken state, decides he is going to put a brick through his window at the squadron. He made a big mistake, he got the wrong window, and bricked the WOS window! A good lad that was a right character!

Again at RAF Gutersloh. This time involving a CPL dog called Rex, the squadron mascot, hated all that wore blue or rode a bike. Rex's kennels were at the rear of the squadron next to the rear door, so no one who was not on the sqn would use the back door.

OC admin had been invited to the Friday beer call, he arrived on his bike, and was aware not to go through the back door. He proceeded to get off his bike, and being clever, was going to climb through the window as Rex's rope wouldn't reach. What he didn't know was someone had extended the rope, as he climbed through the window all in the bar heard a scream as Rex bit OC admin's arse!

David William Ahearn

I'd been transferred across to 4 wing from 16 Sqn (extended my tour at Wildenrath yet again! Sweet) but was still in the squadron block. I was using my advanced Rapier qualification to train operators filling the gaps appearing in the squadron ranks as tours came to an end. One character, name withheld for legal reasons, is not the sharpest knife in the box. Rapier kit set up on the end of the airfield and this character is left to guard it whilst everyone else goes off for some lunch. He's sitting in the land rover and realises he can't see all the kit, so proceeds to move the land rover.

Reversing, following the cable between launcher and tracker, reverses into launcher and snaps off a missile! Puts land rover back where it was, lads come back, Flight Lieutenant Parry goes nuts and this character faints!

Not long after that the squadron is off down for its annual ski trip and he comes into my room to ask advice on skiing—namely what if he gets too fast on them. I advise him to just fall over, ski's come off, no problem. He manages to do this, breaking his leg!

Back to the medical centre. They dislike him so much they make him hobble to the mess on crutches for his meals, so he's not in their way for a few hours. He then gets some complication in the break and gets casevaced to Wroughton. So, the lads have to draw lots to sort out his room, service kit in one box, for storage until he's fit, all his civvie gear in another, to be sent to his home address. Now this guy's personal hygiene was questionable. And when bottles full of piss were discovered in his locker, it was confirmed how minging he was. And he had a big stash of porn, some going to the lads, and the really bad stuff laid open on top of his civvie stuff so when his family open the box they were in for a surprise. Some blokes just aren't regiment material.

Steve Mullan

On 48 Sqn, in early 90s, I recall a visit to Fort George ranges for annual APWT on the rifle (sa80) and APWA on the LSW.

A certain chiefy has the great idea that if you take your zeroed SUSAT off your rifle and place it on the LSW, then it should be zeroed to you! So, complying with this bizarre logic, we removed the SUSATs from the LSWs and placed them on the bonnet of Chiefy's land rover, as instructed.

At some point, someone got in said land rover and drove off back to Lossiemouth. Oops! Rest of day searching range roads for lost SUSATs ... Last one handed to us by a postman—he found it on a public road as he was driving past!

David Jeremiah

On one of my many Belize detachments, the woofers took over and, when a new battalion took over, they always tried to put up the taxi fares. They were told only pay $10, so four guys get to the big C from APC, big argument ensured as to the cost, they gave him the money, he then chased them into the big C brandishing a 9mm

Beretta, and he started shooting at the army guys the band leader said, "Here we go 234," and started to play the trumpet and was shot in the chest. It killed him. Two women were lightly wounded, one in the leg, the other in the arse. We all just dived for cover. He was eventually arrested and things returned to normal. All that for the sake of 50p extra on the taxi fare!

Albi Pinnion

A Rock ape and his mate one evening, after copious amounts of warstiener, decided it would be a good idea to go skinny dipping. Afterwards they had the bright idea of taking the pool lane divider and hoisting it the squadron flag pole 63 Sqn.

Next morning on parade, guilty barstewards take pace forward! Right the warrant officer wants a little word, off to see the warrant, his first words, I might have bloody guessed! "Right, you pair. Down to the swimming pool return the lane divider and take your toothbrushes!"

We had to scrub the whole surround of the swimming pool all day! It was a nice, sunny day, the pool was open. With plenty of fine-looking women, who felt sorry for us and brought us beer all afternoon as the mally was across the Road, and at that time open at dinner times!

Mike Riggs

We were in Germany doing a NATO ex and airfield defence of USAF Bitburg. I was Det Cmdr of a Rapier fire unit deployed on the edge of some German farmer's field. In Germany many farmers plant their crops and then have a 2m strip around the edge where they grow their peas, cabbage, etc. for home consumption. We had made a bit of a mess of said peas by planting our nasty Rapier and blindfire units on this strip.

Along come the irate German farmer who tells us to move and that a certain Herr Hitler didn't cause so much damage during a war that shouldn't be mentioned.

I tell him that we cannot move as we are on a NATO ex. "I send my son to move you," say farmer Fritz.

About 20 mins later, said son appears, has a rant, and gives me one hour to go or he will come back with 1000 litres of pigshit and spray it onto us. Quick radio call to zero and inform them of problem.

Zero comes back and amongst the fits of laughter in the background tell me that, "Sunray says not to move and that pigshit will be good for your complexion."

I reply that, "Message understood, and we will await delivery with bated breath."

Commanding officer arrives within 30mins, accompanied by US Military Police and German Civilian Police plus US German Liaison Officer. "Where is this German farmer?" asks the commanding officer. At that moment there are sounds of a tractor labouring up a hill, clouds of exhaust smoke, and finally the tractor with farmer Fritz Mk2 pulling what looks like a slurry bowser.

"Here he comes," says I (I'm sure they hadn't believed me about the 1000 litres of pigshit). US, German Police, Liaison Officer, etc. intercept farmer—lots of shouting, pointing at me, and fist shaking. Fritz Mk2 turns around and heads off, and German Police tells us that he has warned the farmer that he will be arrested for interfering with a NATO ex (apparently a criminal offence in Germany) if he comes back.

"Every country has its assholes—that was one of ours," says Politzei Pete as they head off.

David Jeremiah

While doing MPC in the Hebrides as the AIG (artillery instructor gunnery) on 19 Sqn, a young LAC was crapping himself as he was waiting to fire his first missile. He asked, "FS, what's it like to fire a missile?"

My reply, "It's like having sex, the same sort of thrill, but the missile lasts longer." Everyone just cracked up as it went over the speaker, so LASO heard it. It took about 20 mins to regain composure of the situation to carry on firing as everytime someone talked on the speaker there was fits of giggles.

John Bailey

1983 RAF Wildenrath 16 Sqn RAF Regiment Christmas function. What a great time we had but it was time to go home, time to catch the bus back to Gilencirkechen. Oh shit, it's gone. So myself and my wife, Gus and his wife, and my good mate Stitch Courser and his wife are now stranded. Drunken thought, W*ell we can tab it?* Wife's thought, *Can't put on as I would be banned.* Well only thing for it—phone MT.

"Hello, who's that? I'm Flight Lieutenant AIG 16 Sqn. Why has my men and their wives been stranded at Wildenrath? The transport was not there when they arrived, get it sorted now."

With that, a very fat, sweaty flight sergeant on a bike came hurtling round the corner.

"Is the Flt Lieutenant here?"

Flight sergeant, "Yes, can you explain?"

"Sorry, Sir, I've got a Sherpa coming back, it will be here in about five minutes." I thought brilliant, got home safe, had a brilliant weekend. Monday morning, parade was taken by Ac IG gentleman, just received an apology from MT officer about the problem on Saturday night, I didn't know I was that drunk I could be in two places at one time? Does anyone know of this situation, comment from the back, "It must have been Santa."

Got away with that one, but on a training day with AIG he whispered in my ear, "I know it was you, you rogue, I remember your stag night in NI." That's another story.

David Jerimiah

Falklands '82, on 63 Sqn, was being transferred to the Rangitery boat for a spot of RandR with Abby and this gunner called Bungalow

Bill. Bill leapt out of the boat onto the ramp of the ship— it was like something out of a cartoon—fingertips on the boat, toes on the ramp, and in slow motion, they separated, no one made a move to help him.

I just pissed myself laughing as gradually he went in the water which was -10C, he went down but took a while to come up. When he did, he still had his beret on his head. We just found that so funny and couldn't stop laughing, my sides and jaw ached.

RIP Abby, we had some laughs

Kevin Bell

Round about the same time. I was on 48 Sqn shooting team. I was training at Fort George. Shooting away and a nimrod flew low and slow down the Morray Firth, west to east. That was the one that came down in the drink, just off shore opposite the Skerry Brae.

The order came at the range, "STOP!" First worry, although the aircraft was well out of range of 5.56, was that we'd put a round or two through the side of it. Unlikely we'd hit it, as it was an Air Defence squadron, and couldn't hit a cows arse with a banjo!

Chris Pacey

I was on lighthouse site tracking it at the time, Kev, Stu was the TC, and Geoff the DC. I reported a large marrow, coconut matting, friendly nimrod, in cover. "Errrr Stu, I think that nimrod is on fire!"

He said, "Nah mate, it will be the landing lights."

"No Stu, it is deffo on fire, GEN!"

He said it would be the search light on the wing.

"Wrong wing," I said and this is coming out of the engines!

He switched the monocle on to say, "Fuck me, it is as well!" He got on the battle net and NO DUFF called an aircraft fire. That was one on the most surreal days of my colourful career.

Kevin Kinghorn

Falklands, early 1983, whilst serving on 16 Sqn as B Flight Commander's Driver. I was tasked with collecting three large post office sacks. I was given strict instructions not to open but to return to Back Eagle ASAP.

As we all know, this is as good as telling us to help ourselves, as it's got to be worth something. On collection, I managed to make a slight detour which resulted in a full inspection of the sacks, which revealed they were bursting with fags, king Edwards, and rolling tobacco.

I spent the next twenty minutes stuffing smokes in every friggin hole I could find in my 1 tonnie, knowing full well the lads are likely to gain little from this priceless bounty. Needless to say, the following days saw a few extra packs of smokes go out to the fly away sites and some hand delivered to the drive sites too.

Mac MacDonald

48 Sqn duty driver, early eighties. There were two duty drivers, living in and living out; each had a duty to inform their respective areas of a callout (of which there were plenty!) or Russian invasion (c'mon it was the Cold War).

They both had to carry a folder with everyone's address and phone number, also the living out had a huge bag of two pence pieces to go to the phone box and call people in. The rules are simple: no drinking, and you must stay within the confines of the camp area.

The Gunners remedy to this boring duty was the M.A.M.O.O.D.D club (Make A Mockery Out Of Duty Driver). Entry to this club required you to get as far from camp and as drunk as possible. I was still dripping wet from the Lossie Raft Race, having a beer or ten, when my detachment was driving out of the hangar—living in duty driver, whoops!

Yozzer Hughes on guard! 1983, a group of LACs are posted to 48 Sqn. A penal squadron if ever there was one. It was full of drunkards, reprobates, career SACs. If that wasn't bad enough, the warrant officer was called 'Nutty' Ralph (Smith), who was not a man to be argued with—I know he hit me over the head with one of those huge old phones once, but that is another story!

During one exercise in the Lossiemouth woods, a bright young man (me) was attached to HQ, where the the worst career examples hung out. Whilst trying to keep out of any trouble from the SAC, I was told to get 'Yozzer' out of the back of the land rover, as it was his turn for guard.

I then found out the SAC Hughes was in fact a crudely painted hardboard cut-out of the TV character (Boys from the Black stuff). Now I was just about fed up with being sent for a long stand/bump start the generator/your turn for the brews again, etc, so I pulled the 'Yozzer' effigy out of the wagon by his head ... which snapped off!

The full wrath of the squadron warrant officer, 'doing the Nutso' came my way as he (Yozzer) was actually on the guard roster, which the warrant officer wrote, so I would have to do his shift as well as mine. I was also ordered to have it fixed by the morning, and it had better look good or else! LAC season was in operation throughout the year in those days.

The veiled threats worked, I made a good effort at the repair to Yozzers untimely beheading ... but to this day I wonder what ever became of him? Does anyone out there have a photo of the real Hardboard Yozzer?

David William Ahearn

I'm sure this is a familiar occurrence to most who served in a certain part of Germany. Trip across the Dutch border for beer and a watch of the fit girls riding their horses, then into Roermond for a pub crawl.

On this particular occasion I got separated from the other lads, got chatting to some Dutch folk who invited me to a party. Moving on to the next morning, waking up in a strange bed, hangover, with a very disheveled Dutch girl sharing the bed. "Where am I?" I ask.

"Venlo," she replies. No money in my wallet but luckily she has a car so drives me all the way back to Wildenrath. Drops me at the gate and it's the long, sobering walk of shame back to the billet. To this day, I have no memory of the party, or how I ended up in Venlo.

Wayne Holliss

Many moons ago, in south block at RAF Lossiemouth, a group of 48 Sqn Rocks decided to have a play with some fireworks. At first, we practice our anti-tanks drill using the 66 tube I'd brought back from Belize to fire rockets into rooms and down the corridor. Next we decided to try out the grenade range, this being a rather sleepy and drunk Jock, so in we crept banger in hand and threw it with great accuracy, it landing on the pillow next to his head. "BANG!" it went, no movement from Jock, but the pillow burst into flames. Jocks room mate shit a brick seeing this and rushed to put the flames out. Never I've seen a sight so funny as Taff stamping on the thing, flip flops melting, bath robe smoking, coughing his guts up in the smoke, as we stood there pissing ourselves.

Next, all the fireworks that were left were lit, filling the corridor with smoke and flame, yes it was stupid of us but he who is without sin, as they say, and to this day, I still can't believe we got away with it.

Albi Pinnion

Similar story, after a beer call, someone had a load of sparklers.

Running about the block with them, a certain Rock got a whole packet and lit, ran the length of the corridor, turned around to see the carpet smoldering.

Monday morning in to see chiefy, "I've got a confession, I've done some damage. In the block!"

"What?"

"I've burnt the carpet!"

"How much?"

"All of it," for his honesty, chiefy sorted it out. The German workers had had part of the wall out repairing pipes and welding! Nothing more was said, but cost a beer every time chiefy had an empty glass!

David William Ahearn

Here's a dog story from Bruggen. There was a rather mysterious compound out on the airfield, (something to do with the Americans?) surrounded by a double fence and the space between the fences was where a couple of big fuck-off dogs ran free.

We Wildenrath lads were playing enemy against the station and a group of us went to attack some dispersal area, only to find no one about. Banging on a window that was showing a light, a lad sticks his head out. "Where the fuck is everyone?" we ask.

Lad replies, "Pne of the dogs from (aforementioned) compound had escaped and everyone was told to stay indoors until they caught the fucker. Everyone but us was told.

Chris Taylor

63 Sqn in 1980. Drove over to the other side of Gutersloh airfield with a new LAC to do a comms check on one of the station Rapier sites. Comms check done, we both jumped back into the LWB land rover. Into reverse gear, thought I would show off my driving skills and booted the engine and reversed at high speed ... straight into a

storm drain about 10 foot deep! One LWB land rover had suddenly been converted into a SWB land rover, and the LAC and myself adopted a position not unlike Virgil Tracy when he takes off in *Thunderbird 2*!

Spoke to the MT controller and it cost me a crate to get it fixed and not a word about it to anyone!

Barrie Griffiths

I think Dick (Bod) Barton may be on here. He was such a charmer without realising it. One morning, as duty driver on 48 Sqn, he went to collect the squadron inspector general from his house. Bod duly knocked on the door and waited patiently. Speaking to the IG's wife, he said, "I'm here to pick up your dad." She was made up for years after that ... the inspector general less so!

John Shearson

While on duty driver, and collecting a signal from Comcen, I went by the block, as you do. I went into 48's south block and found a new station arrival getting changed in a squadron room. He claimed that the guard room had told him our block was the transit rooms and he was innocent. I dragged him to the land rover and took him to see the warrant officer. I told him I had caught the Guin stealing from our rooms. The warrant office actually believed me and gave the guy a good nutty bollocking.

John Brown

16 Sqn. So we had ceased fire and returned to Wildenrath after yet another just got in from on the piss call outs, the sound of that call out hooter still gives me night terrors, and as usual the turn around routine started, wagons washed, refuelled, kit unloaded, and cleaned things seemed to be going fairly well and it was looking like a quick knock off. It would appear the word was spreading to

the guys down at the wash too, because the fire units were coming back in thick and fast.

Now for those of you that remember, the right hand gate to the compound kind of had a life of its own, and the normal routine was duty bod would open the gate to let vehicles in and close the gate again. However, on call outs, the gate was usually left open due to the traffic flow, so things were going along well then all of a sudden there was this almighty bang followed by the proverbial barrage of, "FUCK!" "SHIT!" And other routine profanities along with the hysterical laughter that usually accompanies any disaster.

An unnamed but well known SAC had been a bit keen to get through the gate with the FUT and hadn't noticed that the aforementioned gate had sprung into life and as he was coming through, the edge of the gate hit the righthand launch beam square on and promptly lifted the wagon and launcher off their wheels and reshaped the launch beam. Let's just say it would never pass toe in on Ts and As ... Oh, how we laughed.

Stephen Headey

Remember when on 48, we were deployed to Cyprus in '86. Well we had a stand to when armourers decide to test a GPMG at the rear of our location—wise move that was.

Anyway, the next day our commanding officer decides to visit all sites, as a morale booster, I suppose. Just before his arrival, I put cam cream on the binos to catch out one of the sprogs.

Well, up comes the commanding officer unannounced, says hello whilst I am in the optical tracker seat. To my horror, the first thing he does is pick up the binos and scans the horizon. Upon lowering them, it was a classic black eye look. I was crying with laughter whilst my TC had to talk to him, biting his lip, and trying not to laugh. I believe he went round all the sites like this. Sorry, boss, if you're reading this.

Chris Taylor

48 Sqn back in the mid eighties. New LAC posted onto the squadron and, as a newly promoted CPL, I was tasked with showing him his new 'home'. Cue the fun! Sent him around the station to acquire a new fallopian tube to replace one of the Rapier launcher levelling bubbles. He was away for about four hours, then the squadron received a phone call from the Wg Cdr OC Med Centre who happened to be a female. She wanted to know who had sent this hapless LAC to her medical centre asking for a fallopian tube! My name was mentioned and I had to make a grovelling apology, which she accepted with good grace, and once she had heard and understood the joke, she promptly sent the LAC on his way, telling him to see if the MT Section could help him out with his quest!

Geoffrey Herschell

Whilst in the Hebrides with 37 Sqn one year, we were waiting in the bunker for a 'window' in the weather. We had the usual visit by the Stn Cdr and AOC. The AOC asked, "Who's firing next?" We pointed to a young SAC. The AOC asked him, "Are you excited, Airman?"

"Not really, Sir," replied young airman.

The AOC persisted, "I'd be excited if I was firing a missile."

SAC looked at him nonchalantly and said, "You can have my bastard if you want, I've PVRed."

Barrie Griffiths

I joined my first squadron, 48, with a pilot officer who was always in more shit than I was and deflected it off me. He is now the commandant general of the RAF Regiment. The inspector general was delighted when said pilot officer did a recce of all of the sites with the very delicate surveying instrument, the artillery director, thrown into his Bergan and bounced around as he tabbed around the sites. Needless to say, he was then posted to CVRT! Must be a message in there somewhere!

OA on 63 Sqn took a VIP out on a tour of the Rapier sites without realising he was on permanent send, and proceeded to broadcast all our secrets ... on the battle net! Of course, if you have never served on Rapier, the significance of the 'self-jamming' of the second to second 'fighting' net, by the squadron cdr may not be immediately apparent.

A certain SAC shit the bed in a hotel in Carlisle, sneakily checked out without owning up, to carry on with the road party move to the Hebrides from Germany. Thought he had got away with it until he realised that he had left his passport in the bedside locker, apparently!

Mick Cundy

1980 at Arborfield Rapier Eng training. After twelve months of training at Arborfield, with all that army bullshit, I was determined to have a souvenir. At the last minute, with a friend driving his car, keeping the engine running for me, I, in my No 1 uniform, marched myself to the flagpole in front of the headquarters building, saluted, and with due ceremony, lowered the REME flag that was flying, folded it, and marched myself smartly to the car and we departed rapidly—I had my souvenir.

One day I got into work at 63 Sqn, Gutersloh, to find a fellow Guin already there. I was surprised as he had never been that early before. He was also, unusually, wearing a knitted hat with his denims. I asked why he was there so early and why the hat? He told me that the previous evening, after his wife had gone to bed before him, he had decided to give himself a haircut but had bodged the job so much he had decided to shave his head. He then went to bed. His wife woke up in the early hours to find a bald headed man in bed next to her. She went absolutely apeshit in her shock and anger. When she eventually realised it was her husband, she threw him out of the house. He had to sleep elsewhere for several nights after that.

Another from 63. A Rock friend and his wife were going on leave to UK and they lent me their video player to use while they were away. When they returned, I told his wife she would have to clean the heads of the player as we had been watching 'dirty videos' on it. She did.

John Brown

48 Sqn, Belize, '88 or '89 (can't remember, it's an age thing). A certain CPL of north east descent has a reputation of being a rough tough, no shit kinda NCO, but had one big flaw when it came to Belize, he was, by his own admission, shit scared of the local wildlife, of the crawly type. So, one night, after the usual sesh in the squadron bar, Chris Shepherd and I come up with a plan. Earlier that day, we found a dead bat outside the block. So we leave the bar a bit early and retreive the said flying rodent, attach it to a piece of fishing line and, as you do, pin it to the inside of Geordie's locker door. At the same time, we get Shep's Davy Crockett hat, purchased in Gander on the way down, stash it under his pillow, also attached to a length of fishing line. So the scene is now set, all we need now is the half-pissed Geordie to return from the bar.

So, in he comes and straight away, we start telling him about the news report he just missed about the spate of sudden random attacks on locals in the city by bats, for reasons unknown at this time, but attacks are viscous and a number of locals have been badly bitten, and leave it at that, knowing full well he's gonna go into his locker fairly soon. And, as predicted, in he goes, only to be met by a bat flying out and smacking him straight in the face, immediately followed by hysterical, girly screams and, of course, the rest of the guys pissing ourselves. Once he eventually calmed down and called us everything under the sun, he lays down in his bed. I think you might know what's coming now.

Shep shouts, "Geordie, what the fuck's that?" and points to his pillow, at which point I tug on the fishing line, and the black and white tail of the hat starts wriggling out from under his pillow. Up jumps Geordie, screaming like a girl again, and starts to beat and kick the shit out of his bed. Rest of the block in total hysterics. Probably wouldn't have been as funny if it wasn't Geordie ... Not too sure if he's actually forgiven us to this day.

Chris Pacey

During a spell at the RRS at Mount Pleasant, HQ flight thought they would seize an opportunity to fuck us over by moving our Landy a km down the road during our resupply run. Fair one, good banter, but they overstepped the mark when they came out to visit our site and took the TV cable and remote! We got a box of 48 frozen kippers, and on a quiet Sunday morning, we set about skiffing the whole building. The OC's office drawers, bodge taped under the 2 IC's bin, behind the FN, behind a set of blinds in the inspector general's office, in one of his Pams! Radiators, video recorder, HQ wagon air vents, lockers, they all got it. My favourite, and the present that just kept giving, was the toilet cisterns, they fucking stank so bad, every time they were flushed it came back! HQ, you had talent, but you were no match for the sites!

Gus Dunning

26 Sqn, FI, '86. Managed to wangle a night off site at Sapper Hill as I managed to trap off with a NAAFI hairdresser. Spent the night in the main hotel in Stanley, hot bath for two, etc. Meanwhile, a couple of gunners from each site had been dicked to practice ambush drills in the sand dunes—that turned into a farce. Driving snow, huge storm for the South Atlantic all night, guys dropping

like flys due to the cold. Meanwhile, I was snug as a bug in a double bed and a Doris.

Come the morning, walked her back to her accommodation and, as the storm had passed and it was a cracking sunny day, walked back about 5km to Sapper Hill with a spring in my step. Upon reaching the site entrance, I saw Garry and another busy repairing the barbed wire after the storm. I then regaled my night's adventures in a hot bath, bed, and woman—and very pleased with myself I was indeed. Upon which I was refused entry to the site and bombarded with anything the guys on site could throw at me.

To be fair, how was I to know about the fiasco in the sand dunes some of the lads had suffer, nor was I to know the meadows generator on site had gone tits up, so the remaining members of the crew gad spent most of the night awake trying to fix it and freezing their balls off to boot, as due to the storm, the artic heater had also failed. Last thing they needed was Mr Smug turning up, with tales of having to turn the heating down in the room as it was too hot. It was quite a few hours before anyone would speak to me, but shit happens. My visits to the hotel became a regular trip. Happy gunner.

Nick Day

Spring/early summer, '86, saw B Flight 48 Sqn deployed on ops somewhere in the sun, with a bunch of heroes from Eng Flight in tow, live missiles on the beams, live ammo in the gats, what could go wrong? At least we, the squadron in general, shot no hillsides down ... wink. Sorry Bob ... couldn't resist the dig!

Occasionally the fire units went to battle stations—weapon system at arm ... Radar turning and burning with firing lines connected ... waiting for the hydraulics to slew the turntable towards a hostile target.

Orders were, "This is a highly classified op, cabinet decision, blah, blah, blah, you cannot tell anyone who wasn't involved in the op where you have been." I remember thinking, *Why on Earth would anyone who was involved with the op ask where we had been?* Never mind ...

>Your address is: Number, Rank Name
>   48 Sqn RAF Regiment
>   BFPO XXX

First mail arrived, commanding officer's address written as:

>   Number, Rank Name
>   48 Sqn RAF Regiment
>   *Place name*
>   BFPO XXX

That's okay then, it's still a secret where we are ...

Nick Day

"Right, troops, too much ammo is being lost, it is now a 'chargeable offence' to lose any."

10 min later a young PO can't remember his name or appointment bimbles into the ACP where the Eng FRT was based and asks, "Err um, anyone seen a 9mm round, err any spares here?"

"No, sorry, Sir everything bar 20 rounds or a mag full had been taken from us."

Then there was B1 fire unit, hadn't worked properly since it arrived on 48 in '84. Brian Fleming was playing with the problem of it 'dancing' either side of the Radar Test Az ... Finally he came to the conclusion it was picking something up on a signal earth ... long story cut short, the BBC were asked to switch the local transmitter off for a couple of minutes around 1300 the following day, think the transmitter was near the Salt Lake. BBC answer was that they cannot cut their broadcasts for any military reason, it was gently explained to them that as we had lots of PE4 the cut in, their broadcast could be a lot longer than a few minutes ...

Message received and understood, a break in the BBC World Service about 1300 the following showed B1 Launcher was picking up BBC World Service on medium wave on its earth causing at least one problem …

Towards the end of the exercise—err, operation—for some reason, I was manning the alternate CP late one night … The phone rang, some twat called Sergeant Cxxxxx says he was in the CP:

Twat: "Air Raid Red. Air Raid Red. Six hostile aircraft heading south to north, heading this way, standard attack profile, low level one mile apart."

Me: Thinking, *And exactly what am I supposed to do about it?* But saying: "Okay, Sarge where's the commanding officer?"

Twat: "Commanding officer is in bed."

Me: "How far out are they?"

Twat: "Overhead shortly."

Me: "Okay, I'll wake him up," but thinking, *Waste of time, by the time I've found him, he'll have been woken by the biggest bang he's had for awhile.*

Twat: "No, no, no, don't bother him."

Me: Penny drops—So I say: "Fuck off ." Maniacal laugh from the twat as my phone hits its cradle. Those were the days …

Nick Day

Operation, having to take an engineering air Commodore around the sites … Upshot says, "Why aren't the missiles tied on to the beams when firing lines aren't connected, as per the Falklands?"

"No idea," says I, with very little interest.

"You what?"

"WTF are you on about, Al?" Then he explained that I had to take a roll of red para cord and devise a way of tying the missiles to the beams so they wouldn't ungracefully slide off the beams if the shear pin broke during Ts and As. etc. But it had to be able to be removed quickly at battle stations, plus it had to show that the shear pin had broken by letting the missile move forwards a bit but without sliding off the beams ... So, using the fuze protector and tying a bit of para cord to it through the safety shutter viewing hole and fitting it onto the missile then tying the other end of the para cord to the beam using a slip hitch (I think it's called), pull on the free end of the cord and the knot opens, a pull on the other end tightens the knot ... Showed Al what had been devised. "Very good," says Al, "But what happens if the knot is tied the wrong way round?"

"Dented pointy end of rocket," says I.

While I was looking for Mr J Beagle and his fecking cameras, trying to tie missiles on the beams, Al came back with the commanding officer ... and said the commanding officer wants a quiet chat with me ... *Fuck, what have I done now, what haven't I done*, etc. Trying to concoct an excuse about something I had no knowledge of, all I knew was from Al's tone was that I was in the shite again ...

"Nick," says the commanding officer, "Have a look at this missile, is there anything that can be done to repair it?"

A quick inspection showed that it had been jammed against a missile beam elevation lock which had been incorrectly stowed so it got jammed between two missiles, damaging one.

First thought was, *2lb 8oz of PE4 will sort it* ... but bottled out of saying it. A quick inspection showed one of the gutters down the side of the rocket motor had been damaged, possibly damaging the wiring which ran through the gutter ... and there was no way I was going to dig around in the rubber sealant to find out, plus if the wiring had been damaged, there was no way I was going to wave a soldering iron around performing battle damage repairs on something containing 80-odd kgs of high and low explosive so, "Sir, I don't think we brought the 'red' EMERs with us, so can't really help ...

Al to Nick, "Go round the sites and tie their missiles to their beams." Thanks a bunch, Al ...

Steve Webb

48 Sqn, 1993. Belize det. Soldier V was a gunner on our crew, with the japes and banter throughout the tour being sound, and a right bloody laugh. One day, whilst on site one, I had an idea and after bobo time for the sleeping gunners, I snuck in and set the air conditioning to heater mode.

After the fine adjustment, I retreated to the comfort of my air conditioned room nearby, setting it to a comfortable UK simulator setting.

It worked a treat with the room gradually heating up through the night to a fantastic temperature, resulting in an explosion of sweating, overheating Rocks out of bed at early o'clock. Now, here's the beauty about us Rocks, a natural disaster or an accident, we handle it. Rico Ryan's got it sussed, you make sure you tell them that you did it and, well, things can get hairy.

Well, once five Gas Mark 7 Rocks knew it was me ... war was declared. Retaliation was swift, with my bed sheets coated in crushed Weetabix. But the opportunity to doctor Soldier V's Bergan was just too good to miss when the patrol opportunity appeared. His Bergan, packed for a week's patrol in the jungle, was then left on the site, ready for the early start.

Cue CPL Moi with a bag of goodies ready to swap. Billy Young and the other lads witnessed first hand the sabotage out on the ground. Foot powder was swapped with custard powder. The tin of Off (An excellent mossie repellent) was exchanged ... for an empty one. Add one extremely heavy iron, you remember the ones in the block ironing room cupboard that were made out of an old anvil and very few people used? Yep, that's the one Soldier V got ...

I'm told it's still in the jungle now where he chucked it out of disgust. Just in case he had the chance of a night out ... snigger ... I put an expensive top of his in there, and I filled his container of petrol for the Peak One stove ... with water. That didn't cook too well, so I heard. Either way, it was fun to do.

I'm sure Soldier V loved the experience. No, I'm lying ... I sort of got a hint that he wasn't too keen on the special treatment by the way he shouted my name on arrival at airport camp.

From me to yourself Soldier V ... thanks for being a good sport.

Falklands. RAF Stanley Canopus Hill.

Gareth Burton

As a DC on Poon Hill in the Falklands. It's footy Sunday, so the duty drivers drops me at the mess. Half way through the game, I get a call from nutty nuttal. He's dropped a missile and damaged the launcher after doing weeklies. Ha, I get one of the guys to draw a fake bill for £750,000 and take it to him. His face when we arrived back was just a pearler. Bless, great tour to see, the site off to the Pongos though.

16 Squadron, RAF Regiment.

Stephen Headey

We at 16 had just returned from our first tour of the South Atlantic and were, shall we say, a little miffed to find out we would be back there within months. Morale was low. So we improved it by going to the bowling club, Pop's and Eddie's, and then finally home.

As it was pretty warm that Sunday night, we decided to pay a visit to the station swimming pool. Great time, splashing around, trying to drown each other, before someone who shall remain nameless dropped a log in the pool. CPL, no sense of humour plod tried to arrest us all as we ran in different directions. Back up was called whilst they recovered the said log as evidence.

Well, Monday morning parade. Half of A Flight not there, as we were parading in the lovely accommodation set aside by the SWO at Wildenrath. The commanding officer, I swear, flew down there to have us released ... Great more bollockings and a charge to boot.

Falklands, '83, our second tour that year. My, we were lucky.

Day started fantastic as I had a day off. Fantastic, down to the shower ship, clean, and scrub up and get a meal other than compo. Well, set off back to HQ to have tea. Food duly eaten at 5p.m. Now waited as the squadron bar, which doubled as the mess hall, to open. As per SSO, we were allowed two beers a day but you could save them up ... I did and got hammered.

Feeling a little sleepy, decided to checkout the officers' and SNCOs' mess which was next door. Went in and saw what I thought was heaven. Married quarter soft, comfy chairs. *Well,* I thought, *I just might try them out,* and with that sat in them, pulled my parker hood, and closed it tight. It was, as far as I was concerned, only five minutes before I felt someone shaking my arm gently. "Chiefy ... Chiefy, go to your bed." I pulled my hood down and Warrant Officer Bryant (RIP) stared back at me.

For a moment, we were both like two rabbits in the path of car headlights. This soon evaporated, and to the chuckles of the commanding officer and officers present at breakfast was somewhat amusing. I never moved so fast out of that portacabin, I can tell you. Needless to say, I volunteered my extensive ditch-digging skills that morning as well as a host of other little treats the warrant officer had for me.

John Brown

The night I thought I died! Usual thing, on the piss in Roermond. On the way home went via Bruggen to finish the night off with a few of the lads there. Needless to say, never made it back to Wilders that night. However it was the morning when I had my 'died in my sleep' moment.

Woke up, totally disorientated, pissing sweat in total darkness, and had that clostraphobic feeling in my state of WTF! I threw my arms in the air to hear screams from the corridor, I sit bolt upright to even more screams, then it hit me. I had only fell asleep in a triwall box next to the fucking radiator in the corridor, and scared the shit out of the couple of guys standing there by the box!

Paul Grimley

16 Sqn, RAF Wildenrath, Taceval, 1977/8. I did not witness this but a certain scouse airman (whose name was opposite of night, but shall remain nameless!) came good at last. The umpire called a gas attack and said that one of the Rapier crew had been too slow to put on his respirator. The sergeant IC was told to pick one of his crew to be that man. Inside the tent was said scouse airman, still shaking like a jelly after 'drying out' from his habitual pissed state! Instantly, the sergeant picked him to be that man. The umpire was absolutely impressed by his 'acting', as though he had been infected with a nerve agent! RIP, JD.

Dan Smale

16 Sqn, while on detachment to Nordhorn to set up the Rapier kit next to the live firing ranges and practice tracking A10s coming in on their attack runs. Meanwhile, back at the ranch in Wildenrath, the commanding officer calls one of HQ's lads in (no names, no pack drill) gives him a piece of paper and the instructions, "Take *this* to Flight Lieutenant Burt at Nordhorn, ASAP." Several hours later, I'm stood next to Burt when the bright young SACs in question arrives, salutes smartly, and hands Burt the piece of paper. Paul Burt looks at the paper, looks at the SACs and says, "Right, where is it then?"

"Where's what, Sir?"

"All the kit on this list that you were supposed to bring me."

Paul King

My first 252 on 37 SQN RAF Bruggen, in the late '90s, didn't just get me into trouble once but repeatedly until the officer that had me done left the Sqn.

One Saturday afternoon, enjoying the delights of Dorty, I got in a wee fracas with a JT. I sorted it and carried on drinking, no harm done. Monday morning and I'm front of the flight cdr and am to be charged for my drunken stupidity. CPL 'Brummy' Edwards (God rest him, a super guy) did the honours, and Chiefy was going to march me in. As the officer read the charge out, Chiefy started laughing, somehow he marched me out, finally stopped laughing, and off I go again. It took three attempts before I managed to plead guilty. Can't remember what I got but I did it anyway, think it was seven days restrictions and 100 quid?

It's done and by with so I forget all about it, couple of months later there's a flight cdr block inspection, bull night and the usual shit because a sober officer is entering the block, well inspection over. Young flight cdr appears back at the Sqn and immediately I'm summoned to his office, he pulls out a picture frame displaying a 252 which that morning was by my bed. He asks me if I think it was a joke, my punishment, and did I find it funny? To which I replied, "No, Sir, I never thought it funny, it's the FS that can't stop laughing, Sir." Chiefy is sat at his desk, pissing himself.

The charge read, "SAC King is charged with repeatedly and vigorously hitting a JT of the Royal Air Force about the head with a phone receiver." It never mentions I apologised to the person on the other end, or that a Guin doesn't tell a pissed up Rock to Foxtrot Oscar. I still have the 252 framed and hanging pride of place in the bog.

Dave Vickery

Remember the whole of RAF Lossiemouth out on the piss—about '84, I think—enjoying the annual raft race. Even the station commander was on the pop as well. Rocks had just won said raft race and the prize was 100 cans of beer, so well ratted ... guess what? A TACEVAL was called! Ensuing mayhem saw loads of pissed Rocks driving very slowly to designated spots, towing 1.5 million quid's worth of Rapier kit while totally wasted. Rest of station didn't do particularly well either. Not a lot of fighting, the kit went on but loads of sleeping. Don't think we passed!

Chris Taylor

48 Sqn B Flight Belize detachment 1985 and having recently passed my FT1. I am sent out as an acting CPL on B2 detachment with James Little as my DC. Now normally, Jimmy used to drive the fire unit back to camp after swapping over on Site 1 on a Sunday evening, but on this occasion, he left it in my more than capable hands to drive it back. Now, on changeover at the site, it was discovered that the oncoming DC had a US lighting bar on his launcher so I said that because there was still some daylight left, I would take his and leave mine behind for him to use. Bad mistake!

With SAC Stephen Headey as my passenger, we set off with said launcher in tow. Managing to navigate across the 'yellow brick road' with no problem, we got onto the main road towards camp and I turned to Steve and said, "Wouldn't it be funny if the launcher fell off now because I wouldn't be able to see it!" Within a minute of my offhand comment, we heard an almighty grinding noise behind us. Instinctively, I put the brakes on and we were thrown forward in our seats as the uncoupled, free-wheeling launcher slammed into the back of the land rover! Oops! We got out to inspect the damage and saw that the transit locking bolt had sheared, the turntable was pointed at a jaunty angle, the lighting cable was in tatters, there was a nice V shape in the tail board of the land rover, and I was beginning to sweat a bit!

The pin was missing from the towing bar so we improvised by wiring the launcher onto the wagon and wiring the turntable into a less jaunty angle and made it back to camp.

On arrival, there is Jimmy in the hangar asking what took us so long to get back. I told him why and he surveyed the damage and told me to go to the squadron bar, have a beer, and start filling out an FMT3! Next minute up comes one of the techies who says the beams are twisted, so it's fucked and you are in the shit! I lost a weeks RandR and had to do daily, weekly, and monthly Ts and As on the kit, which was fine once a replacement transit locking bolt was fitted and the lighting cable repaired!

The cause will never be known as I am convinced the pin for the towing hook was rusty and probably snapped due to metal fatigue, as they were hardly ever checked or replaced. The end result didn't affect me, as four years later I was promoted to sergeant!

Mick Townsend

On one of my many, many, squadron sets to Belize, remember coming back from Site 1 one afternoon in the land rover, being driven by a techie (Gen Eng). As we approached the CP, the 2 Para GSM jumped out in front of the wagon, pointed his stick, and shouted, "Stop!" He slammed the anchors on, stopping inches from the GSM. The GSM then asked if the land rover was a Harrier, then Puma, to which he replied, "No, Sir."

"Are you a pilot?" he asked.

"No, Sir."

"So, you're not a pilot and you're not in an aircraft?"

"No, Sir."

"Well stop fucking flying along then!" We nearly pissed ourselves laughing as the GSM smiled and said a very polite way, "Now fuck off!"

Wayne Holliss

Remember on 48 Sqn, some of the lads had been naughty in the local café in Elgin—not me for once—something to do with civvies not liking CS for some reason. Anyway, as way of punishment, the squadron warrant officer decided to confine the squadron to camp and put all bars out of bounds and this on a Saturday afternoon.

So, after the telling off parade in front of the airman's mess, we hung around well and truly pissed off. It was at this point that one of the squadron's legal barristers noted that nuttso hadn't made any mention of the NAAFI shop. Well that was it, off we went, and emptied the entire shop of beer.

Martin Cannon

Another Belize tale. Remember the public service announcements broadcast (I think) every Thursday at 11:00a.m. on Radio Belize (broadcasting to you from "de jewel in de heart o' de Carribean basin")? One week they announced, "Will de relatives of de late Leroy Parks o' Belmopan come to de city morgue to collect de body. Thank you." This raised a laugh in itself, but a week later it got even better. The next Thursday, in a rather agitated voice, it was announced, "Will de relatives of de late Leroy Parks o' Belmopan, *please* come to de city morgue to collect de body. Him beginning to smell now!"

David Maynard

While on 15 Sqn, rapier 2000. We had the handover parade at Woolwich Barracks. We had done the practice parade the day before and all the vehicles were lined up ready for the next day's parade. We went out, taken out, and about by James Callow. When we came back to the barracks that evening, I thought I'd make sure that the Pongo of the first vehicle had done the correct DIs in the morning, so I turned the base isolator switch off.

The next morning, we were all lined up on the parade square. We were give the order to mount vehicles, there was a mad dash to the vehicles, loads of engine smoke, bar one! The vehicles were so close together that the Pongos had to start trying to manoeuvre their vehicles, in front of thousands of dignitaries. We just sat there pissing ourselves and then proceeded to drive off, leaving one vehicle on the parade square.

All I remember then was some poor fucker getting screamed at by the RSM and doubled to the guard room on a Friday afternoon. Unlucky Pongo.

John Ross

Seem to remember getting pissed in San Pedro with a certain person and hatching the plan to save money by 'borrowing' a Cessna aircraft from the civi airstrip and flying back to the mainland! Pretty sure that big Belizian airport guard who found us turning the engine over saved our lives that night! Yep, pretty sure that's how it happened!

Dave Thomas

Scene: rapier demo site at Wildenrath, one wet wintery day in the early eighties. The detachment were presenting a demo of the kit in the field, the site was on top of a mound when along came some Bae reps and three Jordanian officers, they alighted their vehicle and began the short stroll to where the optical tracker and crew were waiting. Due to the inclement weather the visitors were provided with wellie boots.

The nice spanking new footwear did a fantastic job, with one exception, the junior of the officers was walking in pigeon steps all the way to the top, lagging behind everyone else—was the ground very slippery and short steps would stop him sliding, NO—he had forgotten to remove the string tied to each boot top which kept the boots together and in pairs ...

Steve Mullen

48 Sqn, RAF Lossiemouth, who remembers the sergeant that drove to the squadron from a local village, parked in the car park, walked

into the squadron through the hanger, and it wasn't until he was in his bay that he noticed his dog had hopped in his car, travelled the 8 miles, jumped out of his car, followed him through the hanger, and he hadn't noticed?

Chris Pacey

While on the subject of Belize, 48 Sqn in '93. Myself and Tonto were sat on a railway sleeper outside the upside down cafe waiting for a taxi when a darkish fella came sprinting past us straight into the moving traffic, turned right, and sprinted off with no regard for his own life.

Seconds later, another darker lad—without exaggerating, 6"6' tall—went gangling after him down an alley. Two or three shots later, the taller fella came strolling back with a revolver in his hand, stopped right in front of Tonto and I and said, "Won' b' doin' dat again," and smiled at us like only a man that has just killed another man could.

We played it cool as we could to hide our nervous smiles back. "Ain't na' w'rass boies, me is d' po-leece," he produced what looked like a home made ID card that looked about as legit as any I had seen out there, and we were shitting ourselves ever so slightly less. He then said, "Com' opstair an' 'ave a drink wid me brethren!"

Tonto and I looked at each other with the sort of reckless regard of 'what could go wrong', and we nervously went and met his equally suspect-looking mates and had a quick drink of Appletons and got the fuck out! I loved that place!

Steve Mullen

48 Sqn, site renovation up on Covesea rapier site, one of the lads remembers that he had seen some hardcore rubble lying around, so off he pops and comes back with trailer loads of the stuff, made a great launcher platform ... Turns out he was taking the RE runway

repair hardcore ... And they were not pleased! No, we didn't take it back.

Len Hames Belize

I used to frequent a bar just over the swing bridge on the right, it was an upstairs bar called 'Wotchis', ran by an old white haired fella and his son Andrew, a big tall skinny lad about 25. Anyways, I got so frequent I started helping behind the bar, not many squaddies used the bar, it was always full of the dark rum drinking locals. Anyhow, behind the bar was a few broken pool cues (just in case of the odd drunken local), a big fridge of ice complete with the good old ice picks, two big fridges full of Charger Beer and Belikin, and a large box which was hidden under the middle shelf. Never knew what was in that until one evening I am serving away, having a laugh with the locals, when two young locals came in off their heads. Steaming, they started off going around, threatening the regulars, then came and had a go at me. I chased them off with the thick end of a pool cue, much to the amusement of the regulars, who all came up and bought me a few beers.

Meantime, Andrew had come back from his house to help out as it was getting busy when who should appear but the two drunk lads armed with two big pieces of two-by-four. They promptly came over and started on me. Started to get a bit rowdy as more of their drunk mates came in and had ago at Andrew, who does no more then bend down behind the bar, opens the big box and gets out an old fricken shotgun. Bang! Lets one of the drunks have it from about 10 feet, the whole bar was about to explode, or so I thought, the kid goes screaming out covered in blood from his legs, followed by his mate, there was feckin blood everywhere.

Andrew looks around, along with myself, none of the regulars had feckin batted an eyelid, they just carried on playing dominoes and cards, they all just looked up and smiled at me and said, "Well done."

Andrew emptied the empty case out the shotgun, puts a live one in, and replaces the gun back in the box, turns round, gets two beers, and calmly puts one on the bar for me and carried on … Feck me, I thought the place would be crawling with cops, but none turn up … Turns out, Andrew was also a part time member of the Belize Police Force and all the police knew what he kept behind the bar … If only I had known too …

Nigel Allen

Went on detachment to Oksbøl, Denmark with 48 Sqn in '87, but consider myself lucky as we went on the civie ferry/ship (unlike the following year when they traveled by an army flat-bottomed boat and just about everybody puked—somebody should tell that story). Wayne Holliss, were you on this det?

Experienced my first Carlsberg Elephant Beer on this ship (overnight trip) as well as a very obliging woman who took a fancy to me (the uniform works) and satisfied me by way of a BJ in the economy seats (a woman in every port, well almost). Won't tell you what else I got up to, just to say I found the local nightclub and sampled a lovely bit of Danish too …

On a Sunday afternoon, I got rather drunk in the squadron bar and had to have a lie down/kip. I woke up thinking it was Monday morning (dusky sky) and squadron leader told me it was Monday morning and convinced me he had drank in the bar all night with the lads and that I should go and have a shave and get into my uniform, which I did. I then found out it was early Sunday evening.

Chris Vipond

Here is something, read it in a book, story told by a Guin SAC who unfortunately got the whole story wrong from start to finish.

In 1994, I was on 37 at Bruggen, and was sitting in the mess when the head chef came to me and said, "Yours?" pointing to the water dispenser. Inside was a goldfish swimming about.

"No, not me," I replied.

"Oh yes, just seen you walking up main drag with said item."

Caught to rights, so his punishment was drive the walking club mini bus for a couple Saturdays. Bummer, no drink from Friday till Monday.

Well the second week, we go to the dams. The dambusters did over problem was wrong map so for an hour or so we are driving round to find the start point with no luck, entering a village. I spot a kraut walking along, so I suggest to the officer sitting next me to ask him where they are. So he did, saying, "We are the RAF Bruggen walking club and we are trying to find the dams."

The German replied, "You could find them in the dark fifty years ago, I'm sure you can find them in day light." I pissed myself laughing. I managed to trace said Guinn and found out he had learned from a gunner who was at 37 later.

Mick Townsend

On a 48 Sqn trip to Belize, Friday night arrived and, as per usual, mayhem ensued. Late on into the evening, we've made it back to APC and the drinking games started. At some point in the proceedings, Mark and I lost a game and off we went to collect our challenge, dished out by those who'd won the game. I nearly shat myself in fear as I woke up on Saturday morning to find the 2 Para Battalion sign resting against my locker.

Very quickly it made its way onto the armoury roof in the Shorad compound hanger where it stayed hidden for the next three weeks. The paras went bloody mental trying to find said item and I lived in fear of my life for those very long three weeks, before we returned to Lossie, whereupon we proudly unpacked the sign and hung it in the canteen.

That waking moment still causes shivers as the realisation dawned what the challenge had been, but more importantly just how bloody stupid and brave you can be with a bottle or two of Caribbean rum inside you!

Wayne Holliss

Talking of Belize, I remember well our crews' last night on Site One, the good sergeant had buggered off for a shower run, leaving us poor SACs and a CPL alone. Well, the next thing you know, it's party on. Before we knew it, we're all in the sanger next to the main gate, pissed as newts, including the gunner who was meant to be on guard (armed).

Well, when the sergeant got back, you would be right in thinking he'd be a bit pissed, but he went and got a crate in.

This is a tale related to me by a great mate who sadly is no longer with us, Mal Popple. Pops was the Flight HQ driver for a certain now Wing Cmdr who was last seen leaving Bastion with a flag under his arm. Anyway, having done the resupply, they're driving along the country lane chatting away when all of a sudden there's the sound of something metallic bouncing down the road, both decided to ignore it not giving it a second thought.

Some miles down the road, the muppet pilot officer looks across to Pops with his mouth wide open and a look of horror in his eyes. He then looks at the SA80 sitting in the rifle mount between them. Pops then looks at him and says, "You can fuck right off, that one's mine." After a quick 180, they found a rifle laying in the middle of the road, slightly scuffed but otherwise undamaged.

Don't you just hate officers who use to show off? Especially when they'd brought the family along. Well, at Leeming, I remember being part of the demo team who's deployed a kit for 11 Sqn's anniversary. Usual thing, full kit, let the kids have a play, etc. Now this was a special event in their history, so their adj had got the Theakstons brewery to supply the beer tent. Well, the sergeant was in his element and spend most of the morning in there. *Why not?* I hear you say. So, come lunch time, he was well and truly pissed. Well, he turns up at the kit, unable to speak and barely able to walk, so we decided to hide him in the front of the FUT one tonnie.

All was going well up until the point when the sqn inspector general turned up with little brother and daddy. So, meat head is showing them around, pointing out bits and bobs, "Oh look, daddy, my men, etc." the knob. When he asks, "Where's Sergeant T?" So, quick as you like, he's told that the good sergeant is off to the mess for a bite to eat. Great, got off that one.

Then the twat thinks it would be a good idea to show daddy the FUT. As he opens the driver's door, out falls a very drunk and asleep Sergeant T, landing at his feet. He opens an eye looks up and says, "Ello, Sirrrrrrr," then falls unconscious again.

There was once a certain SAC who was sent back from Belize, who before he left took advantage of the local ladies in the rose garden. So there he is, sat on the Vicky 10, next to some Pongo officer, when he falls asleep. Now, had he not been wearing bleach jeans, he might have got away with it, but when he woke up, he had a massive discharge stain from a leaky cock. Needless to say, the Pongo didn't talk much during the rest of the flight.

Stephen Headey

Falklands '83, our second tour, Canopus Hill. Days were becoming warmer and hair was getting longer. In fact, we were starting to look like the hair bear bunch. So it was decided that we would all become hairdressers for a day and take turns cutting each others' mop.

I was first and mine was easy a number one. One of the guys did the deed and it was quite good. Now my turn to cut someone's hair. Up steps Bobby, a loveable cockney, who is scared of losing what hair he has left. Now he doesn't want a buzz cut and asks me, can I just trim it above his ears and a neck shave?

"No problem, mate, sit down." Happily clipping away when all of a sudden someone comes in demanding he go to the tracker. As he turns his head around, the scissors close ... "'Whoops!"

Bobby says in his cockney voice, "You what? What do you mean 'whoops'?"

"Nothing, mate," as four other Rocks are pissing themselves as I had removed a sizeable chunk of his precious locks from behind his right ear. Bobby goes spare, but using a mirror can't see the damage, but he was certainly reminded of it everywhere he went asking, "Who the fuck did that?"

Wayne Holliss

For those of you who haven't done the hardship of a detachment to Belize, every now and then someone was given the job of deweeding the wire that surrounded the Shorad compound. On this particular day, muggings got the job. So, off I trot to the POL shed and obtained one can of civ gas and an empty beer can, and very soon I'm burning weeds. About half way along the wire, our CPL Paddy comes up to me and says, "You're doing that all wrong."

"Really, Paddy? Do show me how to do it then," I says. So he takes the beer can off me and proceeds to overfill it, spilling petrol every where. Now, I threw the fuel where I need it, Paddy decided to pour it, big mistake. No sooner had he poured the fuel on the flames then the beer can, his hand and arm were a mass of flames. Well on seeing this, panic set into the mad Irishmen, he launched the now flaming can over his shoulder, it flying through the air like a comet, leaving a trail of smoke and flame to mark its trail. As gravity took hold of it and began to pull it back to Earth, it hit Suggsy full in the chest. Whoosh! Screaming in agony, Suggs began running around the compound, trying to beat out the flames. Paddy, unaware of the ensuing drama behind him, decided the only way to extinguish the now flaming torch that was his hand was to place it under his arm pit. To this day I hate the smell of burnt hair. As for me, I was stuck between a rock and a hard place, which one do I laugh at first?

Now, Christmas leave was always a special occasion at Lossie, especially the trip down south. On this particular trip, several Rocks set off from Inverness by train, and being the RAF's finest, they decided to make good with the buffet cart. On reaching the half way point, it was time for the group to part company and for each to make their own way. Unfortunately for one of them, the drink had taken its toll, and he was as pissed as the preverbal newt. Now the other members of the group, having great concern for their mate and not wishing for his parents to see/find him in such a state, decided between them that the best course of action for all concerned was to put said gunner back on the train to Scotland, where the lad woke up the next morning. The moral of this story is 48 Sqn had some evil cunts on it.

John Bailey

Same tour, 16 Sqn, Falkland Islands, no one knew we were there. We had built an outside toilet but needed the piping to take the waste away down to the sea, where could we get that piping? Ginge knew where. There was a navy detachment at the point building. Ginge, I, and some others decided to do a midnight raid. We got two massive pipes, plus Ginge wanted the cat there, which we called Compo, as he only liked compo babies heads to eat, that's another story ... Snoz was the sergeant at the time, I will dig out my memories.

Well after going back up the ridge, we could hear the generator, were on the right course, but Ginge shouted, "Stop! The cat is clawing me chest to death!" as he had put it inside his jacket. So, we stopped. I looked up and said, "What's that silver triangle?"

"Shit," someone said, "We are on the wrong side of the mine field." It took us two hours to prod ourselves out.

Next day, I was going to Stanley to go up to Black Eagle Camp, I could hear the navy PO going mad, "How could you lose a thousand pounds worth of pipe overnight? There is no one here!"

Second tour, Falkland Islands, 16 Sqn RAF Regiment, same year, 1983, we done two tours that year to do a Xmas tour, I think. Wireless ridge commanding officer and Warrant Officer Bryant (RIP, Sir) rowing over the harbour to give us a Xmas drink. Both on their way.

After eating my cake from my wife, which was full of Brandy, we get a call, "Hello, all call signs, any calls signs, seen Charlie Oscar 16," on going outside and going over to the ridge, a pocket flair was seen. They were drifting out to sea on the kelp, both laughing and singing away.

Ian Portz

June 1986, 27 SQN were sent north to Lossiemouth to use the Rapier training dome. Whilst up there, we watched the World Cup. At the time, we had a very smart, keen CPL in the dorm (the sort with knife-like creases across the back of his shirt). He was squeaky clean, both in dress and reputation. We had all been watching the match in the dorm. The mood was grim, so alcohol was consumed. Too much on my part.

The following morning in the mess, I asked the lads, "Where is Corporal X?" Immediately, Frank, a fellow gunner, fell about laughing and said that last night whilst CPL X was doing radio checks in his sleep, I relieved myself all over his bed. Corporal X is down in stores begging for clean sheets because he thinks he did it himself. He missed breakfast that day and I managed to avoid him. Think I've got away with it now.

Dave King

North Luffenham, 1973, I know years ago, anyway, 63 Sqn had just converted to Rapier and as such had yet to be equipped with vehicles, i.e, land rovers and trailers. I don't know whose idea it was, but presumably from the pained expressions from officers, SNCOs and JNCOs, the commanding officer, Squadron Leader Challoner had the brainwave (many more equally as stupid ideas were to follow, as I'm sure those around his tenure will testify to). Here we go, driver training on the airfield.

Having no vehicles, we were split into teams of threes, one person was the marshaller, second person was the driver, and the third acted as the trailer. I believe I was an LAC so if I and the rest of us sprogs wondered, *What the fuck?* spare a thought for the SNCOs and JNCOs.

Now some of NCOs were hairy-arsed, experienced men the likes of Trev Braithwaite, Paddy Mac, Taff Harris, etc. and some very senior SACs. However, we all had to do it. Some things just don't go to plan, or it wasn't being taken very serious. Most of the trailers were turning in the wrong direction when the said squadron leader came screaming out of his office with a pair of binos draped over his neck screaming, "That trailer is moving in the wrong direction," whilst almost giving himself a coronary in the process. If my memory serves, we had to stay there until we got it right and parked our 'vehicles' correctly. Couldn't make it up, could you? Happy days mostly.

Paul Holroyd

Has no one recounted the story of a certain squadron leader on 19 Sqn who thought it would be a good idea to redeploy several Rapier fire units down the A34 with everyone, including the drivers, in NBC kit, including respirators! How no one was killed I don't know!

Mark Kimberlin

Whilst serving on 16 Squadron at Wildenrath as a newly qualified ASRI, I was detached to the wing to instruct on the basic Rapier courses they were running. The course in particular had two detachments and my oppo was Kenny Sayer.

One fine summer's day, we deployed the kits on the grass near 60 Squadron and we're doing our AD thing, having quite a pleasant, carefree time of it. Away from the squadron, no zobs about, ideal. Anyway, the time comes for mid day nosh! A certain SAC had been deployed early to the mess to get his scoff and had just returned to guard the kits as the rest of us sallied forth to sample the comestibles in the mess or squadron canteen.

Anyway, lunch over we embark the landies to get back to the kits and carry on with the task of learning. As we approached the kits, we were presented with a rather sweaty and flustered SAC who was going off at the mouth in a language which was clearly not English! Once we'd calmed him down, he comes out with the unforgettable line, "I think I've had an accident." *Has he crapped himself?* thinks I.

"Spit it out then! What have you done?"

"I've driven the one tonner into the kit." The sight that greeted us as the kits came into view belied his little tale that he'd driven the rover into the kit. The vehicle in question was clearly positioned to show that it had come into contact with a launch beam, made obvious by the fact that one missile was hanging off and the other lay forlorn alongside it. "Am I in trouble, Corporal?'

"No, son, you'll probably get a commendation for this! What happened?"

"I was reversing the rover following the 55 way cable when I heard it hit something!"

"What's at the end of a 55 way cable?"

"The launcher."

"Well you passed that bit. Stay here, I'll go and let the boss know," casting a glance at the rest of the troops and Kenny, who were trying their hardest not to burst out laughing, but failing miserably. Anyhow, off to the squadron to tell Flight Lieutenant Anderton and Squadron Leader Murphy that they were one kit down. Anderton, not impressed and wanted to flay the SAC alive. Murphy, who couldn't stand Rapier, pissed himself laughing! "Good job we're getting the new field standard next week then, eh?" was his only comment, apart from, "Let's go and have a look then!" Despite the fact the SAC didn't have a licence and he was told not to sit in the rover, he was let off with a number of severe bollockings and still managed to pass the course.

Kev Spike Andrews

In a Rapier tour in the Falklands during the '80s, it was normal for one operator to do a week in 'admin'. This entailed cooking, washing up, general cleaning up, driving into Mount Pleasant to collect water, POL, mail, rations, etc. It was also his dubious task to empty and burn the chemical toilet. Once it was empty, the waste was placed in a 500 gallon drum, doused in kero (because it burned slowly). The CP was called to inform them of the burn, and a clod of peat soaked in kero was spiked with a six foot picket, lighted and shaken off the picket into the drum, the drum was fired.

One particular day, it was my turn. The kero jerrycan was placed by the drum, the waste placed inside but I couldn't be arsed to go get a picket, etc. Now I thought the kero smelled weird but took no notice. I placed the bag in and promptly poured over half the kero (Civgas). I then decided that I couldn't be arsed to get a clod and douse it either. At which point, I lent into the drum, zippo in hand (I had to lean in quite a way). I then struck my lighter and fired the turd mortar. Three gallons on Civgas left sitting for five minutes in a warm drum (loads of fumes), I sparked my zippo and whoosh! Ashes, turds, and foulness went up—and of course bye bye moustache, bye bye eyebrows—and then coated me in shit when it all came back down. I had no choice but strip off, pour the remaining kero over it, and torch it.

Andy Devine

'88/'89ish, went with the inspector general and a young flight commander down to Wiltshire to do some Rapier site surveys. After a few days around Lyneham, we went over to Hullavington. One of the sites was on a hillock but the farmer wouldn't allow us access. As there was a right of way, the inspector general said we would walk up the track and do a quick round of angles.

The flight commander was sent to turn the vehicle around, we had done the survey and walked back to the road side. After about twenty minutes, the young officer came up the road he had been reversing and had hit another car. No mobiles in those days, so a bit of door knocking and a breakdown call seen us picked up by MT and taken to Lyneham. The land rover was shipped back to Leuchars on a Herc, and the commanding officer's short wheel base sent down the next day. On our RTB, the young officer was given a bill itemising: recovery to Lyneham, fuel bill for the Hercules, repairs to the land rover, admin charges—which totalled over £25,000. Luckily for him, it was a Sammy the Pig windup.

Dave King

Squadron Leader Murphy, OC 16, like many before him, he must have wondered why Rapier detachments required so much kit and a detachment support vehicle to transport 'all the unnecessary kit'. The wagon was as we know totally unsuitable for the role and it's not as if there was loads of kit.

Anyway, he ordered one of the detachments to lay out everything onboard the DSV and then explain and justify every item—tent explanation okay, safari beds explanation okay, NBC shelter explanation okay, the list as we know was endless. He accepted everything until chainsaw appeared again, he accepted the explanation—axe okay. Got down to the last piece of kit, which was a small handheld hatchet. "Well you can get rid of that," was his response, "You don't need both," getting rid of that made the DSV so much lighter and much easier to handle.

Spike Cook

66 Sqn, around 1985. I was walking back from Barsham close after lunch with Ginge. A racing bike overtook us with a new officer dressed in sports kit and peddling for Britain. He suddenly leaned back in his seat and shouted, "Don't you salute officers?"

My reply was, "Not their arse, no, Sir." Well, wrong answer ... Warrant Officer Ireland was waiting at the hanger door for me ... I was then politely informed to march the 200 paces airfield side of the apron infront of the hanger, stopping every 20 paces, and saluting different directions each time until he said stop.

At NAAFI break, the squadron led by A Flight had chairs and scoreboards displayed after each salute. They only had a 0 and a 1. At 1700, the warrant officer shouted out of his window for me to join him in his office. A big smile and two cups of coffee in his hands was a shock. What a man! He said, "Play the game, kid, and drink this and go home. Oh, and you are on your FT next month don't **** up!" The officer turned out to be a good egg and helped me and a few lads prepare for building 159 in many ways. Warrant Officer Ireland, Alec King, Pat Sweeney were legends in my personal journey. Four hours of saluting infront of a hanger full of grinning gunners was good for the soul.

Chris Pacey

Bunker Rapier site at Lossie early '90s. A fresh LAC M is brew bitch in the bunker admin area when Bill Young asked the young man to make a brew. Five mins later the Chai Wallah is still faffing around, Bill says, "What the fuck is taking so long?"

"I am looking for the milk, but I can't find the bottle!"

"It's in a silver bag. It is powdered milk, you Biff."

"Okay, Corporal, another long wait, "How much milk?"

"Till it goes tea colour!" Another long wait and over comes a green, plastic cup with this ashen looking brew that is not moving like a brew should. Bill sips it and, "Phehhhh!" spits it straight out, "What the fuck is that pishhh?" LAC M has used powdered mash! You could stand the spoon up in it! "Fuck off on sentry, you biff!"

Wayne Holliss

Remember the squadron warrant officer on 48 had a habit of doing snap inspections of such things as shirts, berets, and ID cards? One Monday he decided to check who'd ironed their shirts, so it was jumpers off. Oh dear, HQ Flight, several members stood there in t-shirts, having cut off the collars and sewn them into their jumpers. Nuttso wasn't happy.

Adrian Walton

Another Paddy Mac episode. While in the FI, bored off my tits on radio watch, suddenly heard 'no duff' message. Paddy's site was on fire. So being concerned gunners, all the crew were woken up, sat on top of the tracker position with mugs of tea, followed by 'ooohs' and 'aaaahs' as the free firework display the other side of the entrance to Stanley harbour took hold. Even today, it is the best firework display I have seen. Worked out everyone was okay, bar one gunner (think Barney Barnard) injured in the line of duty by being hit in the face by a red hot compo potato as the tin exploded. Cannot remember if it was Taff Bald Eagle Jones or Brummie Wyles who asked, "Is everyone out of the burning portacabin?" and Gunner

Mc Nameless asked if he would go in the cabin and get the photo of his wife, and was told in no polite terms to FO.

Following days pissed myself, as on the speaker came across Paddy's dulced tones of, "Is there an off the cuff whiskey callsign I can borrow?" Paddy's own personal delivery service courtesy of the army air corps.

Steve Holland

One resounding memory on 63 was when the RCT came down the block in MPA, banging on the room doors after the NAAFI had shut. They really didn't think about that one, waking everyone up. They fight naked!

Adrian Harkins

37 Sqn, '92ish, we deployed on a Harrier force exercise to Denmark, somewhere near a place called Billund, I think. Well, we were deployed in some farmer's field and at endex, made sure there was no sign of us ever being there for a week. So we buried a week's worth of blue liquidised shit in black bin bags in the corner of the field. When I say buried, I mean deturfed and scraped a few inches of soil out, then the shit was nicely hidden by the turf.

So, a few hours later, HQ flight turns up with a trailer, tells us, "We're here to collect the shit," so we walk over to the little mound, chatting and catching up. So lad gets his spade ready to enter the soil and I tell him it's buried deep. Well, he drives that spade into the ground with all his might and popped them bags good style, covering himself from his knees to his head in blue shit. Oh and he had his mouth open as well. He travelled back to camp in the trailer with the bags of shit, smiling with his blue teeth, and waving to us as he left.

Gus Dunning

In the FI with 26 Sqn mid-80s, RAF Harrier decided to plough into the oggin while attempting to land. Where upon the blue RAF requested Black Eagle contact all the Rapier sites to confirm they hadn't shot it down. There is bloody trust for you, and before you ask, no we didn't.

Mark Kimberlin

Right! Another from the first 37 tour in the Falklands. Some of the lads on HQ volunteered to be 'honey monsters'—emptying the shit sacks out of the chemical toilets, for which they were handsomely rewarded! Gerry Kelly, rather than put the normal black bags in the shitters, decided to put clear ones in. He was subsequently seen, loitering outside the mess tent with a clear plastic bag full of turds, piss, and blue liquid, squeezing the bottom of the bag. Upon exiting the mess tent, the commanding officer enquires of Kelly as to what he was doing! "Looking for threepenny bits, Sir!" he replied. Dickie then realised what Gerry was squeezing and nearly chucked up on the spot! Well worth the shit money in my humble opinion!

Neil Horn

A memory of Warrant Officer Taff Bruton (RIP). Organised the squadron fishing trip as part of AT in the Hebrides. Boat loaded with about ten of us chucking lines in. Well, we couldn't stop catching fish, hundreds of them; the boat deck looked like a trawler. Well, in great regiment fashion, Taff took all the fish and went blaggin. The Messes, the DI, everywhere. Best free squadron BBQ ever. He traded the fish for meat, beer, buns, the lot. Great man.

Kind of Rock-related, well a dig at Pongo anyway. Anyone recall the incident on an inspector general/SMIG course on Salisbury

Plain, mid '90s? Instructors (who I later worked with at JRTU and confirmed the tale) demonstrating correct explosive disposal of a dud Rapier missile. Lay all four charges for avionics, warhead, rocket motor, and guidance (I forget), and the first charge on the det cord should be rocket motor. Anyway, Pongo screwed it up, and first charge was the rear end guidance, which ignited the rocket motor and off went an un-guided missile for the next 6km, just barely stopping short of a village on the edge of the plain.

Seem to remember similar happening with CVRT at Catterick, where someone (many of us know who) screwed up the up the range trace and dropped prac rounds into the nearest village.

Darren Kitchen

I remember 48 on while on exercise in Cyprus, a US pilot for a hush hush plane was unable to fly after a night out with some senior HQ SAC—the US govt didn't take kindly to him having head injuries ... He tried drinking games and then gobbed off a little!

Paul Grimley

Standing on parade one morning at 16 Sqn, Wildenrath, FS Mick Parry going to inspect the troops of A flight comes across George (AKA Agony Bags). George is a trifle 'under the weather', having had a long night with Scouse Day. He hasn't shaved and his kit is minging. FS goes a bit loud at him, at which point George looks at him as best he can through one eye, points at John Day, and says to FS Parry, "It's not my turn for a bollocking, Flight, it's fuckin' *his*." I have never seen Mick Parry turn so red, and remember well all of the detachment SNCOs (Roy Scott, in particular) trying to stifle a laugh.

Chris Taylor

48 Sqn exercise. RAF, Binbrook, back in 1984. I am the DC on B2, even although I was only an SAC but had completed the TC's course at Larkhill. I had to provide a coverer for a site move so thought I would give SAC Hector Bate some responsibility and choose him. Armed with the signs for FU, RT, optical tracker, admin area, tape measure, etc. off he goes with the AIG, who was Bill Morris, to the new site. Hours later we turn up and there is my trustworthy SAC waiting to brief me on the site layout.

I look at the signs and order 'action', as the good book used to say. All is going well until, after positioning the FU, RT, and optical tracker, we come to lay out the cables! Fuck! They won't reach, even with 5 SACs trying to stretch them! "You fuckin' doughnut," I says to Hector, "The kit is too far apart for the cables to reach!"

"But I measured the distances," says Hector, using the tape measure you gave me.

"And what distances did you measure?" says I.

"It's exactly 30 metres from FU to tracker," says Hector, "To a millimetre!" Cue me giving him a right bollocking and having to re-site the whole shebang! Never ever used him as a coverer again! Nice bloke but should have been called Tim. Nice but dim!

Chris Pacey

1115 on a Monday, Stodge walks into the bay at 48 and says, "Can you drive, laddy?"

"Yes, CPL," off we go then. We pick up Badders, Geordie, Fat Taff, and Scouse Hill and shoot off. So we are driving to across the airfield and I asked where we are going.

"Do you know where the Rock house is?"

"Yes!"

"Off you go then." Monday lunchtime, in uniform, drinking in a civvy pub. I was driving so coke for me. Four rapid fire pints later and it is 1245, time to head back. Stodge decides he is not traveling in the wagon, he is hanging off the tailgate road skiing, wearing the soles out of his boots, and another is on the roof surfing it as we drive through the main gate, past the Guins, and back to the squadron! I was proper pooping it, as I was the driver, but I felt relaxed to know there were adults in the wagon. My intro to Skellitor and midday drinking.

John Shearson

A long day in the Hebs, waiting on the kit to start working, the range equipment to agree the kit was working, and decent weather all at the same time. So I went to my flight cmdr and said, "I've not had a bollocking all day, can I have one now while we aren't busy?" He said okay and started shouting at me. A few minutes later, the AIG comes over and says, "You are always in trouble, blah blah, start running between range head and range control and don't stop until I tell you." Eventually tells me to stop running and rants on about me learning my lesson, etc.

Later in the day, AIG is told the full story and then asks me why I didn't tell him the truth earlier. "Because I was bored anyway," was my answer. Seem to remember he just walked off shaking his head.

Spike Cook

Hercules on the way over to Hebrides in November, 1981, a few A flight playing three card brag with B flight on the tail gate. The usual suspects Chris Taylor, Ginge Howell. I win four hands in a row against the odds and win £230 … a fortune. My birthday during detachment and I decide all my winnings will go towards a 21st birthday party. I hire the tea rooms and invite the whole island with the help of their radio station. The squadron assembles and I think we pay a coach driver JB? Anyway, my presents were all purchased from that little NAAFI and I had to wear them: 1 x Baycity Rollers t-shirt. 1 x pair of pink knickers, and 1 x box of 50 super tampax hung around the elastic of my apple catcher knickers. The rules imposed on me involved me having to drink from a dunked tampon. Without touching glass.

Anyway all the islands girls came and had a ball, much to their boyfriends' disgust. Those that were there remember the coach journey back to Ben be flipping peculiar that morning!

Trev Vennard

So many moons ago, I'm on stag with a legendary gunner called Davy Bates, a gentleman from Portsmouth who didn't say much but when he did you either pissed yourself or changed whatever you were doing to the way he said to do it. Well its 0 early o'clock on Site One, Belize, we are both sat bored shitless in the radio room. Those of you who recall Site One in the early '80s, the radio room was half the shack with the kitchen in the other half. Well, Batesy hears a noise and gets up to investigate, he looks through the hatch and I hear, "Fuckin' hell, Mushy, what the fook is that?" I get up to have a look and it's one of those big rat-like feckers trying to get into the freezer. It's about the size of a cocker spaniel if that helps. Meanwhile I hear the distinctive sound of an SLR being loaded and cocked! Batesy has decided to shoot the bastard.

I then spend the next five minutes trying to explain to him that, yes, shooting the interloper would solve the problem, however, the high velocity round would go through it and into the gas bottles out the back, and the resulting explosion and fireball would probably kill every sorry ass on site, including *us*!

He relented and spent the rest of the night lobbing batteries of all shapes and sizes at it through the hatch while it continued to try to access the freezer and ignored the idiot lobbing shit at it, until it got bored and wandered off into the night from whence it came.

Dan Smale

On a tour in Belize, the boss informs us that the paras have challenged the RAF to a game of rugby. RAF have a few reasonable players amongst pilots, etc. (for years I was convinced one of them was Rory Underwood, but I think that was just my imagination). Anyway, they wanted cannon fodder, so half the team was Rocks with only the vaguest idea of the rules. Don't pass it forward and if they get it, hammer them ...

Anyway the Guins must have known what they were doing, because we won, though it seemed like more of a bar brawl than anything else. Most of the paras were too hacked off to come back to the squadron bar for the third half and the following day. Their commanding officer had the lot of them on a forced march in full kit, last heard the screams as they headed into the distance ... "You will not fucking lose to the RAF!"

Albi Pinnion

Falklands, 1983. Me, the sprog of the crew, having joined up in '82, decided I would impress the big boys! In the boffy only one light, I got a steak and kidney pie dish and over a few nights had polished it with a spoon until it was gleaming!

Got the end of the twin core cable coming straight from the meadows generator, and thought to myself, *Easy*, cannot turn the meadows off, so seperate the wires, both are insulated. *Cut one at a time,* me thinks, cut into the first, and bang! And what seemed like forever until I stopped shaking, a hole burnt in my hand, and the rest of the crew now awake, laughing at me.

For about three days, I had the shakes and spilt every cup of tea I had, thanks for the sympathy, JC, Ken Bewley, Spike Cook, Jock Joan Stuart Currie, Ringo Degsy Williams, and Roger Biamonti.

David Jeremiah

On an exercise in Denmark at Oxbol with 19 Sqn and caught the train into Esburg. We had a day on the pop in the John Wayne bar! So, worse for wear, caught train back except Benny Miller fell asleep, so about ten of us crept off the train as its pulling out the station, we banged on the window to wake him. Then ran off laughing, as you do, three hours later, he arrives back at the camp, absolutely furious. We stayed out of his way till he calmed down and saw the funny side of it.

Wayne Holliss

Now at some point during my first time on 48 Sqn, three of us SACs were given the task to take two one tonnies down to Stirling for a re-spray, and then bring three wagons and an MST back. Now in them days, this was deemed to be a good number, an overnight stay, and a rate one, party on. So, off we set, soon reaching our digs for the night—Ma Brodie's BandB—never forget the welcome, "Hello, boys," mad old cow. So she's shown us our room, problem one, one single, one double bed, three gunners. So being the sprog, I knew what one I wasn't getting, but who had to share with me?

So off we go to the carousel boozer where we settle in for a night on special brew. For some anyway, muggins was soon feeling the worse, pissed as newt in fact, with the room spinning. The other two Rocks decided to return to Ma's, putting me to bed in the single pit. Result, can't remember too much about that night except two things. In my drunken disgust at dropping out early, I put hand in pocket and gave the lads some cash for a drink, rather a lot of cash in fact. For some reason, I managed to spend 60 quid that night, which was a lot in 1986. The second was more worrying, a bit of a commotion in the double bed, the drunken Welsh gunner, thinking he was at home and in bed with the Mrs, tried to reach around where no man should when sharing a double bed with a drunk Rock, the dirty bastard.

John Stowell

One morning on the ranges in the Hebrides, otherwise known as Bendracula, all Ts and As done, kit talking to itself, us, and range control, we had been sent for a chill out in the cabin at the rear of the firing point whilst awaiting the arrival of the target tug from Wyton.

As SOP dictated, an operator had been left to look after the kit and was sat in the tracker shelter. The guy that was in our shelter unfortunately was not what you might call the brightest button on the tunic, and boredom got the better of him. I won't give his name but he went by the nickname of Piggy. When we got called to go to the shelter to prepare for the first shooting run, we found that Piggy, in his infinite wisdom, had started to dismantle the SEZ. He had all the bulbs out of it. I'll let you imagine the events of the next few minutes. Piggy was an enigma. One of nature's failures, bless him. It's right to say that he had passionate fingers, everything he touched, he screwed.

Jeremy Frayne

Was lucky enough to serve seventeen years on Rapier as a Penguin, and have quite a few stories to share, but here's mine. I was an AP with 37 Sqn down south in 1992, on my last night Eng Flight frequented Turner's for bingo! It looked as though the whole squadron was there, which was innocent enough until Alan Lomax informed me that I was being taken back to his site for a haircut! I spent the next three hours plotting my escape, I was followed everywhere. I was doomed! Finally last orders was called, my guards weakened, and left for the bar, and I was gone! Before I got over the grass to the road, I heard all the doors burst open and several threats of death.

I went through the FAC front doors like a rocket, RAFP telling me to stop immediately, then repeated that order 15-20 seconds later! I ran past my room and hid in the drying room, covering myself in parkers and coveralls, and held my breath.

About two hours later, I woke up, my tongue the size of a flip flop following accelerated dehydration and went back to my room, I was safe. There was a commotion next door, so in I went, I was greeted by Shag Ball, Bri Finnegan, Minty, et al, "Where the hell have you been?" And instantly all pointed to the corner of the room, I looked over and there was Simon, the LAC mech. They took him instead and gave him my haircut—with a shovel I reckon. He had been draped over a land rover and surfed back to the site, scalped, and brought back. I wet myself, several times actually, he was sat next to me for the flight home!

Dan Swale

Back to Belize, 16 Sqn tour (probably the Womble tour for anyone who still has the t-shirt). In in a club in Belize City with Charlie M. It's been a long evening and we're perhaps a bit the worse for wear, when some pongo takes a shine to my jacket. He's about to leave with it when I point out that it's not his. He's even more pissed than we are and tries to argue the toss. His five mates seem ready to back him up. It seems like it's about to go south pretty fast when a big black guy wanders over from the bar, and in a very relaxed manner, tells the pongos they are making a mistake. The one with my jacket says something along the lines of, "Fuck off, chimp." To which the man in question calmly replies, "That's Flight Sergeant Chimp to you, sonny." Damn near wet myself at the look on the guy's face. His mates had him out of the jacket and out the door in about two seconds flat. Thanks, Winston.

John Crammond

How to crack up the whole CP shift with an innocuous question. 27 Sqn, Leuchars. CPO. Bob Fishwick, at midday, to recent arrival Bill Cock, "Has everyone eaten? What about you?" looking at Bill, "Have you eaten, Cock?" CP disintegrates into uncontrollable giggles and guffaws. CPO looks around bemused, which makes it worse! Not sure if he ever got it!

David Jerimiah

Steve G was posted as the second AIG to 19 Sqn again in the Hebrides, we had a fantastic wind up. With the delivery of the missiles ready for firing. We had briefed the armourer to have the top three missiles as empty boxes and to leave the straps off so that when he came on the range, he turned the corner and the top three boxes flew off the trailer. We positioned Steve so he could see it all happen. In an instant, he flew down towards the missile truck, and I'm sure his feet weren't touching the ground. We were all giggling as Steve was screaming at the armourer but, unknown to us, the commanding officer was watching from the LASO bunker (the inspector general was in on the wind up) "Christ, inspector general, look what's happened," says commanding officer.

Inspector general's reply, "Yeah, shit happens." Next thing we heard was the commanding officer had the inspector general by the throat, pinned to the wall and was screaming, "Not on my range," it was the commanding officer's first camp, so it ended up as a double whammy!

Robbie Robinson

Duty site, Belize. Thor, the lovable site dog, was chained to a centre peg with just enough to reach the entry gate. Every night a local chap would leave the tower and cycle down the runway home. Thor had a thing about local chaps ... so would run to try and play with them.

Well one night, some lad had added some bungle to the chain giving Thor more rope, so to say. Apparently, the look on local chap's face was a picture when Thor got a lot closer than normal, close enough to chew his back wheel.

David Jeremiah

In the Hebrides, doing the firing on 19 Sqn, a newly promoted officer, a flight lieutenant (ex FS), was sent to the point as the firing point officer. "What do you want me to do, AIG?" I said.

"Go into the SAF shelter and make sure the pies are hot and turned regularly, ready for NAAFI break."

"Okay," was the reply. I was only joking! After an hour, went into the shelter for something, and there he was doing as I'd asked, sat on a chair, feet up reading the paper, drinking coffee from my flask! He just winked and started laughing.

Joan Stuart Curry

At Black Eagle camp, we had the officers' and sergeants' mess and the grunts' next door. Them being grown ups were allowed spirits; us being grunts, two small beers a day. Some guy managed to jimmy the mess room door, remove said spirits in to another container, top up the bottles with water, and retire to a large bomb crater and get merry. This happened a few times without anyone cracking on.

Darren Western

Remember a trip to Belize, and our crew were sent to the seaside to trial a new bit of kit for the Rapier system. Anyway, we're out in the middle of nowhere so a guard is posted with the usual ten rounds and the standard SA80. I'm on stag when in comes Kev Hartigan (RIP) and the duty CPL (pervert) both hammered. Anyway, the conversation goes like this, "Gunner Western, I need the SA80 for a spot of hunting."

Now I'm not one for disobeying an order from a senior rank, so I hand it over. Several minutes later, rounds are popping off, and a while later, Kev comes back with the weapon. Only been out shooting at an alligator for a bit of fun in a nearby pool. That's right, wind the fucker up so it comes into camp looking us. God rest his soul.

Andy Duffield

Going up to the Hebs for live firing with 27 in '86. After a few in the NAAFI and take-out on the way, also a few then on the ferry, most of us had a few on by the time we got to the island! We were all put on the bus by a not so nice flight sergeant, who seemed to hate everyone and any type of humour or fun! We were all a disgrace and should be fucking ashamed of ourselves, etc. shouted and spluttered with glee by such man! After giving his bollocking and feeling very pleased with himself, he went to get off the bus, then a thick jock accent came from the back, through the alcoholic haze, "Fuck off, Bad Toad!" The bus full of drunk Rocks then burst into full hysteria! Bad Toad went to about 20,000 ft and was screaming we were all going to be jailed, to which no one took a blind bit of notice. Luckily enough he couldn't jail 3/4 of the sqn!

Mark Duffin

While on exercise with 48 in 81ish, I was in the B Ech at Milltown, it came time for the evening stand to. As a young Guin (non-Rapier trained cannon fodder) on the squadron, I took up my position in the grass on the perimeter. I had just got comfy, ready for half hour's kip (we never got attacked at Milltown) when the squadron warrant officer (the one before Nutty Ralph) came running out of the cooks area screaming, "Fire, Fire!" We all perked up and looked out for the first ever attack. Some of the Rocks let off a few blanks from the SLRs, while we Guins gave the 'bang, bang' signature tune of the SMG. The warrant officer man still kept screaming, "Fire, Fire!"

Everyone one was like, "WTF, well okay," full automatic on the SMG, brrrrrt, brrrrrt. It was only when we saw the smoke coming out of the cooks tent we realized what he was getting at, the tent was on fire. Panic time, save the baby's head pudding that were cooking for dinner. Luckily a couple of the guys near to the tent noticed what was going on and put the fire out before any major damage was done. Baby's head for dinner, a couple of hours out of the exercise and a good topic of conversation.

Robert Booth

27 Sqn at Leuchars. We were deployed on a NATO exercise to Denmark. The first part was a drive to the ferry port, followed by an overnight on a recently commissioned ship called the 'DFDS Dana Regina'. The only accommodation booked was for the drivers so the rest had to fend for ourselves. The other mistake was to trust the Rocks to sign for our food on the back of the receipts with name and number in the cafe. Continental cafes sell beer. Yeah, apparently Mickey Mouse, Hitler, Che Guevara, and numerous others had never drunk so much. Next morning, lads were found sleeping in the weirdest places, worst was trying to get the guy out of the Wendy house in the kids' playroom.

The exercise itself took place on an aircraft live firing range. We were deployed around the edges of the range, no danger there then. The techs even came and fitted CCTV to the mono on the back of the fire control unit. This was so the senior officers could review things at the end of the day. No one had taken into account that outside the range was a naturist colony and nudist beach. After the end of the first day's play and review of the video, we were told that whilst the AOC was impressed by the steadiness of our tracking, aircraft were the priority, and not tits and ass. Can't remember which unit it was, but their exercise was livened up when a G91 aircraft carried out its strafing run and forgot to let go the trigger. A lot of the lads ended up at the bottom of the kitchen pit.

Gus Dunning

There was a flight sergeant in the '80s at Laarbruch who was thoroughly disliked by everyone on the flight and most of the other single lads on the squadron, but will remain anonymous. After the squadron had a dining-in night, where we all had to be in best blues. Said FS got lashed up and decided he loved his lads that much he would come back to the block and carry on drinking with us bedecked in his mess dress. Well, the lads duly filled him full of any booze they could get in him until he flaked out in the TV room. Then some bright spark decides to get his own back, he would pee on him. Well within two mins there was a bloody queue outside the door.

Come the morning FS had disappeared, God knows what he smelt like, and the matter was never mentioned again, and he never ventured outside the squadron bar. Karma springs to mind.

Tony Tom Sawyer

Football final 37 Sqn vs whoever. The said person manages to turn up walking with a bad limp, tells the commanding officer (manager) that he can't play as he's in too much pain. The commanding officer asked how he did it, and was told it was by falling out of bed. The commanding officer goes mad saying, "You can't do that by falling out of bed!"

The said person with a straight face says, "You can if your bed was on the bike shed."

Dave Vickery

So four Rocks from 48 on Belize tour decide to go to Acapulco for a week Gibbo (Twa Heads), myself, Spike, and Jon (can't remember his surname but his nickname was Burt Reynolds). Had a stopover in Mexico City for half a night, waiting for the next plane. We went into a night club and somehow all managed to end up on stage with a Mexican hostess singing 'When the Saints Come Marching In'. Bizarre and I cannot remember how it happened. Anyway, we obviously attracted the attention of some fine looking ladies who took us to another night club, and we all thought we were in. Then three bottles of champagne ended up on the table and we were asked to cough up. Gibbo decides, *Fuck this,* and got to the toilet then shinned down the drainpipe leaving us to do some negotiating ... after some threats, ducking and diving, we managed to get out, only to find Gibbo had felt guilty and gone back inside to look for us!

He was handed a bill for all the champers and thrown out ... didn't laugh much!

Spike Horton

Remember in the early days at Black Eagle as Flight HQ driver. I was on walkabout with B Flight's driver, looking for something that the kits could use. Well, opposite the camp entrance by the camp refuelling point was the catering section, dishing out fresh food for the Guins. We spied through a window fresh rations plus other delicacies, so a plan was devised, and raid planned ...

Well, the window just fell out as we passed, so in we went and emptied the place. One of the items 'borrowed' was an electric kettle. On returning back to Black Eagle, a sharp-eyed rat saw us and enquired about our found items (not the food). "We found it, Flight."

"Okay, give that to me, I want it."

"Okay, Flight, enjoy." Couple of hours later, OC catering was visiting every section telling everyone that there was a break-in at catering section, a load of stuff was stolen, and presented a list of said items which included a kettle. Not just any kettle but *his* kettle. Fast forward "Horton and (can't remember his name)! My office now!"

"Why didn't you tell me you stole this kettle?"

"You never asked, flight. You just said you wanted it."

"Take it and get rid of it."

"Okay, flight," well it saved us having to hide it in our tent. We sent it out to a site with a note, "Hide if anyone visits."

David King

Hebrides, a very good friend of mine, Terry Morton, and another lad many of you know, John Hodgson, getting ready to begin our normal evening activities in the NAAFI. Terry pops next door to John's room to borrow the iron, unbeknown to Terry, the iron had just been used, and I do mean *just*. Terry picks up said iron and presses it against John's chest and at exactly the same time says, "Is that hot?" The scream, well we'll not mention that but I can still see the complete shape of the iron, complete with steam holes emblazoned on John's chest. Couldn't make it up, and it was a genuine accident, his nickname for a while was Ironside.

Alan Lomax

In the Hebs 37 Sqn doing the usual live firing. Saturday night in the NAAFI. The night of the Lennox Lewis Bruno fight. The beer was flowing when some pongo (there were pongos everywhere) walks straight up to me and says, "You're a big lad, I bet you think you can drop me in one."

Couldn't believe it but I was already in the shit back at Bruggen, so I declined and said, "Look, mate, I don't want any trouble." He walks off smiling, thinking he's made his point with no repercussions. The 'boxing' finishes and some army corporal shouts, "All you RAF wankers out!" Next thing I knew the same pongo comes straight up to me and says the same thing again. Meanwhile one of the other pongos attacked a squadron Guin. Enough was enough, so I pointed to a place in the NAAFI where there was plenty of space and said, "Tell you what, let's go over there." I wasn't a happy Hector as this guy was just rooting for trouble and had targeted me. I then proceeded to distribute one hell of a beating to this guy, claret everywhere. There were pongos hanging on to my neck, squeezing, but I managed to finish the job with the other guy, and my white t-shirt was covered in claret. There was fighting everywhere that night and none of the lads took anything like a kicking. We got off with no police involvement or any disciplinary action despite the carnage.

The following morning, we were leaving to head back to Germany when we saw several army blokes fishing, but they were covered in bandages and moving awkwardly. My guess is the med centre was pretty full that night, but not one casualty from the squadron. What a night!

Robbie Robson

Belize, up country, 1978. 63 Sqns tour, shared a bivie with Roger Dory. One poncho for the cover and one for the ground-sheet. It came the time for Roger and myself to stag on, it was pissing down, so a plan was hatched ... Take the poncho used for the ground-sheet, sit back to back, and both don the poncho with one head in the hood part.

After fifteen minutes, drop head, spin the poncho round, other head pops up. Two hours of stag and both dry ... well, dryish.

Andy Devine

Belize '87, CG visits APC, possibly AVM Leech. One evening, all the SNCOs including the Sheriff (SNCO RAFP), SNCO fire, and the officers went to the Chateau Caribbean for a meal. Myself and Chris Law were dicked as drivers, with Chris taking the SNCOs and the flight cdr, and I have the senior officers. Yes for one night only, CG's driver, and his chariot was a Sherpa minibus.

After the meal and several toasts (think the CG like a swally), even the sheriff brought us out a beer while we waited outside. Finally just before midnight the CG, his ADC (a Rock squadron leader) and OC SHORAD (Sammy the Pig) pile into the back of the Sherpa, full of bonhomie or local rum, not sure which.

So I'm driving back to APC when the ADC asks me to pull over as the CG needed to piss. I pulled off the road onto a dirt track and all three of them step into headlights of the Sherpa, tally whackers out and start to water the bushes. Oh how I wish I had had my camera, what a caption competition that would have been!

Glyn Jones

Not so much a Rock story but it was funny at the time. On exercise with one of the Germany Rapier Squadrons (37, I think). We were deployed in Holland and our site was at the end of a farm track, close to a farm with a windmill. We were set up and knew we would be there for several days, so it was pretty chilled—no NBC, just low flying aircraft—cushty.

There were two guys at the farm, the son—who came to see us and brought milk, spuds, and eggs, proper nice guy—then there was his dad, who was getting on a bit. He used to sit outside and scowl at us, and refused point blank to speak. After a couple of days of this, we broached the question with the son as to why, as the Dutch were always so friendly with the Brits. It turned out that during the war he did okay with his windmill, making flour, mainly for the German Army, but there was always enough left for himself and the villagers to make bread. One day a lone Spitfire flew past at low level, saw the sails turning and decided that this was helping the German war effort, did a sharp turn and blew the sails off with some well-aimed cannon rounds. This meant that the farmer lost his livelyhood and had to go to a labour gang for the rest of the occupation—he has never forgiven and hated the Brits or the RAF for this.

Gus Dunning

Now early '80s, Falkland Islands. All the Rapier kits of 24 hr radio watch, with HQ call for regular random radio checks at the duty op officer's whim. There I am sat there next to the trusting 352, when over the net I hear, "I'm bored with this shit," so obviously waking the ops officer up, he has leapt out of his seat as he came on the net instead of the HQ signaller.

"Hello, unknown call sign, please repeat with your call sign,"."

To which the reply was, "I'm not that fucking bored. Out." Next day, Hooker, who was our delightful OC, instructed the SNCO's to find that man. Needless to say it was a fruitless task and he lived to sleep another day.

David Jackson

Xmas '85 in the Falklands. The OC and warrant officer went round all the sites with bottles of rum at Sapper Hill. They forgot said rum when they left signals pit. Me and Gus drank half a bottle. They got on radio, "Can we have the rum back?"

"Too late!" was the shout back.

Wayne Holliss

Belize 1986, drinking with some pongos from 2 Queens, I know, don't make a habit of it, and soon enough they started to throw down challenges to us Rocks, big mistake. One idiot decided to challenge me to two laps of the compound doing the 'Dance of the Flaming Arse 'Oles', the fool. So, for the honour of the regiment, I accepted and went and got the tools needed.

I came back with a roll of issued blue role and a bottle of mossie rep. I then challenged the pongo, heads or tales—loser has his rags soaked in mossie rep. He lost. Now, being a Rock, I'm a nasty cunt when I want to be, so instead of soaking Percy's rag at the loose end, I drenched the arse end.

So it was under starter's orders, blue roll held vice-like between our respective arse cheeks, trousers around are ankles, then off we went. I shot around like a lightning on reheat, leaving a blazing trail and smell of burning paper. Poor old Percy kept up for the first half, looking like a Saturn V rocket. However, as soon as the flames caught the mossie rep, he turned in to the Challenger space shuttle. Whoosh! Percy's arse erupted in a mass of flame. He ran around screaming in agony trying to pat out the flames with his bear hands. All around the gathered crowd pissed themselves as the now scorched pongo limped back to the med centre, his arse one big blister.

The next morning, we're sat at the stims bar, partaking in a bottle of liquid sugar when Percy comes hobbling by with third degree burns of the arse, and after a right bollocking from the RSM for a self-inflicted wound.

Mark Andrew Bowen

A certain Rapier inspector general was heartily disliked by his squadron. He had a lovely dog, a cocker spaniel, he called Gunner. Inspector general and Gunner went with the advance party by road and then ferry from Oban. On arrival, ahead of ferry departure time, the inspector general announces to his SAC driver that he needs to go to the bank to draw some money (no ATMs then). Strict instructions not to feed anything to Gunner ahead of the sailing as the poor lad has a weak tummy. No sooner has the inspector general disappeared around the corner than the driver had his packed ration box open and is shovelling the contents down the dog's throat. Gunner is as happy as Larry, after being fed boring dry food. IG returns and asks how Gunner has behaved. "Lovely dog, Sir, not a bit of trouble."

Skip to the next morning as the overnight ferry is docking in Oban. The IG, who normally tried to appear as he thought an officer should appear, stuck-up and condescending, was on deck really angry and not the picture of the suave officer in complete control; he was almost frothing. He spots the SAC, his driver, "I thought you said Gunner was fine when I asked you?" he asks.

"Yes, Sir, happy as Larry, why?"

"Because all last night the bloody dog was spewing and crapping all over me and my cabin—my kit and clothes are covered in shit and the cabin is a wreck!"

"Can't understand it," says the gunner, deadpan, "Fine when I left him with you." Needless to say, that gunner was an immediate hero and Gunner, the dog, unfortunately became a route into winding-up that cock of an inspector general.

Jim Higgins

On FRT with Dave Parry during Whirly Gig, and sent to fix a REME FU attached to 26 Sqn. Three phase on the launcher but none on the optical tracker. Says Dave, "You have not connected your long 55 way."

Says the lead grunt, "We dont have one."

Says me, "Why not?"

Says the lead grunt, "It isnt our turn."

Albi Pinnion

Another deployment doo do, we deployed on a callout. Set up basic defences and started to dig in, as we were digging in, came under attack! Threw orange smoke to flank the attack, we're deemed by Di staff to have killed the enemy, only to be confronted by something far more dangerous—a German farmer and his son, neither spoke English, and none of our German was up to speed.

Di staff had gone, so had to call out the liason officer. It was all sorted out, German farmer claimed for a whole field of sweetcorn, even though the actual corn was protected by the leaves. I suspect he did rather well out of it, as later that evening he returned in a very jovial state, with beer and snaps and food for all of us, and family in tow. I think we were there for three days and each evening we were treated the same, by a very happy farmer!

Dave Capps

During an exercise in Germany, the squadron had deployed to Sennelager, when it comes time to drive home, one of the FUT (one tonne) Land Rovers has a steering issue. The nut on top of the steering wheel had sheared off, rendering the steering wheel useless (yes, okay, loose nut behind the wheel). As a measure to get the vehicle home, a set of mole grips were attached to the steering column, not ideal, but it worked.

After a precarious drive home, the vehicle entered the camp gates, narrowly missing the snowdrop. He stopped said vehicle, chastised the driver about his directional skills, and was duly handed the steering wheel by the driver who proceeded to drive off, leaving a gobsmacked copper with a disembodied steering wheel stood in the road ... Ahh, the days before health and safety.

Steve Holland

The commanding officer on 63 during the late '80s, early '90s, deployment to MPA (no names, you can work it out) was very proud of the trout he had caught whilst fishing and, in fact, he had frozen a few of them. Anyway the trout were taken out of the freezer and left in the kitchen at HQ to be defrosted ready for a BBQ at the Dog and Badger the following day.

On the day of the BBQ, the commanding officer seemed a bit miffed that no one would eat the trout that he had lovingly prepared and cooked to share with the lads. Excitedly he would offer round the trout only to hear time and time again, "No thanks, Sir," note: not 'boss', "I don't like trout." Not deterred, however, he tucked into the trout like a tramp on chips.

"Mmmmm, delicious," he declared, while those in the know tried not to piss themselves. The trout when he prepared them were much more slimy than normal. Apparently the trout had been given a salty tasting marinade by a person on nights who again will remain nameless (it wasn't me). But I did hear that the commanding officer was a big fan of the Jazz musician Thelonius Monk!

David Maynard

Right, some of you might not believe this. But on a 20 Sqn detachment up in the Hebrides, I got dicked to do the deployment in the morning with the most laid-back, chilled out sergeant who did not give a fuck. Ts and As, and measure and set displacements radar, optical tracker, launcher, all done. Apart from the launcher which is 3200 out. Everything working until the range goes live and the missiles are pointing the wrong way down the range. Laughed my tits off, did try to tell him, didn't get paid enough. Crack on, sergeant. Basic but top bloke and happy days.

Chris Backhouse

It was one of those Rapier exercises where Eng and HQ harboured up for a while with nothing to do but guard our site. So three or four of us decided to see who could go the longest without curling one out—to resist cheating, each first shit of the week would be inspected for size. After about three or four days I was done, so off I trotted into the yonder (further than normal—you'll see why in a minute ...) and did the dastardly deed. Then it struck me, *I can still win!*

I burned the bog roll and said nothing. I then pronto take a shit once or twice a day in exactly the same place (you can see where I'm going here, right ...)

Come the last day of the exercise, I proudly claim victory. My competitors falling by the wayside. Take my last (first!) dump and invite the losers to inspect my week's worth of shit all piled up into what they foolishly believed to be one huge log.

Bill Young

Whilst down in South Atlantic, had a bit of a laugh with another Rock (no names, coz Rico would kill me). Sent off for 'he to she' transformation pack for him. A few weeks later, said pack arrived complete with 'hide your manhood' ladies knickers and stiletto heels up to size 12. He was furious! And said he was going to ask Coy to return initial request so he could check handwriting. I just thought, *Bollox—wish I had typed it ... Help!*

However, he got the last laugh. After a heavy session in NAAFI, I fell asleep, he managed to draw fishnet stockings and suspenders onto me (with indelible, waterproof ink). It was weeks before I managed to get the artwork off! Twat, suppose fair is fair—call it a draw this time.

John Hodgson

Belize '93, 48's last tour. Been there about a week when there was a RAF top table in the mess. Needless to say, the rum and coke was being downed like there was no tomorrow. At some stage, in the early hours, I retired to bed. About 20 mins later, one of the CP staff was banging on my door, "It's a call out!" After a pleasant exchange of words, oh hum, I looked in on Steve Thorp, who was by now perched precariously on the edge of his bed, probably looking for his eyes, judging by the state of him.

If I remember rightly, his crew went to Site 5, which needed the four tonner to get the kit up there, and guess who had to drive the four tonner? Turned out that the call out was instigated by our howling mad FS, who was also at the top table but we put down his lack of drinking to him being a tight jock! Couldn't understand his explanation, but then again, not many people could understand him anyway. Can't name names, of course, but it's an anagram of Millie Weldrum! Had a great tour, apart from the tragic ending. Cheers, had a great time there with all.

Phil Swales

First week from passing a Rapier course in Germany at Wildenrath after a posting from 58 to 26 at Laarbruch. It was a clean up day on A Flight, kit serviced, was a Thursday, vehicles washed, etc. My job (SAC) was to take the dets LR and one tonners to the wash in MT with CPL Royston 'Taff' Jones (a good mate. RIP, bud) in the morning before NAAFI break. We'd just finished the last one, the TRT, when Taff said, "Right, Ginge, it's NAAFI break." So I thought we'd be going back to 26's compound and the canteen, nope, went to the families' shop on way out of camp, picked up a couple of Warsteiners each, and preceded to drive out of the main gate, right turn to Wemb, and drove to behind the church, where we parked up.

To say I was bewildered was an understatement. Then a Land Rover approached us, followed by another two, then another one, and out of the Rovers stepped Chiefy Kavanagh, Sergeant Paddy Mac, Cpls Ally Robertson (all RIP), Paul Compton, and drivers SAC 'Geordie' Hadaway, Magraff, and one other whose name just eludes me, not sure if it was you Noddy Rigby on this, my *first* Wemb NAAFI break) Anyhow, everyone congregated with beers in hand, this at ten in the morning!

I was from field, wasn't used to this, was used to the YMCA at Catericklol. The thing that got me was the 'this is the norm' type of feeling. It was brill. Then comes dinner time, after some scran, it was into the Double LL for vodka and cokes (Taff), Bacardi and coke, Meyers rum (MaGraff). Blimey, this was dinner time. I normally have a cup of tea.

After this, it was back to the squadron and carry on with the clean up till knock off, then it was a couple of crates in the flight crew room—not a beer call, that was the next day, a Friday in the squadron bar, this was for something else. Think someone put the ale on for the birth of his baby girl. What a crazy week my first week was. Excellent times on that squadron, great lads of *all* ranks, from the commanding officer down to the LACs who were on the Rapier course with me and posted in at the same time.

Rob Davies

My first Falklands tour and I'm down on the helipad with an unnamed colleague. A chopper is bearing down on us and I just need him to earth the chopper before I can hook up the underslung net. Instead, as the chopper descends around our ears, he freaks, drops the earthing cable and runs off! I'm a LAC, wondering what the fuck to do next, stretching to reach for the fallen earthing hook before snapping on the load. I shit myself! Wasn't impressed!

Joe Cornes

Whilst sweeping our bay out on A Flight 26 Sqn, we asked Bill, could he shove his hand through the Launcher tow eye? Yes was the answer. But could he get it out? Yes again! With the help of grease, and three gunners pulling, over the screams of pain.

Tony Ryan

Some may remember the dark days of Stanley, when the Rapier sites were a little more basic compared with Mount Pleasant. Anyway, I was on the site known as Fly Away or Arrow Point on the Map, and we were a tadge isolated to say the least. Among our crew, as a new member of the Corp, who I would take over from on sigs duty in the sigs bothy—this was a comfortable little shack were you listened to six hours of static while reading some interesting glossy artistic magazines. Anyway, after getting a briefing from Gatts Gatlin, I would crack on with my stag. It wasn't long before I was finding soiled bits of blue roll all over the sigs pit, as Gatts was quite an excitable chap and held the crew record of six bouts of excitement in the one sigs' shift. I was not a happy bunny as this was becoming regular occurrence and despite my guidance of potential blindness, hygiene, etc. my warnings went unanswered. So, I plotted my revenge.

One of the duties we performed was spending a day on admin, cleaning, cooking, etc. and part of this was emptying the thunder box. I mentioned to Gatts that he needed to stir the shit pit round a bit as we burnt our domestic rubbish in there. As well as our shit the pit was about six foot deep and a fair size in diameter. So Gatts leaps into said pit to spread a lot of the previous unburnt stuff into a neat pile ready for today's rubbish, totally unaware that a jerry can of petrol had already been added. I appear like that scene from *Lord Of The Rings,* running with my piece of burning blue roll from behind the cam net and watched it sail into the pit. Well, up went the Gatt pig, proper on fire, as the fumes ignited under his parka, we watched him struggle in his panic to try and escape the flames, as he struggled the climb the banks that had oil on them for some strange reason. We left him in there long enough for Albi Pinion to get a photo for the album. Gatts was a little bit singed but nothing to write home about. Moral of the story is, if you are going to spank your monkey make sure you *clean it up* if it's sick.

Stephen Headey

Falklands second tour for 16 Sqn. This particular night, I was on radio watch at the tracker and outside it was blowing a real storm, wind, rain the full Monty. All of a sudden, over the net on came a cry for help, as one of the sites radioed a no duff situation in regards to their portacabin roof, as it seemed to be lifting up because of the storm. All of a sudden, a further message was relayed saying it had gone and had blown off into the night.

Cue Rocks off duty in their pits watching the roof bouncing up and down until it flew off.

It later transpired that earlier in the week, the DC kept tripping on the tie-down wire which kept the roof on, and ordered one of the lads to cut them off.

Adrian Harkins

37 Sqn '92ish. We've just finished some Nato exercise in Belgium, Florensee, I think the place was. Anyways, we are having an after exercise piss up with all the other nations finest from pilots to national service types. So as the night went on, the other nations are getting rowdy and you could tell it wasn't going to end well—you got the impression that some of these pissed pilots still thought there rank meant something to us in a bar! Wrong American pilot gets a smack in the chops by Eddie Fraser (RIP) that shuts them up, in fact they all looked shocked, as the lads were now mobilising to take on every nationality in the bar.

We now make a retreat as we are asked to leave, as some sort of security is on its way. So going back to our accommodation, we hear some loud music from a block party and invite ourselves up there. Yanks again, long story short, Eddie Fraser gives the alpha American of the bunch a couple of rapid to the head, for being the big man and getting funny with us, so we legs it from there as well.

The next day, we sleep in for parade—and I think the sergeant comes and gets us—we've had a few hours' kip and are still pissed. We are tasked with filling all the jerrycans with diesel for the trip home, and then told to go to the cook house and make the squadron sandwiches for the rat packs. So, with hands covered with diesel, we start to make them. Big Taff reminds us to lick every piece of ham and cheese we put in. The lads were saying the sandwiches tasted of diesel but were still eating them until we told them we had licked all the ham and cheese. Well that started a spitting contest there and then.

Bill Hayes

I have been keeping this one up my sleeve but have decided to put myself out of my misery before I die. I was a member of 21 JSTU which was the initial Rapier trails unit. We started in Australia and then moved to Singapore for wet weather and battlefield trials. 16 hours a day, day in and day out. It was very tiring to say the least. Well after about two months of this, we arrived on site on day at 0400 as usual. It was going to be a big day as we had a brigadier from the RA flying out from the UK to see the kit in action. I was tasked with DIing the gen set. It was a black as dogs' guts and we had to feel our way around. I went to the radiator and, with what little light there was, could not see or feel any liquid. So I went and filled a kettle with water (very high tech back then) and poured it into the radiator. The whole lot went in without making any difference.

So I went and got another one and was just about to pour it in when one of the REME blokes stopped me and advised that they radiator had been full the night before and we should check it again before putting more water in. Over we went, and much to my gut churning dismay, realised that I had put the kettle full of water into the oil cap, not the radiator. No reserve generator, no trial on that day to show the brigadier, therefore one wasted trip from the UK to Singers, and one very embarrassed Rock. There, I have done it, they say that confession is good for the soul.

Ginge Armour

48 Sqn very early '80s, I ran the station disco. This one night after the disco had finished, drinks begun to flow faster than we could manage, but howling laughter over nothing in particular. This very large gentleman (I think they were a visiting unit or other) approached one of our smallest (Dobbo) and said something like, "You've spilled my beer." Dobbo tries to explain, no not him, just as fist comes swinging round towards his face, which makes Dobbo duck. Dobbo then begins to run away, but towards the window, with it's three foot high ledge, pushes himself off said ledge, and flies through the air without any greatness of ease, and head butts this oaktree of a guy, who hits the floor before anyone can shout, "Timber!"

The melee that followed was a bit of a blur but it involved someone's (other team) head through the fruit machine, part of the bar shuttering wrapped effectively around another, and me waking up with my ear sown to my pillow (I won't forget Frankie the medic for that one). Can anyone elaborate what else happened that night, as after somebody gave me them blue pills, all I remember was 'Golden Brown' by The Stranglers and Skip doing a funny dance.

Stephen Headey

Second tour of the Falklands, '83 AAAD (all arms air defence). We assembled at Hooker's Point to carry out a shoot which involved the MATS team from the UK with their remote controlled flying plane target. Two GPMGs set up on poles, myself on one gun, and Dai on the other. MATS team ready their toy and say we will be lucky to hit it. Seemed a reasonable challenge. Order was given to load a belt of 200 and watch and shoot. From behind us, we heard the whine of a prop engine and hear it take off. Target approached from the right and we were given weapons free. Both Dai and I opened up and kept our fingers firmly planted and let the belt go. All of a sudden, the target began to shake and shimmy, and disappeared into the sea ... Surely not. The MATS Team were shocked and try to pass it off as a malfunction. Once they retrieved the plane, it had indeed malfunctioned ... due to the amount of holes we put in it! So the rest of the shoot was cancelled as they sloped off to repair their baby. Boo hoo.

Wayne Holliss

A certain SAC in the NAAFI, moaning to the old girl behind the till about what a knob the sqn warrant officer was, so she asks, "What's his name?" He tells her. "Oh yes, know him well, you're right," says she.

"How do you know him then?"

"He's my husband."

Joe Cornes

Someone was driving the FUT towing the launcher, but instead of waiting for the hanger guard to open the doors, they decided to jump out and wind the door open themselves. Whilst rolling open, then jumped back in to the wagon flooring it, unfortunately the hanger door rolled back off, end stops a bit quicker than predicted. Well the FUT got through! But the heavy steel door hit the launcher on its half entry ... fuck! The right hand launch beam was now pointing high right compared to the left beam, still in it locked transit position!

I still remember the sounds of many copper hammers ringing out a futile tune in a bid to straighten it before the engineering road party and flight commander arrived back ... well you have to try, don't you?

Gus Dunning

26 Sqn, on the sauce in the block TV room, and the tightest man in NATO CPL Alvin Robinson gets too pissed and goes

off to his room to sleep it off—but he made one serious and tragic mistake. He left his door unlocked. Some scally rounds up as many as you could fit in the room, while he was sound asleep, and they proceed to cover every single inch of his room in shaving foam. It was a total white out and looked like something from Willy Wonka.

Well Robbo was still sound asleep and not joining in the fun, so up steps Ni**er Brown and Tojo with a couple of blank firing pistols, loaded with CS rounds they had purchased in Holland. Three rounds in the room, shut the door, and wait. Just like baking a cake. There suddenly appeared out of the room a drunken, shaving foam monster, going hysterical as he tried to get away from the CS, and couldn't fathom the way out as he was falling over in all this foam. Happy days.

Alan Lomax

Out with Digger Deakin (AKA Skitz, and trust me, he wasn't nicknamed Skitz for nothing) in Reindahlen. Having the usual belly full of beer, dressed in number ones (can't remember why).

Well some geezer verbally started on digger—a pongo, I think, who had a broken leg. Things started becoming heated and I could see that Skitz had had enough of this geezer, but how could he address the issue when the guy giving him shit was in plaster from his knee down. Then Skitz had an idea. "I'll tell you what, I'll tape my leg up to make it even." *Most considerate*, I thought. But no, Skitz wanted to go a step further, "Tie my arm behind my back too." So we bodged him up and there was Skitz, ready to wade in, hopping on one leg with arm tied behind his back. They both went outside and Skitz made an attempted headbutt and then creamed in on the ground. Obviously, it was a debacle but the sight had me and everyone else laughing their gonads off. You just couldn't make it up, but that's what happened.

Steve Mullen

Remember my first (only) cat-board on 48. As an LAC, I was told, naturally, at the end of the day to stay outside with the rest of the goon platoon and take the kits out of action and back into the hanger while the rest of the squadron assembled in the canteen for the top operator presentation. Some humble pie was eaten when they had to come and find me to give me the award!

Dan Smale

A bit of a long one, pull up a sandbag. I promise there's a funny bit at the end if you persevere. 16 Sqn tour in Belize, in the early '80s. On a week randr, I've set up a run to Mexico on a chess set buying mission. I've taken the lads orders sorted out transport, done the shopping, and a couple of the lads have taken the lot back to camp while I head off on my own for a few days in Mexico City. I think the bus ride was about 12 hours or something ridiculous.

Anyway, my crew and Flight Lieutenant Burt were going to climb Popocatopetel, a volcano about 75 miles from Mexico City the following week. I had no desire to make the trip back just to turn around and drive back again. So, after some grovelling, the boss agreed that we'd RV on the road up to the volcano instead. The lads would bring my kit for the climb so I wouldn't need to lug it around on RandR.

Spent two days of my Mexico City jaunt with some serious stomach bug, coming out of both ends. Made it to the RV a day early, hoping to get to the hotel that was supposed to be halfway up this mountain the night before. Got as far as the bus went and started walking up this dirt track from the last village late afternoon. Bad idea, couldn't reach the hotel and had to head back to the village, which was little more than a shanty town of wooden shacks. Nothing like a hotel or even a bar, and the last bus to the nearest town had gone. A doctor, who spent a couple of days a week in the only brick building—what passed for a clinic with one room for the doc and one treatment room—took me in off the street and gave me bed in the clinic for the night. He didn't speak much English but I gathered that while he was in the village, the villagers took it in turns to feed him and he took me along for supper. The elderly couple and what I presume was a grandson who were our hosts, lived in a one room wooden shack, with a dirt floor and an open fire surrounded by bricks on which they cooked a couple of plain flour tortillas. The doctor and I ate them and I'm thinking blimey, not much of a meal, when I realise the three of them aren't eating. Don't think I've ever been so humbled by someone's generosity to a complete stranger. There was one shop in the village and I sent the kids for cokes, twinkies, and whatever other goodies he could carry. You'd think all their Christmases had come at once. Bizarely they had an old Beatles album, no record player, just this album.

Following day, the doc had to go back to Cholula, so I had nowhere to go for another night and after a day spent hanging around with no sign of the climbing party, I headed into Cholula on the bus and with the last of my cash (I had no credit card in those days), I spent the night in a hotel on the edge of the central square, which was our alternative RV. The guys should have arrived by evening, no worries, they were obviously running a bit late (as it turned out, they'd had a blow out and stopped to get it fixed, if memory serves).

So, the following morning, I sit on my case on the edge of the square and wait, and wait, and wait. I'm skint now, not even money for a drink, and definitely no way to get anywhere else other than on foot. The whole day passes and by now I'm wondering what the hell has happened to them. I've spent three days now trying to hook up with them and they are a good 48 hrs late. Actually they aren't, I find out later that because they are running late, they figure I must be at the hotel up the mountain by now so don't bother with checking the alternate RV first, and by the time they get up the mountain, they decide it's too late to come look for me, and Paul Burt, bless him, decides I can fend for myself.

Unaware of all this, I stand around all night, getting a bit dehydrated, twitchy, and generally bad tempered. The first Mexican to approach me is pissed and takes some getting rid of, the second bloke to get in my face appears to fancy me and I'm losing the plot by now. I spend the night stood there, contemplating my chances of stealing a car to get back to Belize. Around mid morning, three lads in their twenties approach me and start chattering away, of course I don't understand a word, and by now I've seriously lost the plot, so I look at the biggest one in the middle and with my best scowl I tell him, "Fuck off right now or I'll kill you."

I'm fluent English he replies, "Oh, I'm terribly sorry, my wife had noticed you standing here since yesterday and we thought you might need some help." This young couple and his boss and his wife put me up for a few days, fed me, and treated me like family and then they buy my ticket back to Belize. I went back a year or so later and repaid their hospitality. Never did get to climb that volcano though.

Rip Eyre

Black Eagle, Falklands, 1980s, SAC Budgie Brown has the task of lighting the Lazyman each morning, and filling the Nob Hill water bowls. During an evening drink (two-can rule?) Budgie is informed that there hasn't been any Batman in the RAF since the 60s. Next morning there's a commotion on the helipad, the warrant has been told by a zob there's no water. Next thing the warrant shouts, "Brown, where's the officer's water?"

Budgie shouts back in a broad jock accent, "Sir, there's no' bi'n any Batman in the RAF since the 60s. If the officers are wanting any water, they'll have to fetch it themselves."

After a couple of seconds, the warrant calls to the zobs, "Officers, go and collect your own water." I'll never forget the look of pride on Budgie's face as he helped the zobs get their fill!

Steve Moore

It was August 1982, Wildenrath transit block. The block was H-shaped and one quarter of it was full of Rocks off 16 Sqn. It was a seventeen-man room with the usual one locker, one bedside table, and, of course, a bed each, plus all the crap furniture that the station WO had the German workers put in the place because it was all the broken shite furniture the SWO had especially selected for us—the twat. We also had about thirty tri-wall boxes, cut and taped to make your own, but not quite, one man room.

Anyway, most of us were fed up with living like the homeless in among broken furniture and boxes, so me, Tomo, Jasper, and couple of others decide to have a BBQ in the gap of the H block between room and the other half of the block nearest the woods. But the problem was that only this side of the block was suitable for digging a fire pit but it faced the building (the CAO) the station SWO had his office in. In the woods behind the block was a giant bivi type shelter, that we think the aircrew did use for survival lessons and such like, and it was covered in a green canvas sheet 12ft x 35ft. So once we had a loan of this (nicked), and it was the same colour as the block, we then cut down three medium sized trees and dug them in and hung the canvas on them so the SWO couldn't see us. After that, we had to decide if we was going to use our metal feet wipe grates from outside the block door or nick two from another block. We used ours and the plan was to swap them with another block once used and burnt. So the pit was dug, and the beer money collected, but some in our room were on leave and if we got too much food, we wouldn't have loads of beer, so me and Tomo came up with this great plan for two reasons. No. 1: Invite the med centre blokes in the next room to us on our side of the block so we have more money for supplies and that all worked to plan. No. 2: I will tell you about later.

So, in between buying the beer, food, wine for medic boys and the one and only bag of charcoal, I found all these road name signs dumped in the woods after the new ones had all been put at the end of the various roads on camp. These we used as decorations around the BBQ area—it looked good. So, we had our BBQ and all went well, and we couldn't be seen by the SWO or any of the the camp because of the big canvas sheet. So the first night was great and it was safe because we had the fire extinguishers out the block. So the next night went okay, as did the third, but then we got through the second bag of charcoal that the medics had got, and I am not sure now but it was either me or Tomo said, "F**ck, going for more charcoal, let's use the naff furniture and burn that, and we will have some more space in the room."

So Tomo and I set about turning tables and lockers into BBQ size bits to cook on. The medics wanted to know what we had done with the money for charcoal, and it was explained that it had been spent on food and drink, so they should shut the f**k up and drink some the shite wine they asked for, and get chopping that pile of table legs up or Tomo was going to shove a table leg up their butt, and they would go to work in the morning looking like spiders. So they soon joined in and asked to borrow my machetes and got it done. So the fourth night to the tenth night went down a treat as did the food, drink, and furniture. On the eleventh night, it all got a bit out of hand and once the last of the food had gone and Tomo said, "Don't know about you, Steve, but I am a bit chilly, let's have a bonfire with the last of the furniture and warm up a bit." And that's what happened, but one of the medics remembered he had a bag of tates in his car, so some of them got chucked in. We had been sitting by this fire for some time and the tates was almost done. We hear sirens and we think it must be the scuffers off to the NAAFI, because one of them is getting a kicking by one the squadron as it was in previous weeks. But no, the fire section burst through the green canvas with the duty officer, at which point I said "We've not got enough tates for lot," and then I saw he was the duty officer and you could almost see the steam coming out of his ears. I said, "Red wine or beer, Sir?"

He said, "Shut the f**k up!"

I said, "okay then," the fire section started laughing.

Duty officer said, "Who's organised this?" So I put my hand up.

Duty officer said, "Can't you speak or are you to drunk?"

I said, "No, Sir, I am the BBQ duty fire piquet here, with my trusty water gas here on the floor next to me, and I've my hand up because you told me to shut the f**k up, Sir!"

Best I can remember, duty officer said, "Do you know that if I can see the glow from that fire while I am doing my late night patrol, so can the soviets from space?"

One the medics mumbling, "Is he patrolling in his phantom?" But duty officer didn't hear that and I was doing my best not to laugh and firemen are laughing now and the officer is getting madder by the minute.

I said "The soviets, Sir, we didn't think of them!"

Duty officer "Yes, the f**king soviets!"

I said, "Next time, we can get some extra tates for the soviets if they are coming." Officer went mental and took my name and then comes the best bit, earlier I told you I had two reasons for inviting the medics from our half of block and this is it! Duty officer has took my name and I confirmed I had collected all the money and with Tomo gone and got the food and drink. Duty officer asked, "Are you in charge then?"

I replied, "No, Sir, but do you see those three wine-guzzling Gerts sat against the wall? They are the three junior NCOs from the medical centre, and the one on the right that's asleep? He is the NCO in charge of our side of the block, Sir!"

Next morning I am in the squadron 2IC office explaining about the BBQ and that the NCO at the block wanted to have a BBQ with us so we thought it was alright and okay to do and when all said and done he is in charge of the block, Sir! At the block with the 2IC, he said, "Did you lot nick all these f**kin' road name signs? You have even got the f**kin' name plate from the station commander's house."

I said, "No, Sir, we found them just over there in the woods, they are old ones that the German workers put there, and if the duty officer is correct, they must be trying to hide them from the soviets, Sir."

2IC: "Are you taking the piss, SAC Moore?"

"No, Sir, ask last night's fire section crew, if you like. I am sure they will confirm it!"

2IC: "Okay then, let's look inside the block next," but we only got a few yards and he asked, "Who cut the f**kin trees down?"

"That was me and Tomo, Sir, because that medic told us to put the canvas screen up.

2IC: "Did he?"

"Yes, Sir, got about fifteen witnesses to that, Sir, in the block."

2IC said, "Not been over here before and this had better be 100% and not like that mess out the back which you are going to clean up on your own." In the room, 2IC asked, "Moore, is this room been like this since you got on the Sqn?"

"Yes, Sir, it has, we have made our own sort of rooms out of these tri-wall boxes and what furniture we have got is all sub-standard or broken, and the German workers use the end or our room to store various bits of busted furniture until they take it away to the rubbish, and about two weeks ago they took the last lot before they went on block leave, all our stuff in here is rubbish, Sir. We live like the homeless here because they ain't got no money to spend on us because they need it to keep an eye on them soviets, Sir."

2IC said, "We will see about that, SAC Moore. You just clean up all that mess and when it's done, I want to know how many cans, bottles, and food packets you clean up, so make a note!"

While I am cleaning the mess up, the NCOs from the medical centre was with the SWO in the station commander's office getting a new arsehole ripped. They never did speak to me or Tomo again—knob heads"! 73 food packets, 47 wine bottles, and 437 beer tins over just under two weeks, we Rocks loved it.

Ian Portz

One dark night on 27 Sqn in the mid 1980s. I was on exercise on a Rapier site off base. Whilst sitting on the Rapier generator, another Gunner and me were comparing the vibration of the generator to that of a washing machine. Conversation went on and we spoke of women having orgasms on said washing machines. Friend gunner and me covered all manner of embarrassing sexual topics. Who would get it and who wouldn't. How we might like to do, and what we had done!

Unknown to us, the radio and developed a fault. The radio had switched itself onto permanent send and had been broadcasting our entire conversation. If that was not bad enough, but due to the nature of the exercise, all conversations were logged in the command post, in case we gave away top secrets to the Russians (we were informed that they might be at sea, listening in spy trawlers). By the time we noticed the telltale send light on the radio, it was too late!

After the exercise, I was expecting a massive bullocking, but when we returned back to the hanger, half the squadron were waiting outside clapping and cheering us home. We did get a slight bollocking, but after all I was told that we never disclosed our missile strength; so it was not all bad!

Marty Richards

Remember on 27 Sqn sports afternoon, told to bring a towel and trunks to go swimming. Swampy had organised this. All in one tonne, and off we went to St As, of course, no fucking swimming pool! Straight into Kate's Bar for a heavy afternoon of drinking, such fun, and this went on until a silly cunt told the zob that there was no pool in St As.

Neil Pilling

One from a Guin who had the pleasure of serving with Her Majesty's R.A.F. Regiment for over twelve years on 3 Rock squadrons. When serving with 27 Sqn in the early/mid '80s, one of the deployed sites for the Rapiers was opposite RAF Leuchars on the other side of the estuary— actually at the end of St Andrews golf course. We (Guins) had been sent to a call sign to fix the broken kit. Entry to the site was guarded by a raised (top of sand dune) sentry point which at this particular time also had a GPMG. Anyway, kit fixed and enjoying cuppa when the field telephone buzzes. A whispering voice on the other end said, "Get everyone up to the sentry point asap—no noise and stay very low as you approach."

Well, we all made our way up to find the two lads on stag, chuckling away. They beckoned us forward so we could see what was going on. So now there are eight heads on the edge of a small sand dune, watching two locals (male and female), giving it max (sexually) in the back of their car. Then in amongst the tittering and chuckling was the sound of a GPMG being cocked very quietly. Sure enough, as the gravy stroke approached, a burst of blank from said GPMG caused the male to literally shit himself. Tittering and chuckling changed to gufaws of laughter and clapping as they re-adjusted clothing and drove off at a rate of knots. I still chuckle at the memory.

Steve Scott

Talking of the odd fight or two ... 63 in the Hebrides for live firing. Those who have been there. Cold. Windy. Damp. Boring is probably an understatement. Having left the bright lights of Germany and Asbach and wobbly, we were invited or gatecrashed the local Kaylee. In stumbles a few lads, 30/40, into this hall. Looking to our left were the females. To our right, the males ... priority, hit the bar. Now after an hour or two ... somehow, a small confrontation began which escalated in seconds to all out war. After battering the locals in situ, there reinforcement arrived as we were being ordered onto the bus. A Scottish gentleman attempted to gain access to the bus ... at the same time bus windows were going in. The local did not like not being allowed to get on the bus. A gunner who was happily sitting on the bus had enough. Picked up a bar from the front of the bus and ejected the gentleman. A good night was had by many but not all.

Belize, '93. Picture courtesy of Stephen Le Roy.

Albi Pinnion

RAFG, Gutersloh, 63, around 1985, there was a Rock's wedding. Reception in the set's mess, one Rock a little worse for wear decided to dance on the page's mini. Unlucky the pardre saw him and knew his name, due to the colour of his hair. The pardre, being a man of the cloth, gave the said gunner a way of not facing 252 action—his suggestion was to attend the church of Scotland for six weeks.

The Church of Scotland, for those not in the know, was in the attic of the Rock block. Every Sunday was the same lots of abuse, Hare Krishna being played as loud as possible. On one occasion, the CPL gen eng (Slic to his mates) was hanging out the window by his toes, screaming as the church goers went to church.

The same wedding, all the Rocks in uniform went back to the block to get changed, one of those was somebody that has lost a lot of pudding and now drives an ambulance on occasions. He ran down the corridor and forgot about the fire doors, but made a good attempt at destroying them. He cut his belly open quite bad, but in good old regiment tradition, a couple of plasters a bandage and some bodge tape, he was good to carry on—funny now that he does the profession he does! Love yah, Dags!

Mac McCarthy

48 Sqn, Belize, 1992. Our crew has been given the only foot patrol of the tour, day six out of eight, and we're getting a bit tired and low on rations. Our location is on the bank of the Sarstoon River, which is the border between Belize and Guatamala (Guatamala are the 'enemy', and any contact with them must be reported immediately).

We're at least a day's slog away from our next stop, which is an abandoned police station below Cadenas OP. Then day eight is a mega-slog up the hill to the OP for our Puma home. Keen to think outside the box and make things easier for ourselves, our two attached Belizian scouts are asked to see if they can find a boat, which we can use to get the patrol up to the police station. Great idea, painless, winner.

In a suspiciously short period of time, the scouts are back, "We got us a boat, man." Brilliant, we all head to the riverbank to our new boat. Ah, it has a crew too, even better. We all kick back as the boat takes us upriver to our destination, it won't take long and we can spend the rest of the day on 'admin'. As we're chugging along, innocently thinking these local 'Belizian fishermen' have volunteered to take us to our destination, it transpires to be not quite the case.

Our scouts had not found a boat, but had seen these Guatamalan fishermen tootling by. The effect of two M-16s levelled at them was all the convincing they needed to comply and change their plans completely! So, an innocent request to see what was available had now turned into armed kidnapping of foreign nationals by British Forces! Was worth it though, we needed the admin!

Stephen Williamson

Late '80s on A Flt 26 Sqn, our comrades on B Flight were getting ready for their FI tour which would be a Xmas tour. The usual banter with them when they are down there, we will be in Holland, drinking beer, hope they don't miss the pizzas too much, and I was probably the worst going on about it.

So the week before they go, I end up in Kev's bar, got chatting to some woman, long and the short of it, the scuffers catch me and her at it on steps of the local church. I hand over my ID and she hands over hers, she is only married to a Guin in Wildenrath. No problems, did not think anything of it until Monday. Flight cmdr calls me into his office ask me about Saturday night, give him my side of the story. Posted to B flight. I got some stick from them when I turned up with my kit. To be honest, it was a great tour.

Chris Vipond

Bruggen, and we just come in off exercise. Well, the fire teams had done there admin and I was swanning over to the squadron bar, looking forward to a few beers, when the DSC chucks some keys, get that washed, refuelled, it's the hire car, and its getting picked up soon. Squeeze me, but I'm fire teams, not HQ flight. No, I'm there, they are too busy, as I see half them skulking in the back door. No amount of pleading, I'm there, and I'm doing it.

So off I go through Elmpt at 50 miles an hour, 1, 2, 3 speed cameras flash there and back, and I've the sun visor down. A few weeks later there's an inquiry who was driving, only name on work ticket DSC's. Who paid the fines? I can honestly say, not me.

Phil Pringle

On 20 Sqn, I was on A1 (John Weston's then John Wycherley's crew) when the squadron first formed, and a few months later moved to A3 with Mick Alexander as DC and Pops Popplewell and Al, Travest as TCs, and Mick and I now are still good mates. He did run a tight ship though, mainly due to the LACs and young SACs on the crew, and if you cocked up, you were liable to get a slap! Earning him the nickname of 'the Colonel'—after Colonel Callen, the Mercenary—which Woody put in permipen on the back of his exercise green director's chair.

One day, after a couple of the lads had had a roasting from Mick, they came into the bay not happy bunnies. We then started servicing the kit. Woody then said, "I'll get him back," and altered every switch and dial on the Klystron and any other he could find.

I did say, "Mick won't be happy." But it fell on deaf ears. We deployed the kit in front of the hanger the next day for TsandAs, powered it up, and omg, beams going up, down, spinning round, tracker head spinning, and 181 (radar tracker) juddering, the lot shaking. The Guins were called, and said it needed to be sorted in eng, so we put it in eng and left it. They worked it out and the flight were assembled and semi-bollocked by the inspector general and AIG, they had a word with Mick also.

We went to the bay and denied all knowledge to Mick, not wanting a punch, and said it must have been B Flight! Following week, we deployed for TsandAs by the 25 metre range, started putting the kit in, and Mick said to me, "Park the FUT over there, Phil."

So I said, "No problem," and jumped in and started off, having to use quite a few revs and a bit of clutch to get over the kerb, as I did this, I was watching Mick get redder than his hair! And words wouldn't come out his mouth and the, "What fuck have you done, you cunt," came out!

I jumps out and said, "What, Mick?" and he just pointed! I had driven over the OCF and not a kerb! Half flat, like a coke can! Mick calmed quickly and sent the DSV to borrow one from another kit. We finished and went back to the hanger. Mick, a CPL on the other flight, was summoned by Mick and he promptly went to get some fibreglass and green paint. They repaired the dome of the OCF and, using a dent kit from MT, knocked out the dents. It dried, was sanded, and painted. It looked like new, took it to Eng, and said it fell from the tailgate of the FUT! It amazed the Guins how much damage could be done by such a small drop, but couldn't prove anything!

The following week, however, servicing the kit, I dropped the small dome at the front and it broke its bracket! Rendering the kit unserviceable, as no spares were held! Inspector general and commanding officer went mad, and wanted me charged, but on a formal warning at the time, Harry Foxley, the squadron warrant officer, said to me I would get a working weekend rather than charged. So I spent the weekend painting all the white car parking lines and all the yellow and white lines in the hanger. The following week, I lowered a launcher jack and it broke and fell off! Thankfully, there was a fault in the casting on that.

One day, when Mick's son is older, I'll tell him about his dad and how he, Gerry O'Neill, myself, and Mark Sherlock, after drinking in the NAAFI, went to the block and was reduced to drinking Ronson lighter fuel and sweet South African sherry!

Stephen Headey

I was driver to PODS PO DeSalis (RIP) on 48 Sqn. Well, one fine day, he asked me to take him to SHQ. We drove over, no worries, and then started to return to the squadron. As we were approaching the turn up the hill, we noticed another Land Rover ahead of us, moving violently from one side to another. Imagine our surprise when the rear wheel of said Land Rover over took it, and went into the fence. I nearly crashed through laughing but stopped the wagon. Out steps Bod, and it just couldn't get any funnier, as his face was a glow of red. Didn't do his checks.

Steve Holland

Many happy memories of standing by the speaker at the NAAFI in Gutersloh at the Thursday night bop. If anyone tried to stand by it other than a member of 63 or invited guests, chaos would ensue. Other memories of the electric wrestling include everyone clearing the dance floor to watch Graham 'Baggy' Trevor doing his interpretation of the moves to Madonna's 'Vouge'. The DJ being banned from playing Lulu's 'Shout', due to over enthusiastic and highly dangerous dancing. The night would normally be finished off with a trip to the Chicken Inn, where one of the favourite things to do was to light the blue touch paper on Michael Bashford by telling him, "That bloke just called you a wanker!" Then standing well back and watching the fireworks.

Mark Hallburton

The street of a thousand bars 1985. Myself and Ian Durbridge having a giggle in a porn vid shop. Around the back, where what I could only describe as what looked like toilet booths. A seat facing the door and room for one. There was a TV screen above the seat facing the door. Very confusing, as if you sat on the seat, then the screen would be behind your head. Penny had dropped—it was a porn booth, by the way, but very confusing screen set up. So I puts me coin in the slot and stood there watching all the action. People passing were geggling in, so Durbs and me squeeze in together and close the door. It was then I noticed a mirror on the inside of door so that was it. You're to sit down and watch TV in the mirror.

So I'm sat there, with Durbs standing in my face, when the cleaner opens the door only to shout at us for having two in the booth, and for what she thought we were getting up to. Oh, the shame as we both scampered out, only to get pissed up that day.

Tony Ryan

I thought I best tell this tale of woe, as this has happened to many a brother of our hallowed corp. I was unaccompanied for the best part of year at Bruggen in the early '90s, as the trout remained at Lossiemouth doing her A levels. I was in the new Rock block next to the med centre, and not block 50 next to the Pig's Bar, where the rest of the squadron were housed.

So I had a fair distance to travel to meet the lads and discuss the meaning of life in the Pig's Bar. However, there was a short cut through the woods, which for a roughfie toughie Rock was just perfect. The journey normally took about one fag and two pisses to get there but for some strange reason, it took a lot longer to get back. It was with horror that I and other fellow Rocks had discovered that some knob head had decided to dig a huge trench through the woods and start to lay some piping. The trench was just over 6 feet deep and about 5 feet across, so we decided to bridge it with bits of pallet ladders and other bits left by the workers as nothing was going to ruin Friday night's Pig's Bar debate.

The problem arose on the return journey, it was quite a lengthy debate which left me in a very confused state as I ventured into the woods. I was very confused by now and, three fags later, I managed to locate the bridge, but some twat had knocked the fecker down. So I decided to run and jump across, as I was practically an Olympic athlete. This ended in tears as I bombed into the bottom of the trench. I eventually got to my feet and tried to climb out, but due to the sandy soil and my confused state, I was going nowhere. So, I decided to sit a while, light a fag, and work out how the hell I was going to get out of this fecking trench. Fag in gob, just about to light it and this voice said, "Giz a fag mate."

I nearly shat, "Wot the feck!" It was some Guin, close to tears, who also had attempted the mighty leap also without success. He had been in there for about hour. So I said, "Tell you want, mate, you help me out and I will pull you out."

"Feck off, you will leave me, I know what you Rocks are like." So I had to give him my word that I wouldn't abandoned the poor twat. Those who were at Bruggen at the time will no doubt remember that fecking trench. The moral of this tale is 'a Guin in the hole is better than a bird with a bush'.

Wayne Holliss

South block bogs, Lossiemouth, 1986. On this particular night, I like a lot of the single lads on the squadron were in their room, watching telly, doing their admin, and generally going about their own business, when all of a sudden, a herald came a shouting along the corridor summering all Rocks to the bogs. So, off we trotted to the said place, and when we got there, there must of been half the block, all gathered at the door to trap three. I managed to make my way to the front, and as I peered in to the cubicle, I saw the wondrous sight. For there in the pan was the largest, thickest turd I'd ever seen. This thing look liked a brown short 55 way cable and just as long, there must of been at least 8" of piped shite above the water line, the rest of its length disappearing under the u-bend. Comments a plenty were being expressed by the lads, all without consideration that somewhere out there was a brother Rock who could be in desperate need of medical attention. All of a sudden the crowd parted, as if Moses himself had done it. There at the trap door stood the squadron turd expert himself, Gunner Shitson. He glanced at the turd, eyeing it in only a way an expert in his field can, and with a small smile and a hint of wickedness in his eyes, he said, "Bloody hell, need a closer look at this." He then bent forward, hand outstretched. Alas, gentlemen, this is where this tale must end, as there was one hell of a mad rush to get the fuck out of throwing range PDQ.

George Bray

Whilst at Laarbruch on 26 Sqn, my wife and I attended the Thursday night bingo for the ladies, and dominoes for the men weekly session in the sergeants' mess, having arrived there on our push bikes. It became a bit of a drawn out affair as the dominoes always came to a stalemate, meaning we had to have another game upon game, and several more drinks whilst all the time the wife is nagging in my ear, ready to go home. The winner of the dominoes was eventually found and we made our way out to the bikes (wife still nagging). Having got on our bikes, the wife took off like Mansell, right up the bike lane. After 500 meters, she is well ahead of my wobble bike, and yelling back at me. I thought, *There she goes again*, and I started to speed up in order to catch her. As I sped up, I didn't notice the large tree trunk that someone had duly laid across the bike lane.

As I lay across the bike lane with the bike on top of me, and with a few cuts and bruises, someone said, "Told you but you wouldn't listen!"

Trev Vennard

I was in Belize in the early '80s with 27 Sqn, and being young and dumb, I thought it would be a jolly jape to go 'up jungle' with the resident infantry unit. Tony 'Rico' Ryan said he would go too, which was a bonus. Now the resident infantry unit was the Royal Irish Rangers and the sergeant major. Thought that it was appropriate that these two young gentlemen from the RAF regiment should be afforded the rank of lance corporal for the duration of our time with them. *Nice*, we thought, so off we trogs, up through the jungle, toward tree top op on the Guatemalan border.

About half way, the sergeant major wants to change the scout up front, who was armed with a loaded shotgun. Tony offered to take point and the paddies were all nodding approvingly as he moved up through the patrol. It was then I pointed out that Tony was of the Papal persuasion, which for some reason changed the attitude of the patrol. This resulted in the sergeant major taking the shotgun, unloading it, and then giving it back to Tony, and in a broad Belfast (Sandy Row) accent says, "There's no way I'm giving a Fenian a gun with bullets!" The look on Ricos face was priceless!

John Stowell

One of my postings was GDT at RAF West Raynham ('84–'86). For those of you that may not know, Raynham at the time was the home of 66 Sqn RAF regiment and the Rapier training unit, as well as being a UK Air Defence base, with the HQ of 85 Sqn, which was equipped with the Bloodhound SAM. 85 Sqn was split between three bases, the other two being North Coates and Bawdsey. Collectively, they liked to call themselves the '85 Sqn Bloodhound Force'. Each base had its own GDT Sect. Ian Hutton was at N. Coates, Bob Laughlin at Bawdsey, and myself at W Raynham, with OC regiment, who was a young FO.

On one occasion, he decided to call a meeting of all his regiment staff at W. Raynham. The day arrives and meeting done, we hot-foot it into Facebham for a few sherberts. At closing time, head back to the mess for a few more, where we invited the boss to join us. One thing led to another and at o'now starting to light o'clock, the boss was a bit under the weather. In fact, he couldn't speak or stand unaided. Not wanting to see him in the proverbial, Bob and I take him back to the officers' mess, only to find the doors locked with a combination lock. The boss was in no state to tell us the code, so on looking around, we found a small window open at about shoulder height above ground.

After some effort, we managed to lift him up and pushed him through, and on hearing him thud to the floor inside, we staggered off. The other two duly RTU and I went back to work having been stood down the day after the event. The boss didn't turn in for work and, after a couple of days, I started to get a little twitchy as on asking around. No one had seen him for a few days. Eventually I phoned the officers' mess to find the same. Not seen for several days and not booked out. So I asked one of the stewards to check his room where he was lying in bed, still ill.

Several days later, he turned up for work, sore and battered, with no memory of what had gone on. "What happened," he asked.

"Er dunno, boss, you wuz okay when you left." And as far as I know, he never found out I ain't used his name but if you're reading this boss—Sorry!

Keith O' Sullivan

After a week on exercise, as part of exercise Spring Tiger. We were recalled early back to Gut. Friday lunch time or there abouts. As we approached the squadron compound, we were informed that all squadron personal should be in the main lecture room for a briefing. The commanding officer came in, said that we had received orders, 48 hrs, prepare to move to UK, and that we were going to the Falklands. Well that was it, the whole squadron was a hive of activity, be borrow or aquire kit needed.

Finally, finishing at about 21:30 that evening, all the single lads went straight to the Malcolm Club for beers. Can't remember much else of that evening! Bit of a beer blur. The sunday morning, we had to be in work for 08:30.

John Stowell

Another one from my 16 Sqn Wildenrath days. Those that were there in the late '70s will relate to this. Every year, we had the annual migration to Bavaria (week about by flights) for some skiing and fun, written off as cold weather training. On the first occasion we went, we arrived at the destination—if I have it right—a small German, army training camp named Gastor—pardon the spelling—to find that there was a unit of German Army conscripts already there, under the control of their regular NCOs and some officers. So, in the interest of further cementing our commitment to the NATO alliance and showing our allies that we were prepared to back them up in the event of a Warsaw Pact invasion, some of us (Grub, Maggot, Agony Bags, Jappy, and myself, just to name a few, sorry if I missed your names out) got talking to the NCOs, which lead to the inevitable piss-up.

At some time in the early morning our flight cdr—Flight Lieutenant John Tunnah—comes bursting into the room and, on seeing us still there, did not go via the SCRAM button, and went straight to critical mass and started to melt down. A few short hours later, whilst getting the kit ready for the day's events, he informs us that for our sins we were to spend a day each in turn working in the cook house, with me nominated for the first day. So, whilst every one else is out on the slopes being coached on the trick of skiing, where required, I was in the cook house scrubbing pots and pans, and peeling spuds. The result was that on the next day when I got out there, every one else was doing fairly good impressions of being able to ski whilst I was doing one of not having a fucking clue.

After I had mastered the art of the T-bar ski lift, the next problem was coming down, which I can only describe as being an uncontrolled descent with a few falls and somersaults, that I have since been told any Olympic gymnast would be jealous of. It was after one such descent that John Tunnah skied over and swishes to a stop and says, "You frighten' the effin life outta me! Everytime I see you start your descent, I cringe and can't breathe until I see you stand up again at the bottom. Do me a fucking favour and stick to what you can do," and instructs me to go to the ale house down the road, upon which he hands me a 5 nark note saying, "That's for the first drink!" I thought, *What a bonus*. So there may be truth in the saying 'what goes around, comes around'. I never did learn how to ski!

Black Eagle Camp, Falklands.

Stephen Headey

16 Sqn, '81, Ski exped, Southern Germany. Hilarious times on this, especially watching OC 16 using the T-bar on the slopes as though it was a ski rope instead of putting it under his arse, much to the Germans disgust and laughter from us.

Eating ice cream loaded with alcohol, or drinking Gluwein and then becoming the Franz Klammer of the slopes, convinced you were now a black run expert when you had never even strapped a pair of skis on.

Germans flying everywhere to the shouts of, "Banzai," as camoflaged DPM Salopettes-clad lunatics shot down the hills over the moguls, knocking kids flying, and hitting the tree that jumped out in front. My, what a sight we cut, and did wonders for international relations. Carry on movies had nothing on us.

CHAPTER 5
AIRBORNE: A BAR TOO FAR

Ian Black

Regiment CMPC team, 1984, and on this day, each team set off at 5 min intervals. Para regiment team, that is made up of all there DS from 'advanced Wales' don't take too kindly to being passed on the first big hill, and make reference to our 'mickey mouse wings'. Chris C, who was team sergeant, had to be restrained from ripping their WO2s head off. Anyway, we leave them in our wake and the storm blows over. Next night, we have a horrendous night navex in the Elan Valley, where the para regiment team get lost and got choppered out. Oops. We get wind of this, and as we pull into the RV next morning, we see the reg team heads bowed, eating their scoff. Chris C couldn't help himself and says, "A'wite, lads? Good chopper ride last night?" It was hilarious.

Anyway, last day, after digging in the night before, having a section in defence shoot from the trench the following morning, followed by a stretcher race to the finish line—we ended up spanking them on the stretcher race too. But fair play, they came up to us at the end and we made peace.

Andy Cullen

I remember on 2 Sqn, I was a part of the Bergathon Team. We had just set a new world speed march record in the London Marathon. The warrant officer puts a slab of Guinness on the floor and says, "Well done, lads. One fuck'n can each!"

Ian Boyce

'79-'82, Young Ian is now on the harrier force at Gutersloh. Ostensibly, I only exist at time of war/exercise, so initially I am attached to the GDT section as an extra sergeant, then Dereck Dale decides I should be attached to 33 Wing. As such, I travel to Laarbruch, to run a pre FT for lads, due to head for Catterick for an FT1.

Mick Gant is an SAC on the wing and he is at my disposal, helping me with admin, demos, etc, I also got him to help me with physical for the course, this he loved. I asked him to have a suitable route for a 'demanding' run one afternoon around 1600. He had just the thing, leave it to him ... I had the troops parade in OGs boots and sweat shirts, Mick and I had Bergans, think they had belt kit. Mick led us out the gate through Boar Wood for miles. The lads were knackered, but Mick was not done. We headed back into camp, to the swimming pool, to do a 'river crossing'—this was the middle of a German winter, it was *freezing*! After this, the lads were finished for the day. I do not know what they remember from their FT but I bet they remember Micks wee run.

Robin Flack

Late '73. Colerne in the block. C130 jump due the next day. A certain Aussie jock is knelt on the floor, handful of grass in one hand, small amount of water cupped in the other. He begins to rock back and forth chanting, "Oh, Odin, bring us wind," throws grass in air), "Bring us rain," throws water in the air, "Thank you, oh Odin, the powerful one," gets up, "Sorted, lads," jumps off, walks away.

Sure enough, next morning, pissing it down and blowing a good one! He smiled all day.

Robin Flack

Colerne. Thickwood Families' Club. We are hosting a darts match against the camp married guys. I'm chalking, my GSD laying next to me, Chiefy Deeley (bless him) is throwing. A dart bounces off the wire and, with a thud, sticks point first in the floor about an inch away from my dog Tasha's nose. She doesn't flinch, but the look he got!

Later that night, sat at the tables, Chiefy sat at the next table. Tasha crawls quietly forward, places her wet nose in the palm of his hand. He went up in the air, proceeded by the table, four pints, and some other glasses, only to be first down. He copped most of it. Tash had resumed her position by my chair, still giving the look, but with a little smile.

Picture courtesy of Robin Flack

Richard Stubbs

Lad in the 2 Sqn block at Barnham, with a particularly minging and obscenely short dressing gown. Two lads decide to nick it while he's in the shower, dowse it in petrol, and burn it on a stake so he can see it from his bedroom window for a bit of weekend boredom relief.

Cue RAF coppers or other do-gooders heading into training area. They see a burning effigy and report it. 2 Sqn all on parade Monday morning for a mass bollocking and accusations of KKK style racist intimidation. Touch awkward.

Briefing before a jump.

Richard Coleman

2 Sqn was in Cyprus covering ops for 34, who'd gone on their annual field firing packages. Our stay coincided with that of an ATC summer camp. It was either the first or second night and we were in 34's bar, drinking. Sat at a table with a bottle of KEO when a cadet warrant officer storms up to me and takes the bottle off the table, telling me I can't drink, and need to leave. I told him to fuck off, and thought nothing of it. Walking back to the transit block with a few others when a Land Rover pulls up next to us, and out jumps the cadet and a clutch of cadet officers who try to bundle me in the Land Rover whilst telling me how bad I'd been drinking. It's fair, I looked about twelve years old, and they were convinced I was a cadet and wouldn't believe me. Of course, my GNR colleagues did *nothing* to back me up other than watch on and laugh. Had to show my ID!

Garry McCormack

So, it's a wet, miserable Saturday night in Brecon as I arrive at Dering Lines for my platoon sergeants' battle course. I'm the oldest student by a country mile, 37. My 'colour boy' instructor from 1 Scots Guards was only 32! I dump my kit in the barrack room and the duty gobshite pongo from the '1st Queen's Own Gortex Rustlers' pipes up, "Fuckin hell, 'Biggles'. What the fuck are you doing here?"

"Well," says I, "I saw the course advertised in DCIs, so I thought I'd apply. I'm particularly looking forward to the hill walking phase, I've heard so much about the Pen y Fan that I can't wait to see the views."

Pongo, gob smacked, "No, no, for fuck's sake, Biggle, it's not that kind of course! This is PSBC, the infantry promotion course, it's a thrashing, blah blah blah. What do you do in the Crabs?"

Me: "Have you ever been on an airfield, like Brize Norton and seen all the different coloured lights in the ground marking out the runways and taxiways and where the aircraft park?"

Pongo: "Yeh."

"Well I change the bulbs in them when they go out, it's quite a difficult job, especially in the dark. You've got to get out there fast, glass cover off, bulb change, glass cover back on, as quick as you can in case an aircraft is about to land."

Pongo, in absolute hysterics: "Ha ha, fuck me, Biggles, don't make your bed, sleep in your doss bag tonight because you'll be going back to Crab Land tomorrow night!" Now I apologise to those who have had the pleasure of PSBC (or indeed SCBC/PCBC) for awakening those nightmares hidden in the depths of your minds, however ...

On the Saturday evening, you have map reading and tactics exam, they are pass or fail, you get your result Sunday evening ... Sunday morning, early breakfast parade and draw weapons, get given a number and jump on your respective Bedford to the training area. Form up in your platoons and smash straight into the army CFT. When you finish, you are given a quick admin break, and then directed to a farm, given a brief, and sent off on individual navex. Once finished, grab a brew from the 'Norgy', warm kit on and onto the wagon, as soon as the Bedford fills, it departs back to camp. As they say, it pays to be a winner, scoff in the cookhouse, finish at 1700hrs because it's a Sunday.

So it's clean rifle, clean me, and into clean uniform, ready to be in the lecture theatre for results at 1900hrs. 1850hrs, there's an almighty crash. Percy smashes through the door to our room, looking like he'd just done a days Somme reenactment, kit all over the place, and sweating like a tanky on a spelling test ...

He looks at Biggles with his puppy dog eyes as I walked past him with my blue wings on my para-smock, with my RAF regiment 'mudguards' on my shoulders, proudly wearing my blue beret and RAF cap badge ...

Pongo, panting and shaking like a shitting dog: "You don't really change light bulbs on airfields, do you?"

"No mate, I don't. Oh, and I'd use your doss bag tonight if I were you!" *Per ardua ad astra.*

Robin Flack

Bridlington, sea descent. Holiday-makers all sat on the beach with their ice creams, etc. Suddenly the air is full of a C130 as it flies past about a half mile from the beach. And then ... OMG! People start falling out the back with big hankies on their backs! The holiday makers went wild! Waving, clapping, ice creams and candyfloss going everywhere! And as for the two girls getting changed behind towels, I can only say sorry but the friends holding the towels were to blame for turning to watch the fun. As we climbed off the recovery boat onto the pier, we were met with crowds applauding, asking for autographs ... and one or two young ladies asking for phone numbers ... just another day for an airborne warrior.

Bridlington, sea descent. The brief was, after canopy deployment and nearing the sea, as you feet hit the water, hit the strap release button, lift arms skyward, and slide out of the harness, thus avoiding a soaking wet canopy dragging you under ... simple! Except for 1, who at about 150 feet got out of his harness, hung onto the straps with one hand, and started banging his chest with his free hand making monkey noises and Tarzan calls. Oh we did laugh! Well the PJIs didn't ...

So were sat on this C130 minding our own when we get, "Stand up! Hook up! Here we go again!" The side doors slide open, PJI does his checks, No. 1 gets to the door, looks out and briefly down, has quick convo with PJI, PJI radios to the pilot, "Are you sure correct height? I can see the rabbits ... in fact, I can see the feckin' voles on the deck! ... Okay, okay, okay ... Lads, pass it on, jumping low today, not a lot of time."

We got out and had just enough time for the chutes to deploy before pile in! No time to assess drift, etc. Turns out the pilot had set his altimeter wrong and we went out at 350 feet rather than 800. Oh, we did laugh! The pilot got one hell of a chatting to when he got back, and warned to stay away from us ... for a long time ... Forty years later, he's still staying out of our way, probably for the best.

So I'm laid up in Wroughton after back surgery. Been there two weeks, not allowed out of bed, laying on my stomach only, Nurse comes in and infioms me that a squadron jump had been a bad one and two guys were in the next ward a bit broken. The despatchers had sent them out at the same time and they met under the kite at a bit quick speed, lots of broken bits. I demand to be allowed to get up and visit. "No."

"Yes!"

"Okay, I will get you a chair."

"No! I will walk." So round I go (with help). One guy is still out of it on pain killers, etc. The other, a tall Scotsman, is awake, "What happened?" I asked.

"Eyeee, the twat tried to kiss me on the way down, I'm not having that," he said, "So I thumped him." Two days later, he decided to visit me. "Chair."

"No!"

"Crutches!"

"Okay" ... So with compoud fractures of his leg, numerous ribs not in the correct place or piece, I get my return visit. Later that day, the same nurse came to my bed and said those imortal words, "You lot are fooking nutters!" He now doesn't want crutches, says a stick will do. "Fookin' nutters!" and walked away muttering ...

Dean Gray

When we closed Catterick down (still gutted about that), we ferried all the flight's kit down to Honington. Now there weren't many HGV drivers on 2 Sqn, so I found myself driving up and down the A1 most weeks. I wasn't selling pallets to people like some were doing though, no names, no pack drill. Now most of the time, I'd be on my own, happy with that, tunes on and left to my own devices, make the most of it and all that.

Now and again, I'd have a passenger, more often than not it was Dave 'The Bastard' Knight. Fair play though, he'd be straight to sleep and leave me to it. Now the old four tonners were easy to drive with no hands required in the slow lane on the A1, so feeling a little naughty, I'd have a tug whilst DK was asleep. Well as he was a very, very, very popular member of 2 Sqn, I thought

I'd give him some of lad's payback. Well I had to get rid of my Harry Monk somewhere, so I used to smear it around the inside of his beret. It used to soak in nicely. We'd get to the main gate at Honington, I'd wake DK up, we'd slip our berets on, and I'd be rather chipper, obviously with a cheeky little grin on my face. That's normal, right?

Scott Ramsay

2 Sqn Nordic skiing trip to a small town called Sweitzel. No names. Each chalet was allocated a senior man (none were me). In one particular chalet, the senior man decided to treat all his friends (I was not in his chalet) to champagne and lap dances all night on the stop-over in Brugen—with the money that was given to each senior man for food and water shopping for the whole trip for his eight fellow house mates.

A young LAC was made to use the credit card his dad gave him in case of emergency to buy eight hungry men food and drink all week to cover this up! Said senior man was seen shouting on that evening, "champagne and whores for all my friends!"

Bill Hayes

I was going to tell you the story about my 'cherry jump'. The ninth jump that you do is your 'cherry jump'. That is the first jump that you do after your wing's parade, and therefore the first jump that you can be charged with 'Lack of Moral Fibre' if you refuse. Up to that point, you are a trainee and if you refuse during training you are simply RTUd. So my 'cherry jump' was a balloon at night. I was already bricking it and to get a balloon at night was another brick in the wall for me. Over time, I came to love balloon jumps. Anyway, I was the last man in the stick and the blokes in front of me were all very experienced and left the cage making all sorts of screaming noises and, "Oh shit!" exclamations.

With each jumper I was becoming more and more edgy. To make matters worse, we had a trainee dispatcher who, it seemed to me, was also a bit unsure of himself. When he called me to the door of the cage, I walked up, hands over the reserve, heard him breathe in, and I was gone. I was already falling when I heard him say, "Go," poor bugger. I will never forget my 'cherry jump', and the piss that I had taken out of me by my mates that had jumped ahead of me that night. Bloody Rockapes.

Photograph courtesy of Bill Hayes.

Dean Gray

Last night in Cyprus in '95, and 2 Sqn are in the Aki Arms. It's getting late, we are wrecked, and we are on parade at 5.45 the next morning. Sensible thing would be to go home … nope not us. Myself, George Ireland, Big Bird (RIP), Daz Roby, and a couple of others that after twenty years I can't recall who they were, decided to pool all our Cypriot pounds together and head down to Limassol. We head to a club with about twenty-five people in there and before we know it, its 3.30 and we need to get back to camp. We get a taxi back to the main gate, it's now about 4.30.

I'm asleep on the floor in front of the gate guard when the duty driver picks us up and gets us back to the block for about 5.15—obviously sober by now. Squadron on parade and I'm hiding in the back row, and Mick Knight asks if anyone wants to guard the baggage whilst they all go to the mess. My right arm has never moved so quick, well maybe a bit quicker, and I'm guarding the bags. When I say guarding, I'm using them as a mattress and I'm straight to sleep. Squadron come back and we are off to the terminal, I'm straight to sleep.

As we walk across to the Herc, the commanding officer, Kirk (or as he was known *insert word) ambles alongside me and says, "Okay?"

I'm like, "Yes, obviously."

He says, "Go and have a look in the mirror on the plane."

Someone had written c**t on my forehead in permanent marker and I'd been wandering around all day with it there.

Robin Flack

Salalah, part of the boxing tournament organisation, all 2 Sqn boxers. 5 rial entrance fee, which included eight boxing bouts, free curry and rice, free cigs, and a few cans of beer. First four bouts go well—short break for a karate demo, smashing wooden blocks, etc. Smallest guy on the squadron climbs into the ring, well up for it, squares up to the karate king, hits the deck. Suddenly a (sorta') woman screams from the back, "Leave my bubba alone, you bully!" This 6`3" long blonde haired thing sprints to the front—wearing a pink crochet string mini dress, high heels, stockings, and sussies—and climbs into the ring, lays out said karate king to cheers from the audience. She triumphantly struts round the ring and spies the CO, "What you fucking laughing at? You're next!" climbs out of the ring and chases the CO out of the theatre, shouting, "Come here, you hunk, I need some man love!" All in a day's work ... we're here to entertain you.

Germany, mid '70s, in a wood (if I told you where, I would have to kill you. Haha). Rumours are rife that there is a local all girls centre not far from where we are hiding. Sure enough, on day two, OC site gets a visit from a representative from the school, expressing her concerns as to safety, etc. OC site draws himself up and states, "Ma'am, you have my word that no member of this site will at any time put your girls in any form of danger or compromising situation." (yeah right!)

Madam OC centre's reply, "Thank you for your assurance ... but ... ahem, I'm more concerned for the safety of your men. It's a corrective school and, putting it delicately, a lot of the girls are not ... tame." Oh that was a great site briefing the next morning ...

Ian Boyce

Following on from Robin, 2 Sqn parachuting at Catterick. We had not been there long, there was to be a visit from some American general, so 2 Sqn will put on displays and demonstrations to impress the VIP—midmorning balloon parachuting, several cages up and down, lots of blokes doing impressive drills, bound to impress—except it was too windy. Instead of cancelling the jumps, we went ahead, balloon cage right over by the A1, we jump at 800 (perhaps

700 due to angle of the cable, balloon was pushed by wind). Several of us had minor injuries and a couple had broken bones, one bloke was dragged down the runway, para helmet worn down, and reserve pack full of holes, toecaps of his DMS worn through. He was concussed by his head bouncing off the runway.

After this, we went onto a log race around the assault course, my section against another, I was one bloke down (injured from the jump). Yank general asked if I could still win with one man down, naturally I replied, "Sir, yes, Sir!" He was suitably impressed, thinking I was at a disadvantage (not realising being one man down meant one less man to go over each obstacle). Naturally, my section won and got a crate of Newcastle Brown from him. NQNP.

Paul Hazzard

Our last night in Goose Bay after doing Frozen Rock, I think '95, someone thought it would be a 'good idea' to see what the consequences were of snorting brandy and tequila. The affects are the same: eyes go bright red, tears flow freely, and facial muscle twitch uncontrollably ... except tequila makes your nose bleed as well. After a many snorts and shots, spirits were high and more daring challenges were made. Bear in mind it must have been at least, minus 15 and all done naked ... as per SOPs! In no particular order, these are some of the challenges that were made and undertaken by the twelve foolhardy people—sorry I can't remember who most of them were, but those that were there know who you are.

- Run around outside and dive into snow drifts.
- Nick a bike, ride out of the block, down the steps, and get catapulted over the handle bars to see who could get thrown the furthest.
- Run around the WRAF block.
- Jump out of the first floor window into snow drifts (I remember jumping out with Taff and jumping out with the WRAFS

watching from their rooms from across the block. I jumped out of the second floor window with a towel above my head in an attempt to reduce my speed. How I never broke my legs, I will never know, as it must have been at least 30ft! I couldn't wear boots for three weeks after as I bruised my heals badly).
- Run along the underground corridor from one end to the other, about 200 metres, WRAF block one end, officer block the other.

About 23:30, four of us—myself, and I believe David O'Brien, Chris Brown, and Stuart Reid (Brains)—thought it would be a good idea to see if the officers' bar was still open. It was, and just as we were about to open the door, OC detachment opens it first and in front of him, stood naked, four Rocks in a multitude of skin colours, looking at him. In true Rock style, he looks at us and then says, "Suppose you wanted to be invited in for a beer?" So all four of us walk into the bar and, unknown to us, the wives of the regular officers were there as well, and a look on their faces is something I shall never forget.

Being the gentlemen we were, we struck up conversations with all and I was stood at the bar, chatting to this wife, without a care in the world. It took her and the rest of the wives a few minutes to forget that there was four naked Rocks standing around chatting and acted if it was the norm ... maybe it was for officers!

The pilots of the Herc who were flying us back the following day were more shocked than anyone else and they tried to cower in the corner, wondering what the hell was going on. I thought it would be only right to go and speak to them and explain to them that if they were offended by our attire, "Tough fucking shit," OB, being also ex 2 Sqn, addressed the young FO who was also ex 2 to inform him that, "These hats had been out of the window before he had so he had better get the fuck out as well." So without hesitation he strips off, jumps out of the window, comes back with a big gleam on his face, only for OB to comment that his hook on was shite, his exit was diabolical, his PLF was non-existent, and he was still dry from the waist up, so he had better get it right this time. Back he returns, soaking wet, with a cut above his eye as he hit a road sign!

It was now our turn to form up as a stick and run along the length of the bar, onto the chair, onto the table, onto the window ledge, and jump out of the window, being dispatched by the flight lieutenant. Somehow all five of us had managed to jump between two skidoos and this road sign. How no one got injured that night jumping out of windows, getting frost bite, embedded into walls or snow drifts is a miracle in itself and if Carlsberg did nights ...

Further to my post about that trip. I think it was Bear or Chris who got a Red Cross parcel delivered when we living out on the frozen lake, and in it there was a bar of laxative chocolate. One segment of you constipated, two bits if you heavily constipated. They put nine pieces in my drinking chocolate! Pissing out of my arse for twelve hours into a bucket under the trees. Even boss knew what happened and kindly offered a medi vac chopper back to camp, which I kindly declined. Didn't find out till day before we left what had happened, as I thought I just had a stomach bug ... Bastards!

Robin Flack

So we are at Catterick doing balloon descents on the airfield. A lovely bright day with hardly a whisper of wind. Plans are hatching, only to be scuppered by the order, "No stand ups allowed!" Oh crap!

Some of the ossifers allowed to go up in the cage, I can only think that all the other ranks' wives must have been busy scrubbing floors or something. Anyway, half way through the day, the PJ I decides to get out first, and with a, "Despatch yourselves, lads," disappears into the 800. On executing a perfect stand up on landing, he is greeted by an extremely red face WO, eager to bollock whichever airman who had dared to disobey his order. Realising he couldn't, the WO immediatly changed tact and bollocked him for leaving four of his men up 800. The guys duely despatched themselves and, yup, all did stand ups, and all answered the same question with, "Well he did one, Sir!"

"Oh feck it, go on then, but I will charge any man who breaks anything!" Happy days jumping!

How did Davey 'Shovel' Hill get his nickname? A long, long while ago, at a camp that some will remember, after a hard day's exercise and an even longer session at the Great Bustard Inn, we retired for the night in our Nissan hut billet. Roy Barlow was last in and turns the light on to get undressed. Dave Hill got up said, "Get undressed in the dark, Roy, we're sleeping," and turned the light off.

Roy turned the light on again saying, "'I can't see."

Dave got back up, said, "Fecking try," and turned the light off . Roy, giggling by now, turned the light back on. The 'click' was followed by a 'clang' as a shovel hit him square across the back of the head and shoulders.

Roy rubbing his head, whirled round and said, "What you do that for, Davey?"

Davey (sobering up rapidly) said, "Just a reminder to turn the light off when you're undressed, mate," and went back to bed. Oh, happy days.

Picture courtesy of Bill Hayes.

Picture courtesy of Bill Hayes.

Si N Becks Lloyd

We had a zob on 2 Sqn that used to bring his black lab in. He let slip not to give it chocolate. Needless to say everyone rushed to their little stashes in the CVRT cages and fed the poor thing stupid, as you do. He enjoyed all his 'treats'. Needless to say the inevitable happens right outside his office door, and it stank to heaven—really gagging shit. As it happens though, the offending, massive, and soft pile outside his office was also adjacent to the swing door connecting two parts of the corridor which when pushed open, smeared it all over the carpet, doubling the gagging factor. By now several SNCOs were asking, "What the fuck's that stink? Smells like shit!"

I think some poor Lac got lumbered to clean it up, and the dog never made it to the squadron HQ for some reason or another.

Andy Cullen

Remember in the USA, on an exchange with another 2 Sqn lad, the US jumpmaster says, "You boys jumped steerables?"

I said, "Yes," the other lad murmured and said to me he hadn't. "Easy, mate, just land into wind," says me. Out the helicopter we go, down I go, towards the smoke on the DZ. All of a sudden, I am bombarded with abuse as my mate has the wind on his back, heading in the wrong direction.

"How do I turn this bastard?" Safe to say, he creamed in big time.

Robin Flack

2 Sqn, mid '70s. A well-known, lovable Welsh rouge goes AWOL for a week, decides to return. Arrives back on a brand new civi police bike c/w blue lights radio and nee naws, claimed to find it in a box on a police truck, and 'borrowed it'.

Are you all sitting comfortably? Nobody need the toilet? Good then I will begin ...

Long, long ago, in a far off land (that lost 2-0 but still thinks it's superior), 2 Sqn had just finished a tacival and returned to the holding base. Deep joy! There was a BoB dance in the NAAFI that evening, shave, shampoo, and ... ensued. I popped over to see my cousin, who was on the base, with promises to return before the end of the hop. I turned up at 2230 to view a sea of carnage, blue light flashing, and lots of uniforms with white hats running around. Oh dear, the boys had been at it again.

A fight had started about a girl (oh, surprise!) and the two involved where slung outside. Then some clever sod on the committee decided to stop the disco and turf everybody outside, where the fight was still going on. Well, what happened next, you ask. It hit the fan big time, resulting in twelve 2 Sqn guys being charged for offences including: 5 counts refusing to stand still when told to (what!); two counts refusing to stop hitting a RAFP when told to. One count sniffing acetaline, foaming at the mouth, and chasing a RAFP officer round the camp with a 6' piece of angle iron; one count showing the custody sergeant an offensive weapon whilst under arrest. The other two I really cannot remember. I, for some reason, was escort for the accused on all cases. On the offensive weapon charge, a guilty plea was entered, with mitigation. "He asked me to show him what was in my pockets and the flick knife open on its own." Fined £50, the other eleven were fined similar amount but refused to accept the punishment and elected for court marshall!

Well (told you all you should had gone before I started!) back in jolly old Blighty a couple of months later, I again was escort to them all, and a party of RAFP where flown in to testify. The lads had chipped in and hired a civvy lawyer to help then. He ripped shit out of the statements with things like, " I'm sorry but 'stand still, you're nicked', is not an acceptable caution in any law book ... in a scuffle, after a long exercise, 'stop hitting me' cannot be conscrewed as an order, mearly a request, and what were they doing in the middle of the scuffle anyway? ... On the foaming at the mouth one, no description was entered for the assailant, and why was access to the bottles allegedly so easy made?"

The end result (phew) eleven court marshall trials concluded with not guilty or insufficient evidence verdicts. Result! Well nearly, there was a few behind the sceanes bollockings to come.

I woke up the next morning with the right arm of my civvie shirt in tatters, and four deep scratches from my shoulder to my elbow—when measured they fitted the exact proportions of a fork. I have no idea where I got them from! Oh happy days.

Wesley Bardoe

I can recall the whole of 2 Sqn being asked to assemble on the mats for a warning order regarding an op in Kuwait. The commanding officer was standing there waiting for everyone to arrive when Lewie—I am sure it was Lewie—walks past, hand out towards the CO's face, and says, "Fuck off, boring." Commanding officer casually starts the briefing with, "See me in my office afterwards, Lewis ... Right, fellas, listen in." Anyone else remember that or has my Mrs been feeding me magic mushrooms?

Ian Black

After a hard day on pre-para in the Cairngorms, we set up camp for the night. The PTIs had two land rovers and went to the pub but left one of the Rovers. I happened to notice they'd put the keys under the seat. Fancying a pint after a long hard day, I asked who was up for going to the pub, got a few volunteers—who shall remain anonymous, unless they want to fess up!

Anyway I drive and we head to the pub the PTIs haven't gone to, I forgot to say that we roped an officer into coming with us as well. We're sat in the pub, enjoying a cool beer when in walk the PT staff, well and truly rumbled, and one of them was a Rock hater. That night and for the next few nights, we got driven to the middle of nowhere and dropped off separately to sleep in a ditch by the roadside, then the staff would pick us up in the morning to start that days tab. After each big mountain day when the rest of the course got picked up, we had extra tabbing to do and, last thing at night, dropped off in the wilderness again. This went on for a few days—can't remember exactly how many—but I was convinced we'd failed. On our return to Catterick, we finished the last few days and on the Friday, when you get interviewed as to whether you've passed or not, the land rover incident never got a mention.

Fair play to the PTIs, they gave us shit, we cracked on with it, and all was forgiven. If you told that to the kids of today …

Robin Flack

2 Sqn. A young, shy SAC is in a queue for a taxi in Bath with his girlfriend. A knobhead walks to the front ofof the queue and announces, "The next one's mine!"

The young, shy SAC says, "Excuse me but there is a queue."

"You want it, pal? Well you're gonna' have to stop me," at which point, he hits the deck, hard.

At the civi court hearing, a PC, who stumbled apon the scene, stated, "As I rounded the corner, I saw a man, who I now know as Mr X, stamping on the victims head."

Judge: "Tut tut, Mr X. Is that what happened?"

"No, Sir. He caused me to lose my balance while try to avoid his blows, he stumbled and fell right where I was putting my foot down."

WO acting as a good character witness, "I have known and trained SAC to a high level where winning is the only way, he assures me that his only aim was to protect not only his girlfriend, but all the other innocent people present. It was only when the supposed victim started throwing punches that his military training kicked in, in order to protect all about him. I would expect no less from any man under my command!"

Judge: "Case dismissed!"

SAC: "Thank you, Sir."

WO: "There *will* be a bottle of scotch on my desk tomorrow, you dick! Next time check for coppers!"

Ian Boyce

Early '70s, young Boycey had not been on 2 Sqn long, typical squadron display for some visiting general or politician. I was looking after the signals stand, just by the main entrance to the hangar. Across from me was a weapons stand, manned by Mick Gant. Pride of place on the table was the IWS, the box lying open on the table, the various mounting brackets being used to demonstrate how the site fits to SLR and GPMG. The AR15 mount was left in the box, as we did not have a use for it then.

A junior officer came along to check we all knew our stuff prior to the visit and did not recognise the AR15 mount, so he asked Mick, who convincingly explained that this was the mount to fix the IWS to the 9mm pistol. Young Rupert moves along and checks all the other displays. Visit now ongoing, VIP stops at the IWS stand and asks Mick what the mount in the box is for, before he can reply, young Rupert keenly jumps in, explaining that this is how the IWS weighing nine pounds is mounted onto the SLP.

OC II turned a funny colour and as VIP moved off, loudly muttered, "Gant, you're a cunt!"

Si N Becks Lloyd

2 Sqn with the armour, late '80s. Doing ranges with it, Germany in the summer months, which as you well know, is beautifully hot and dry. Brief goes like this: Spartans drive down these tracks to this

point, engage targets with mounted gimpy, supported by Scorpians, whilst troops debus. Told to fire all gimpy rounds. 'Get rid of it' was the phrase.

Duly get to the allotted location and give it rooty toot. At this point, something akin to a mega angry, fiery devil starts whizzing around the range, setting fire to everything it touches. In seconds, the whole range is ablaze, smoke and flames everywhere. Range binned, fire brigade called, not very happy Germans or range officers, oops. 7.62 mm hitting a 20mm incendiary round lodged in a tree didn't really help.

2 Sqn late '80s, early '90s, Salisbury plain ranges. Now the lighting of people's kit had been pretty rife of late so, never one to miss a chance to get revenge on a fellow gunner, I grabbed the opportunity with relish. We're all stood around, waiting our turn to go down the range, kits all prepped. Just bomb up and off you go.

There's me standing next to Gary thinking, *Right, ya bastard, revenge time*, and promptly lit him up and stood back to watch the ensuing chaos, like you do. How the fuck was I supposed to know he'd been and bombed up with loads of gimpy link, etc. Got in the shit for that one.

Richard Devlin

Training wing cinema, March-ish, 1996, approx 1100hrs, 2 Sqn, exercise purple star Fort Bragg pre-deployment briefing. Sitting there in the cinema next to Warby and Scruff the Cat (Les Burns), listening to Saff Sergeant from 82nd Airborne telling us all not to go near or try playing with the snakes and other assorted wildlife we may encounter. All through his lecture, he would keep stopping to ask if anyone had any questions. So after about an hour of this and no one interacting with him asking questions, I decided I would take it upon myself to ask him a question in the spirit of international airborne relations. I raise my arm. "Soldier, what's your question?"

"I was just wondering, are we knocking off early this afternoon cos we ain't had an early Friday knock off for ages, and I have a thing on in Liverpool to get to."

"Shut up, Devlin," said the C.O. At this point, the heads of the Four Horsemen of the Apocalypse all turned in unison staring at me. Death: F.S. 'Beefster' Mick Knight. War: F.S. 'Mad Dog' Andy Ramsey. Pestilence: F.S. 'Goldenballs' Chris Blackman. Famine: F.S. 'Madasaboxoffrogs' Ian Boyce.

Now Beefster seemed pretty upset that I had asked this question to our Yankee cousin. End of lecture and Me, Les, and Warby exited the cinema like fucking lightening and jumped into my Audi GT5S and tore off to the mess, and could see Beefster smashing through Trg Wg doors looking for me in rear view mirror. Chuckling away, Warby points out the fact that, "Beefster is gonna fucking kill you when we get back to the hanger after lunch."

"I know, mate, I hadn't really thought this through, it was a spur of the moment thing." Les just sat there giggling uncontrollably.

1315 hrs, standing on C Flight lines in the hanger, and the Beefster screams my name so loudly I think the yank's mates in Bragg could have heard him. So off I go for a pep talk with Michael. Now, I had had a few bollockings in my time, but this was a different fucking league. You know when the person bollocking you is so angry that they start making up the weirdest swear words. So after being suitably pepped by Michael, he informs me that I am key orderly for the next week, and so I can forget about Liverpool this weekend (I wasn't even going to Liverpool that weekend) and that if I was a second late to open the hanger, I would be charged and could forget about the States.

0555hrs Monday morning and I get to the hanger and Beefster is stood waiting for me checking his watch. "Morning, flight sergeant."

"Shut the fuck up and open the hanger."

"You are here very early, flight."

"I will be here at this time every morning this week, you Irish Fenian prick," that was the pet name that he used to call me when on our own).

"Well, do you want to pick the keys up then? No point in both of us being here early." Another Pep talk and rest of the week goes without a hitch and I go to States for purple star.

Turns out that it would have been better to be locked up cos then I would not have had to witness Lewi and Tibbs having a wanking contest at Bragg to see who could jack of the fastest and quickest.

Six nations, 1999. Ireland vs. England, Landsdowne Road, Dublin. I am in Jury's Hotel near the ground watching on big screen with a few mates. I am waiting to start in the fire brigade in Dublin after leavin 2 Sqn late '98. Match over, England win, and a load of the crowd pile into Jury's for more drink. An English couple come and stand next to me, wearing England hats. So having a good bit of banter with them and the female saying how she comes to Ireland often to see family and friends as she grew up here and went to school here. A very nice couple and after about two hours, she asks was I in fire brigade in UK. "No, I was actually in the RAF."

"Oh, my brother is in the RAF."

"Well I was RAF regiment, so probably don't know him."

"He is RAF Regiment too."

"I was mainly on 2 and 58, so if he's Rapier, I probably don't know him."

"Oh no, Michael is 2 Sqn, flight sergeant."

"You have to be kidding me." Husband gens it and I go to the bar to get a round where something hits me. So I go back with drinks. "So you spent a lot of time here and went to school here?"

"That's right," she replies.

"Where was Michael when you were living here and going to school?"

"Michael grew up here too and went to a boarding school in Dublin, if I remember rightly."

"He used to call me a Fenian and other Irish bad names that I will not repeat in front of you, I don't believe the cheeky bastard turns out to be more Irish than me."

"I will ring him and you can ask him yourself." She whips out the mobile and rings him and says she has met a friend of his at the match in Dublin and hands me the phone.

"Beefster, me old mate, how the fucking hell are you?"

"Is that you, Devs?"

"It certainly fucking is, and I have just spent the last few hours with your delightful sister who has told me of your early years growing up, you big Irish lying Fenian bollix!" Beefster and me had a good old laugh, and he made me promise never to tell anyone, which I have not. Karma.

Picture courtesy of Bill Hayes.

Picture courtesy of Bill Hayes.

Ian Boyce

1976, 2 Sqn is now in the province, AandB at Aldergrove, SW at Bishops Court. After a while, Mick Gant is sent from Bishops to hold with us, something to do with a 'misunderstanding'. over a loaded/cocked weapon (Mick did have lots on his mind, from the domestic front).

Around midday on a day off, Mick informs me he has wangled us an invitation to the RMP Corps function at Alexander Barracks, so I have to borrow suitable attire—as a young CPL, I generally wore t-shirts, jeans, and dessy boots. I do have a fine pair of cream trousers of my own and borrow a squadron blazer, squadron tie, and blue bri-nylon shirt (it was the '70s). We set off on foot to ally-pally, only a five minute walk, and gain entrance with our 1250. We pop into the guardroom, where Mick in his loudest posh-officers voice declairs, "Eh hellea, my name is Gant, I believe you are expecting me?"

Moments pause, then everyone in the guardroom slams to attention and the sergeant salutes us, I am looking at all these monkeys with broken noses and slashed peaks. *Fuck, fuck, fuck, what has Mick got me into?* We are now being escorted by a redcap CPL, to the NAAFI, where the function is being held. I quietly ask Mick, "WTF is going on?" he explains that everything is okay. He phoned the guardroom earlier and asked if we could attend the function, he was OC Special Forces and I was his adj, just up from Armagh for a spot of RandR. To say this was a bit of a shock to me was an understatement.

Robin Flack

You've already heard about my worst para descent (night entanglement) 2nd worst, Catterick balloon windy. Side right, side left, oh, shit type windy. Hit the deck, bounced, dislocated my left shoulder, bounced again, put the bugger back in! Now that hurt! Must be some more horror stories from my fearless bros from the sky …

Steve Bateman

This tour of RAF Goose Bay in Canada '92 by 2 and 51 Sqn was a cracking month's worth of fun with top brothers. The amount of goings on could fill a book on its own. Not to mention the powers of Dr Labatt's, which on a nigh time cured all the aliments of the sickies. One incident was the pizza van raid. We made a load of orders for pizzas from the local town. The pizza man turns up with a van full of pizzas in arctic boxes. Goes to the block across the road first to deliver a pizza to some Canadians. When he returns, all his pizzas have gone. Hands up me, Les, Smudge, and others have whipped the lot. The irate pizza man came in the block kicking off and got smacked by one of the 2 Sqn's most mellow Rocks, who knew nothing of about the raid. The pizza man leaves and an hour later the regional police with pistols drawn burst into the block, but by then all the pizza have gone.

Robin Flack

Germany, mid '70s, in a wood, mid tacival exercise. On a night off, a few lads popped down to the local town to sample the local fare, three decided to get a taxi back. The taxi pulled up by the woods and the guys dismounted, melted into the foliage, without paying! The next morning, all ready for the day's fun, all cammed up, grass and twigs sticking out from webbing when we are called to parade in single line order. A local copper and angry taxi driver appeared to try and recognise the three naughty boys. FFS! We couldn't recognise each other! He stood no chance! They walked up the line and back, at which point the taxi driver threw his arms in to the air and stormed off!

ABOUT THE AUTHORS

Stephen Headey

Having served in the RAF Regiment for thirteen years on field, Rapier, USAF, and helicopter squadrons in various locations throughout the world helped make me the successful businessman and company director I am today.

The regiment gave me discipline and the fight to see things through, even when times were tough and I lost a limb, I never gave in. I credit this to the training I received in my career.

Today I am now the owner of an import company for British expats. This book was born out of wanting to help my fellow brothers in arms, and it was a pleasure to be involved in this from start to finish.

Tim Parker

Joining the RAF Regiment in 1980 helped shape me as an individual. The things I learned and did on the Queen's Colour Squadron and a succession of Rapier and USAF squadrons are very much a part of who I am today. Throughout my life, if a notion or observation strikes me, down on paper it goes, usually in pictorial form. I am flattered that many of the quick, rough, and ready cartoons I scribbled out on NAAFI breaks or slack time on guard are still retained today by many comerades. It is an honour to have provided old and new images for this work.

I've never fully turned my back on the Air Force, and despite an absence after twenty-four years regular and reserve service, I have recently come back to the fold. Watch out for more artwork.